WALKING ON DARTMOOR

Clapper Bridge Nr. Lower Cator, Widecombe. Walk 25

WALKING ON DARTMOOR

John Earle

CICERONE PRESS
MILNTHORPE, CUMBRIA

ISBN 0 902363 84 0

CONTENTS

Stone Circle, Scorhill Down. Walk 33

Introduction

Very often people have asked me when I return home after one of my expeditions to the Himalayas, Tierra del Fuego or Baffin Island, whether I do not find Dartmoor rather tame and unexciting after the great mountain ranges of the world. Settling down to write this Guide Book to Dartmoor has made me pause, think and try to justify and back up my claim that I find Dartmoor a most exciting, interesting and intriguing corner of our varied world.

Dartmoor has been called rather glibly the last great wilderness in England. This, of course, is true for whatever that really means. It is indeed a huge, largely uninhabited, lonely area of moorland of some 365 square miles. They also say that you can be, on Dartmoor, further from a road and therefore I presume civilisation, than any other wild area of Britain south of the Scottish border. On the North Moor near Cut Hill and Fur Tor it is over three miles to a road, if you count the military road from Okehampton Camp and on the South Moor, near Stringers Hill and Erme Pound, the nearest road is again over three miles away.

So that is one reason why I find Dartmoor attractive. I love the wild, lonely, remote areas of uplands and mountains. Even at crowded holiday periods you can still get away from the masses and walk all day without seeing a soul.

Then, even if I have only been away for a few days, when I return to my home near Widecombe-in-the-Moor, as I get out of the car I take a deep breath, for Dartmoor has a strange, indefinable scent that changes with the seasons. Sometimes the misty air is full of the smell of damp, peaty moorland, at others the pungent scent of gorse; in March when the farmers are swaling (burning the moor to improve the grass for grazing), the wind brings a waft of burnt heather and gorse or the smell of the smoke itself.

The rolling, sweeping horizon of Dartmoor with its huge skies always thrills me. Except in a few steep-sided valleys you are never shut in on the moor; you always have the feeling of distance and vast open spaces. Everywhere, except in prolonged summer drought, there is the presence of water; quaking bogs, small streams and the peaty, moorland rivers tumbling down over water-rounded granite boulders, while high overhead the skylarks pour out their own evocative liquid song.

Of course a lot of the landscape, certainly on the margins but also in some of the remote river valleys, where the tinners have been at work, is fashioned and changed by man. Man has lived, hunted and worked on Dartmoor since pre-historic times and obviously has left his mark, from hut circles, stone rows and megaliths, to tinners' spoil tips and blowing houses, to newtakes, peak cuttings and ancient fields, to china clay works, forestry and dams.

I find the history of man on Dartmoor, especially the pre-historic period fascinating. I still feel a strange, prickling sensation in the scalp when I am alone in one of the areas of hut circles or stone rows. Almost I sense the spirits of the Bronze Age people of 4000 years ago. It is no wonder that Dartmoor has its share of legend and folk lore and up in the deep peat hags of Cut Hill you could almost believe in the stories of pixies!

Sadly there are very few of the true, old Dartmoor farmers and their families left in our modern times. Men and women for whom a trip to Exeter or Plymouth was a once a year outing, who thought nothing of travelling to market in gig or cart, taking two or three hours there, and back again, whose slow, hard life revolved around the seasons and the harsh taskmaster Dartmoor.

Life and the old ways have changed from the days when every small village had its bakery and blacksmith, when the grocer, the butcher, even the fishmonger from Brixham, the haberdasher and tailor delivered to the door of remote farms by pony trap; when harvest suppers and whortleberry gathering parties were part of the year's major social events. Modern farmers on Dartmoor, are a different breed, but just here and there are a few folk whose memories reach back into the old days and the ways of their fathers and grandfathers before them.

The wild life on Dartmoor is not outstanding but when you do come in contact with the secret inhabitants, it is all the more exciting. The buzzard, I suppose, with its moth-like wings and the mewing call, like a kitten, is the most common big bird on the margins of the moor and in many ways epitomises Dartmoor with its soaring, wheeling freedom or sitting like a sentinel on a pole or bare tree surveying the world. Then there is the thrill as a couple of red grouse get up with a clatter and their loud 'go back' call, or the excitement or the brief glimpse of a reddy-black, arrogant hill fox loping off in no hurry. But it is the skylark, that minute speck in the blue summer sky, with its bubbling song, that brings back a surge of happy, childhood memories of walking or riding on hot, breathlesss days into the heart of the moor and I still scan the skies trying to find the little, soaring creature pouring out its ecstasy.

I hope therefore to share with you, through this Guide, some of the magic and mystery of Dartmoor. I should like to show you places to visit that I think will interest and fascinate you, so that like me, you will become a person who loves and appreciates this lonely wilderness and will return to it again and again, for it has a haunting almost hypnotic influence on those who walk here.

The Geology and Formation of Dartmoor

This Guide is no place to give a full and detailed description of the geology of Dartmoor. For those who would like more information, it can be found in some of the excellent books listed in the bibliography. However to appreciate and understand the moor and its landscape, it is a pleasant little scrap of knowledge to know how Dartmoor was formed and something of what happened over the milleniums since its creation.

At a time when the Earth began to look green as plants and even small trees evolved and the seas were full of vertebrate animals such as primitive sharks that eventually led to the existence of the first amphibians, where Devon and Cornwall are now was part of a huge flood plain. The sediments in certain areas of this plain became the early rocks seen now, such as the Dartmouth slates and Devonian limestone. This time in the development of the Earth was known as the Devonian period and occured 400 million years ago and lasted some 50 million years.

As the warm seas encroached the southern areas of what was to become the British Isles changes took place. Coral reefs grew in the seas and volcanoes erupted here and there. Sediments, mud and sand, accumulated round the coral reefs and volcanic debris and we have the beginning of the Carboniferous period, 345 million years ago, which overlapped with the previous Devonian period. It was, of course, the chief coal forming age associated with the coal seams and carboniferous limestone.

Then as this period came to an end, about 290 million years ago, both the Carboniferous and Devonian deposits were subjected to mountain building pressures and foldings known as the Armorican movements. The rocks and soils of Devon and Cornwall as we know them now were formed at this time. The limestones and sandstones appeared caused by the great folds and upthrusts.

It was about this time too, 290 million years ago, that the granite of Dartmoor probably arrived from below the earth's crust, though dating such events is fairly difficult. Granite is an igneous (Latin; fiery) rock and is formed under conditions of intense heat. Dartmoor granite arrived as an igneous intrusion into those overlying sedimentary rocks, in which, because of the violent folding they had been subjected to, had many faults and cracks. Some of the granite was able to follow these weaknesses to the surface while in other areas the granite welled up under the Devonian and Carboniferous rocks like water in a blister. Some of the sedimentary rock even became absorbed into the granite itself because of the ferocious heat. So we have the characteristic dome-shaped mass of rock, in area some 365 square miles, in the centre of Devon.

Because the granite was protected by the layers of rock above from the cold air, the molten rock cooled very slowly resulting in large visible crystals; the slower the cooling process the larger the crystals. Gradually the protective layer was eroded and destroyed by the weather during the Permian period and in time the granite boss was exposed.

Later during the millions of years that followed a layer of granite itself between fifty and two hundred metres thick was also eroded, until we have Dartmoor as we know it today.

Dartmoor granite is composed mainly of three types of crystals. First, quartz which is the glassy grey substance that in its pure form produces the distinctive six-sided crystals with pyramidial points and striations on the sides. Next the small dark, glistening specks of black mica, a crystal that occurs in many of the massive rocks, and lastly felspar, which gives granite its colour, red, white or grey. These are the larger crystals seen in granite. It is felspar, when it has decayed or been decomposed by weathering, that becomes kaolin or china clay.

For several different reasons there are a variety of granites to be found on Dartmoor.

Surrounding the moor like a ring there is an area called the metamorphic aureole where the encircling rocks have been changed in composition either by the intense heat of the igneous intrusion or by steam, geysers and hot springs associated with igneous activity.(I shall be writing briefly about the ancient tinners of Dartmoor and other mining activities later. Suffice to say, at this stage, that most metallic ores are associated with plutonic rocks or areas of metamorphosis.)

On the margins of such granite masses as Dartmoor, super-heated water or gases forced their way into the cracks and deposited layers of crystalline minerals including the ores of metallic minerals. The way that this process led to the present position of the various areas of minerals is very complicated. Put in simple terms the mineral bearing fluids and gases started deep down in the granite mass and as they were forced up to the surface the minerals crystallised in the order of their crystallisation temperatures. So obviously minerals with the highest crystallisation temperature became solid near the hot granite and the others followed in order as the temperature decreased towards the surface. However, the erosion mentioned earlier has resulted in the following simplified diagram of mineral deposit on and around Dartmoor.

This period of mineral deposition probably took place 190 million years ago but the process might well have been spread over as long a period as 115 million years.

A final word must be written about the tors (Celtic-*twr*, a tower) of Dartmoor. They are after all its most distinctive feature, sometimes described as 'cyclopean masonry'. It has even been suggested that they were put up by the Druids! They are, of course, residual features left after both chemical and mechanical weathering has taken place. Controversy surrounds their origins and which of the two methods of weathering is the most important.

(i)   Chemical weathering is the actual rotting of the rock itself and depends on the composition of the crystals in the rock and how they react within themselves.

(ii) Mechanical weathering is really straighforward erosion by water, frost, freezing and heat.

But however they reached their present state they are fascinating features that are fun to explore and scamble on, each one being different from the next.

Surrounding many of the tors are large areas of rocks lying scattered over the slopes leading up to the tors. These rocks are called clitters and were broken off the main mass of the rotten tors as they became exposed, by water freezing in the cracks and joints and finally pushing them off onto the slopes around.

Finally I refer you once again to the geology books if you want to follow up more details about the tors and the formation of Dartmoor.

Vegetation

Dartmoor usually conjures up thoughts of mists and quaking bogs; Great Grimpen Mire of The Hound of the Baskervilles. A lot of the moor is indeed bogland and while there are a few areas, usually very small pockets, where a horse or a bullock could sink in and I presume human beings, there are no bottomless pits, like quicksands covering large areas of moorland. After rain a lot of Dartmoor makes for wet walking and you have the extraordinary situation of bogs on the top of the moorland - not just by the stream and in river valleys. This is the blanket bog found in areas of eighty inches of rain in a year. Here grow bog asphodel and tormental with sphagnums also a little heather with sages.

Peat made up of fibrous dead roots forms in areas where the angle of the ground is less than 15 degrees and again where there is abundant rainfall.

Then you find areas of valley bogs; marshlands with reeds and the sources of streams and rivers. Here also is found sphagnum as well as cotton grasses, pale butterwort, bog asphodel, sundews and bog violet.

The wet areas of moorland that are not blanket bog have got cotton grass, ling and bell heather and puple moor grass.

On the drier moor it is heather and in other areas whortleberry that thrive. Bracken grows in profusion also on the lower slopes of the drier moors and after swaling or burning the heather, bracken will colonise large areas.

On the high moor itself the three ancient woodlands of Wistmans Wood, Black Tor Beare and Piles Copse are fascinating. They are all three found on the west facing clitter slopes and the trees are mainly stunted oak, never more than three to five metres high, with a few mountain ash. On the floor of these woodlands, on or among the rocks are mosses, ferns, wood rushes, lichens, liverworts and whortleberries, while epiphytics festoon the branches of the trees themselves.

Even the barren granite tors have mosses and liverworts in the deep crevices and lichens on the rock faces.

Finally there are the delightful wooded stream and river valleys that run down from the granite moorland. The vegetation in them in often profuse; golden saxifrage and sphagnum, stonecrop, daffodil, wild garlic and St.John wort.

Fauna

In my Introduction I mentioned briefly a few of the creatures you can see on Dartmoor; buzzards, red grouse, foxes and skylarks. If you are lucky you might also come across badgers at dusk or the shy almost extinct otter by the rippling streams and rivers. Stoats, weasels and the ferocious mink that has now colonised certain areas having escaped or been let loose from mink farms, can all be discovered. Rabbits still breed and live in profusion in spite of myxamatosis. The harmless grass snake and the not so harmless adder basks on the warm rocks in summer, as do lizards.

Kestrels with pulsating wings hang on the air and the sparrow hawk also hunts the moor. Ravens, carrion crows and rooks are all inhabitants of the margins of Dartmoor, the crows and ravens hated by farmers at lambing time when they are quick to see the weak, helpless lambs and move in for the kill. On the higher moor the wheatear starts to arrive in March from Africa, to breed here; in Victorian times these small birds were considered a delicacy on many dinner tables.

By the rivers, the dipper, that remarkable little black and white bird that seems to fly underwater and builds its nest on overhanging rocks just above flood level, darts about with low flitting flight.

You will often disturb an old grey heron fishing in the streams and rivers and off he will go with long, languid flaps of his great wings.

The moorland streams themselves are the homes of the brown trout and salmon and the beautiful salmon trout called peel in Devon.

Finally black slugs will appear on moist, damp days and probably the Dartmoor midges. A vast number of insects are found including honey bees, dragonflies and spiders while butterflies and caterpillars including the Emperor Moth catch the eye with their bright colours.

Man has grazed his animals on Dartmoor from the time of the Bronze Age and herds of cattle still roam certain areas, while large flocks of sheep, including the Scottish black-face that has done so much damage to the whortleberries, are found almost everywhere.

But it is the ponies that most people associate with Dartmoor. They are called 'wild ponies' but they are all owned, in fact, by the farmers who have commoners grazing rights and if you look closely you will see that they have brand marks on them. They are rounded up twice a year but the most important 'drift', as they call it on Dartmoor, is in the autumn for the local pony markets. When you look at the ponies on the moor you soon realize that they are a mixture of many different breeds that have been introduced to the area. However, there are a few studs that are trying to purify the strain and get back to the thoroughbred pony, the true emblem of Dartmoor.

Man On Dartmoor

It has often been said that Dartmoor is a landscape fashioned by man, which up to a point is true. Man probably first wandered onto the uplands of Dartmoor as a hunter as early as 8000 B.C. when the moor was a wild, mountainous region of towering tors, very different from that which we see today. These men from the Old Stone Age actually lived in the limestone caves and rock shelters of the coastal areas of Torbay and Plymouth, but they left hardly any signs of their visits and certainly did nothing to change the landscape of Dartmoor.

Neolithic man also came up onto the moor and may well have settled there but archeologists have found no evidence of this. What is clear however, is that forest clearance had started on Dartmoor before this period and certainly continued through the Bronze Age when man first came to live on the uplands.

So it is with Bronze Age Man, from around 2000 B.C. until about 500 B.C., that we have the first evidence of man's dwellings and activities on the moor, by which time the topography was very much as we know it today. One of the great delights of walking on Dartmoor is that it gives you the chance to visit some of the many Bronze Age remains to be found there. Dartmoor is perhaps one of the richest areas in the world for pre-historic sites. Even on the shortest walks one usually stumbles on some evidence of Bronze Age Man. There are the hut circles that usually occur in groups, sometimes within a surrounding wall or pound. In recent times archeologists have shown great interest in the old reaves or long earth and stone banks that mark ancient fields and territorial boundaries. There are many barrows and cairns, the old burial sites where in some cases the earth and stones have disappeared leaving the actual burial chambers themselves called kists or kistvaens, looking like large stone boxes. Near these burial mounds you can often find the mysterious stone rows and standing stones or menhirs. Nobody is really sure why they were put up but the stone circles may have been places of worship and the stone rows often lead towards the bigger barrows or burial mounds. There have been attempts to explain them as markers for the seasons or the solstices or even phases of the moon, but for whatever reason they were erected, the larger circles and rows are well worth visiting. The longest stone row on Dartmoor, by the way, is over two miles long, near the River Erme and Erme Pound.

Early Iron Age men were next to live on Dartmoor as the remains at Kes Tor proved, where a whole community dwelt with an iron-smelters house and workshop nearby in its own pound. The date has now come up to the fifth century B.C.

Then there appears to be a gap in the human occupation of the moor from about 400 B.C. until the coming of the Anglo-Saxons about 700 A.D.

It was at this time that the houses changed from the round hut circles of the Bronze Age to rectangular shapes with their surrounding field systems. The remains of these houses are stone-walled but excavation has discovered that very often below the foundation are the post holes of wattle and turf huts from earlier times, the sites having been rebuilt on many times. The medieval village at Houndtor is perhaps the best known example. By the various dating systems used it is interesting to find that the early Saxons built in wood though there were large quantities of stone available and there must have been evidence of earlier men building in stone. It was not until about 1200 that stone buildings appear.

All through the early days of the Saxons and into medieval times Dartmoor was not actually claimed by any group but plenty of people took advantage of the good summer grazing and drove their sheep and cattle onto the moor as the many lanes leading up onto the high land indicate.

It was the Normans who made Dartmoor one of the royal hunting forests and so began the organisation of administration and allocation of land on the moor. The name Dartmoor Forest has persisted from this time and can be misleading. It was a term used for a royal hunting area and did not necessarily mean that the land was covered with forests. It was also about this time that the ancient Dartmoor tenements were founded and the whole conception of 'commoners' who had grazing rights on the moorland started.

Tin was mined in Cornwall in the times of the Bronze Age but we first find documentary evidence of alluvial tin streaming in the year 1156 near Sheepstor and Brisworthy. In that year about 60 tons of smelted tin were produced. Within fifteen years or so the production had risen to over 300 tons a year.

So the early tinners used an opencast mining system working in the broad, shallow, river valleys where the rich tin deposits had been carried by floods and were contained in the sands and gravels. The larger stones containing tin ores were crushed in primitive mills and then washed or streamed with the other tin-bearing sand from the river bed. Smelting took place over a peat fire which produced impure lumps of tin but there were also more refined smelting centres.

By the thirteenth century blowing houses had been introduced for smelting where charcoal was used as the fuel and the molten metal ran from the furnace into moulds. The name blowing house comes from the fact that huge bellows were used, powered by water wheels, to help produce the intense heat needed. Quite a few remains of blowing houses can be found on Dartmoor though not many have the moulds and wheel pits to be seen.

The output decreased over the years and by 1243 only 40 tons were produced, but tin streaming continued until shallow adit mining began in the fifteenth and sixteenth centuries and later still this method was changed again to shaft-mining in the eighteenth and nineteenth century.

So all over Dartmoor you have the evidence of the work of the tinners throughout the ages, from the mounds of rubble left behind after the early streaming, great gullies of opencast mining, to the old ruins of the buildings, wheel pits and engine houses of more recent times.

The tinners themselves in medieval times were probably small farmers who tried to add to their meagre living by forming small groups to search for tin. However, during this period the tinners were a powerful and favoured group of workers with a large number of privileges which included exemption from certain taxes and dues, and from serving on juries and with a right to form their own militia. All these privileges seem to stem from the formation of the stannaries which controlled the tin industry and taxed it for the Crown.

Dartmoor itself was a stannary and was almost a self-governing country with its own laws, courts and even a jail. So it was that the tinners had rights, privileges and protection as providers of royal taxes which put them beyond many of the laws of the rest of the land.

Each of the stannary areas has a town where the taxes or coinage were collected and these towns were around the edge of Dartmoor; Tavistock, Chagford, Ashburton and so on. The countryside under the control of these coinage towns covered vast areas even as far as the north coast of Devon but the boundaries all met at Crockern Tor in the middle of the Dartmoor stannary. This led to the Great Court or Parliament of Crockern Tor sitting at this windswept part of the moor, the first recorded meeting of which was in 1494. It was here that the huge task of setting the laws and rules of the tin industry were worked out. The day to day administration was dealt with by courts in the stannary towns where they also heard legal cases to do with the tin industry such as wrangles over ownership of land, bad management, even common assault. As I said the tinners were a law unto themselves but they dealt impartially with all cases and handed out punishment equally impartially.

The Parliament of Crockern Tor was also aware of its duty to the rest of the country, for in 1532 they discussed the problems caused by vast quantities of sediment and waste, caused by the tinners works on Dartmoor being carried down the rivers Dart and Plym and silting up the harbours at their mouths.

But over the years the importance of the tin taxes for the Crown lessened and the power of the Great Court of Crockern Tor decreased and many of the privileges for the tinners were withdrawn. The last tin coinage was in 1838 and by 1896 the stannary courts were abolished. The tin industry in Devon was dead and so were the powers and privileges of the tinners, men who knew that in the early days they could defy the laws of the land because the king depended on them for a large part of the royal income, but in return created their own laws and rules often more severe than common law.

Farming on Dartmoor is another huge subject that I can only touch on here. Clearly prehistoric man herded his animals on the moor. In the twelfth century the Cistercians from Buckfast Abbey drove their own sheep up onto the moor near the Abbey to graze there and indeed travelled across the moor by the Abbots Way, (described later), to Tavistock Abbey with their wool.

I mentioned earlier the Ancient Tenements of Dartmoor which came into being with the Normans. It was the increase in population at this time that made more and more people look for farming land on the higher areas of Dartmoor, and this is clearly the start of farming settlements on the moor as we know them now. Most of the land was owned, as a lot of it still is, by the Duchy of Cornwall, and the tenants had to pay their rates to the Duchy and agree to certain feudal duties.

Most farmers look to increase the acreage of their land and on Dartmoor the system called newtakes had been operating since well before the fourteenth century. The average farm on Dartmoor at this time was about forty acres. This old system of newtakes allowed the farmers on the ancient tenements to enclose and reclaim eight acres of rough moorland every time a new tenant took over the farm.

The modern Dartmoor farmers of today still have to contend with the harsh conditions faced by the tenants of years ago. Many of the farms are still rented from the Duchy and occupied by the same family for generations. Cattle, sheep and ponies are still all important; keeping livestock is the way that they make their livings. If the farm has some good enclosed pastures they may keep a herd of Friesians for milk. Lower down, maybe in a sheltered valley, the less harsh climate will allow farmers to grow a few cereals as well as keep dual-purpose cattle, sheep and ponies. A few pigs and chickens, usually managed by the farmer's wife, may all add to the possible income for the typical mixed Dartmoor farm. At the other end of the scale there are a few high moorland farms which might really be called small holdings which in these hard days are not really economic to run even with the subsidies that are given to hill cattle.

Hay, of course, is an important crop for all the Dartmoor farmers who have large numbers of animals to feed in winter, but with the high rainfall and uncertain summer sun it is not surprising that many now make silage instead of hay.

Several of the old moorland farms have the word 'warren' after their name; Ditsworthy Warren, Huntingdon Warren and there is the Warren House Inn, the third highest pub in Britain we are told. These were all farms where rabbits were bred commercially, the oldest being Trowlesworthy Warren which dates back to 1272. If you visit these 'Warrens', which I hope you will, you can often find the remains of the old burrows that were constructed of stones and earth where the rabbits lived and bred. Nets and dogs were used to catch the rabbits and at Ditsworthy Warren you can still see the stone dog kennels made in the walls of the yard behind the farm.

I need to make passing reference to a few of the other industries that have brought man onto Dartmoor and in all cases have changed the landscape by his exploitation of the resources.

Peat-cutting, quarrying, china-clay mining and forestry all fall into this category. Of these five only peat cutting is no longer carried out on Dartmoor on a commercial basis, but the remains of the old workings at Rattlebrook are well worth a visit and there are many large areas near the tinners works and mines and the old farms where there is plenty of evidence of the peat cuttings of the past.

Obviously I have not been able to mention all the activities of man such as the moormen, the pack-horse routes, the cutting of the peat-passes, the building of the prison at Princetown, the Dartmoor crosses but I hope to make up for some of these omissions in the Guide itself. However, I need to end with what many will consider a highly controversial use of Dartmoor by man and that is the activities of the Military.

Of course it is nothing new and there were military manoeuvres on Dartmoor as far back as the 1860s, and from that time on firing and exercises have taken place on the various ranges that have been created. I need not dwell on the various licences and Bills that make it possible but all of you who walk on Dartmoor have to be aware that on quite a number of days of the year large areas of the north moor are closed for use and that you need to check always in newspapers, local Post Offices and other centres to make sure that there is no firing taking place; a subject I shall return to later.

The Legends of Dartmoor

As man has lived on Dartmoor since prehistoric times and as the landscape itself is often mysterious it is no wonder that there are many legends and folk tales to be heard. Many of them of course are to explain some of the wierd features of the moor or to give an explanation to some unaccountable occurrence. Again, as might be expected, many of the stories are linked to the Devil and perhaps the best known comes from my own village Widecombe-in-the-Moor.

However, this legend starts in the Tavistock Inn, Poundsgate where some of the locals were enjoying a pint on the morning of Sunday, October 21st 1638. They heard the sound of a galloping horse approaching and then suddenly the door burst open and a tall, dark stranger entered. There was something sinister and foreboding about him but the people in the inn shrugged it off as the stranger ordered a tankard of ale. He paid with gold and raised the tankard to his lips. As the beer went down his throat there was a loud sizzling noise and the locals drew back in horror and astonishment. Within a moment the pot was empty and the Devil, for it was surely him, swept out of the bar and the sound of his horse galloping off towards Widecombe could be heard in the silent inn. Later when the landlady opened her till, after drawing a great many pints to calm the nerves of her customers, she discovered that the gold given to her by the stranger had turned to withered, autumnal leaves!

The scene now shifts to Widecombe church and a young, dissolute tinner called Jan Reynolds who was a heavy drinker and gambler with a weakness for the cards and the girls; something of a 'no good boyo'! It appears that he had sold his soul to the Devil for money, to pay his numerous debts, forgetting, as is often the case, that eventually there has to be a day of reckoning.

On this particular Sunday Jan had spent quite some time in the Old Inn before the service and now was slumped at the back of the church very much the worse for drink and playing cards to while away the time during the sermon. But quite soon, with the combination of the drink and maybe the sermon, Jan fell asleep. No sooner had he dozed off, than with incredible suddenness, a terrible storm blew up with ferocious winds, thunder and lightning. The congregation cowered in their pews and then with a loud explosion and, I am sure, fire, brimstone and a smell of sulphur, the Devil appeared through a hole in the roof of the tower, seized Jan by the scruff of his neck and before anyone could move, shot back to the top of the tower, where he had tied his horse to one of the pinnacles, taking the hapless Jan with him. With a final thunderbolt the Devil rode off with Jan in tow, sending the pinnacle to which he had tied his horse crashing down into the churchyard. They were sighted passing over the Warren House Inn, the last hostelry Jan Reynolds was ever to see and then he vanished forever.

Take the story as you will but there are parish records of a terrible storm on Sunday, October 21st 1638 in which four people were killed and sixty-two injured in Widecombe Church. This storm has a place in the Guinness Book of records as the worst tornado ever to have taken place in the United Kingdom.

I could fill a book with the numerous other legends there are but let me whet your appetite by mentioning a few more in the hope that you will be able to find out the stories yourself.

Jay's Grave on which, it is said, there are always flowers to be found.

The Hairy Hands seen and felt, it you are to believe the legend, where the Cherrybrook flows under the road near Powder Mills.

Childe the Hunter, who in Norman times was caught in a blizzard while out hunting on the moor near Fox Tor Mires. To try to protect himself from the freezing storm Childe killed his horse and crept into the carcase but to no avail; his body was found by the monks of Tavistock Abbey, who because of the conditions of his Will written in the horse's blood, were left his lands at Plymstock for giving him a Christian burial. A 19th century cross over a kistvaen marks the spot where Childe was supposed to have died; Childe's Tomb on the map.

Then there is the Coffin Stone near Dartmeet.

Or the story of Benjie of Cranmere Pool.

The Dewerstone or Devil'a stone where he is supposed to hunt with his pack of Whist hounds, coal black creatures with eyes of flame.

Hound Tor has the same legend.

Near Hound Tor is the Bowerman's Nose another hunter, turned to stone this time.

Branscombe's Loaf and Cheese, Lady Mary Howard, The White Bird of the Oxenhams, The Hound of the Baskervilles. The list is endless.

Dartmoor Today

Dartmoor was one of the first National Parks in the British Isles and dates from October 30th 1951. The Headquarters and Offices are at Parke, Bovey Tracey, Devon, TQ13 9JQ, telephone Bovey Tracey 832093. This Guide is no place to enter into the controversies and politics that surround the National Parks in Britain and in particular the Dartmoor National Park. The pressures on such areas of wild beauty are enormous from those of you who, I hope, will want to walk on the moor or the many thousands who just drive up here in their cars and coaches and look for parking space, through to those with commercial interests such as farming, forestry, military training, china clay works and dams for water, not to mention building roads within the boundaries of the National Park. I read somewhere that more terrible things had happened to Dartmoor since it became a National Park than ever before it was designated! Clearly as the pressures of urban life build up, more and more people will want to escape into the quiet and peace of the countryside, but do they really want that? I sometimes doubt it when I see the crowded car parks at Dartmeet, Princetown, Widecombe, Postbridge and New Bridge. So there has to be control, discipline, money and understanding care to make sure that Dartmoor still retains its beauty and wildness without, on the one hand, stifling and thwarting those who have to make a living on the moor or, on the other, making the National Park like some awful exhibit never to be changed, with tight controls for entry and concrete paths to walk on as you find in some of the American Parks.

For people to come on Dartmoor means that in many cases they have to be educated as to how to use the countryside and this includes the open moorland which many regard as land that is not owned by anybody. This is in fact not true. Dartmoor National Park does not belong to the nation as the name implies; it is all owned by the Duchy or by the farmers who have common grazing rights (the commoners) or other landowners. There are however a few small pockets of land owned by the Devon County Council one of which is around Hay Tor.

To start then you could find no better advice than the Country Code.

1. Guard against all risk of fire.
2. Fasten all gates.
3. Keep dogs under proper control.
4. Keep to paths across farmland and then only if there is a right of way.
5. Avoid damaging fences, hedges and walls - particularly by climbing over them.
6. Leave no litter - take it home.
7. Safeguard water supplies.
8. Protect wildlife, wild plants and trees.
9. Drive and Walk carefully on narrow country roads. It is

important to know how to back your car and be prepared to do so!

10. Respect the life of the countryside.

Coupled to this last one I should like to add one more.

11. Do not make unnecessary noise.

I feel that I should also mention the notices put up at many points that state that there should be 'No Vehicles beyond this point.' This is not a National Park Law but a Highway Law that states that no vehicles should be driven more than fifteen yards from a road. Following on from this I would urge all car users to park sensibly and with consideration. Do not block gates as local farmers and other users of the moor may need to come and go without hindrance. Do not park in narrow lanes or on busy roads.

The other problem is caused by Dartmoor ponies. Obviously the visitors are intrigued by them especially the younger ones and there is always the temptation to feed them. But this is a most dangerous thing to do. Firstly it attracts the ponies to the roads where they loiter hoping for titbits. Driving at night or in mist or pouring rain with bad visibility, it is a fearful hazard both for the pony and the driver to come on a group of ponies suddenly, tucked round a blind corner. Secondly, by feeding them, it gives them food that is not suitable and also make them less capable and determined to fend for themselves which they must do during the long, hard winter months.

Access can also cause problems. No wonder many Dartmoor farmers still regard the tourist as a scourge. I have seen people tramping across a fine crop of hay to have a picnic. All too often groups will climb the dry-stone walls to cut off a corner. Once one rock is disturbed a great many more usually fall. I have heard farmers complaining of gates left open and animals wandering on the roads or in fields where they should not go. We have all found empty tin cans and broken bottles left lying around; a terrible danger to livestock. Cigarette packets and butt ends, fish and chip papers and fried chicken cartons all litter the popular areas of the moor and often private land.

Many of the Footpaths and Bridle Paths are clearly signed with boards and the Rights of Way are well marked on the maps that you will be using. Please stick to and respect the Rights of Way and do not stray off them. As a good, general rule you can assume that all enclosed fields are private and that you should not enter them unless there is a marked Right of Way.

If you have any doubts, the Dartmoor National Park Headquarters, at Parke are always very happy to help and advise. There are several seasonal Information Centres at strategic places on the moor including Parke and at Princetown, Postbridge, New Bridge, Steps Bridge, Okehampton and Tavistock. You will also see, going about their work quite a number of the Park Rangers who, amongst their many jobs, act as a liaison with the Public.

Public transport onto Dartmoor these days is sadly almost non-existent. Gone are the days when the railways circled the moor and the one splendid line to Princetown took you across rolling moorland to well over 400 metres, and every moorland village had its bus service. However, there are still a few local bus routes and in particular the Pony Express and the Dartmoor Link operated by the Dartmoor National Park Authority. You can get the details of these services from Parke or local bus companies. But I must assume that most of you will come to Dartmoor by car.

Where To Stay

As you drive across or around Dartmoor you will often see farms and small Guest Houses advertising bed and breakfast and you may be the sort of person who likes to try places on the off-chance that they will have vacancies, but at the peak holiday periods you would probably be better off booking.

There are many excellent hotels in the area ranging from the large and expensive to the small and not so expensive.

There are Youth Hostels at Steps Bridge on the Teign, Gidleigh on the edge of the moor and at Bellever near Postbridge. The Dartmoor Expedition Centre offers full board or self-catering bunkhouse accommodation in the off-season.

As I have mentioned all Dartmoor is privately owned and permission must be obtained from landowners before pitching tents or caravans. Some farmers will allow you to camp on their land for short periods; a few have recognised sites. The National Park Authority has a leaflet that gives you further details about camping and also lists the various sites on or near the moor.

As well as the information you can obtain from the National Park Office in Bovey Tracey, a most useful little booklet is issued by the Dartmoor Tourist Association which lists a great number of hotels, guest houses, farms and other services in the area, including a Phone-a-Bed service on Tavistock 3360, but this is not for advanced bookings. For more information and a copy of the booklet contact The D.T.A. 8, Fitzford Cottages, Tavistock, Devon, PL19 8DB.

Dartmoor Weather

As with many upland regions on the west of Britain you can expect a high rainfall on Dartmoor. The prevailing westerly winds come in from the Atlantic loaded with moisture and as Dartmoor is situated on a peninsula between the English Channel on one side and the Irish Sea and Bristol Channel on the other, the rainfall of over 80 inches a year at Princetown and much of the surrounding moor is only to be expected.

This oceanic climate coupled with the fact that much of Dartmoor is between 200 and 600 metres high means that there will be strong winds as well as heavy rain and of course the notorious mists which can blow up in minutes. I shall be writing about clothing for walking and the use of the map and compass in a later section, but all walkers on Dartmoor must be prepared both physically and mentally for mist and bad weather with hard frosts and snow in the winter.

You can telephone for recorded Weather Forecasts on Plymouth (0752) 8091 or Torquay (0803) 8091. These are updated twice a day. (On (0898) 500404 there are more frequently updated regional forecasts.)

One final word about flooding rivers. Dartmoor is like a great sponge which retains water until saturation point is reached and then it releases huge quantities with amazing suddenness. The rivers can come up several feet within an hour or less. The power and weight of the water of a river in flood is something you would never imagine unless you try to cross. The rule is don't! It is far better to walk extra miles to an easier crossing place or a bridge rather than attempt to wade across especially with young people. Hopping from boulder to boulder is also to be discouraged at all times, even more so with a river in spate, it usually ends with wet clothing or worse a sprained ankle or broken bone. If you have a light rope, then in a real emergency you might feel that you would have to cross using one of the correct safe-guarding methods found in Langmuir's book mentioned in the Bibliography.

Clothing

Let me start at the top. You lose an enormous amount of heat from your head and therefore some form of headgear is extremely important all the year round, for even in summer, warm, sunny days can quickly become wet and cold on Dartmoor. In winter a balaclava is well worth carrying. It is also worth mentioning that a broad brimmed hat is a good thing to have on hot summer days for with a slight wind, sunburn is another hazard coupled with heat exhaustion and even heat

INTRODUCTION

stroke.

For winter walking thermal underwear is excellent but not essential and a woollen shirt. For summer lighter shirts will be sufficient. The rule is that several light layers of pullovers are better than one large, chunky sweater. It means that you have more control of your body heat and can shed one layer at a time when you are wearing several. Thermal, fleecy jackets are very popular these days and to wear a light sweater with one of these jackets to put on or take off, seems a good combination.

I like to wear breeches with a pair of long socks but some of you may prefer trousers. Whichever you choose, for winter walking, they should be made of a thick material such as wool or woollen mixture and loose enough to allow easy leg movement; jeans are too thin and usually too tight to be ideal walking clothing but for summer they will do. There are plenty of excellent lightweight trousers designed for walking on the market these days.

Next thick socks or stockings; loop stitch are very comfortable. Now perhaps most important, boots. The choice here is vast and nearly everyone has their own preference. Lightweight boots are very much in fashion these days and for long days of walking they are far less tiring. However, the boots that are partly made of fabric cannot be said to be really waterproof unless you wear with them the type of gaiter that has a rubber rand that fits into a special groove round the welt of the boot. So probably I would suggest a lightweight, leather boot with a cleated rubber sole to be worn with gaiters, especially those with the rand. The sole should be flexible so that it bends with your foot as you walk. If the boots are well treated with waterproofing wax and you wear gaiters you should then be dry to the knees and I hope you do not go any deeper than that! I see no need for the really heavy, leather mountaineering boots for Dartmoor. You should get adequate ankle protection with lighter boots and there are no long scree slopes to descend.

I shall probably incur the wrath of some experts, but to be honest a good pair of wellingtons are excellent for a lot of Dartmoor and there are quite a few types of rubber boot on the market made with studs that can be taken out when not needed. Obviously it depends on your feet and whether you feel that you can walk comfortably all day in wellingtons.

Then you will need an outer layer of waterproof clothing. I am afraid that you will certainly need both jacket and trousers if you are going to walk a lot on Dartmoor in summer and winter. For summer walking a jacket only will be sufficient, but I do feel that a hood is

27

essential to stop the wind and rain going down your neck.

I am not going to enter into the arguments about the breathable fabrics, there are so many on the market now but it seems that whatever you wear you will be very lucky to remain completely dry if you are out for several hours on Dartmoor on a wet and windy day. Either the garment will leak or you will get wet with sweat! In any case water will seep up the sleeves and down the neck! But do not be tempted to leave your waterproof and windproof garments behind, they are a life-saving and essential part of your equipment. The choice of which one to buy must rest with you. Gortex, Entrant, Ventile, Waxed Cotton, Nylon proofed with rubber or PVC. The best answer is to visit a good equipment shop and look at the various makes available.

Finally gloves or mittens. I prefer wool for inner gloves and indeed most of my other clothing such as shirts, sweaters and breeches; wool stays warm when wet. Again it is useful to have a waterproof and windproof outer glove for winter walking.

It is not really clothing but you will need a small day rucksack to carry your food, spare clothing and all the other little bits and pieces I shall be suggesting in another section. Obviously if you are thinking of camping then you will have to consider a 65 to 70 litre capacity sack but for a day walk, up to 40 litres will be sufficient. A sack is useless if it does not keep the contents dry and it is usually a wise thing to put all your clothes into a polythene bag inside the rucksack.

Equipment

A final word should be written about some of the other small items of equipment that I feel might be taken with you for safety and comfort. Food for the day obviously is needed but it is a good idea to take a little extra in the form of 'emergency rations' such as chocolate, sultanas, nuts and raisins, Mint Cake and flapjack. On a hard day's walk you will need some 4000 calories and in cold, bad weather even more.

I usually take a water bottle or a Thermos flask. Drinking from moorland streams can be dangerous. So often there are dead sheep or cattle in or near the water and many people find the peaty water upsets their stomachs in any case.

It is always wise to carry a spare sweater or thermal jacket.

A torch might well be of vital use if the walk takes you longer than you expected and you have to finish in the dark.

I hope that you will never have to use it but a whistle to attract attention if needs be, could save a life. The International distress signal is six long blasts on a whistle or six flashes with a torch in quick succession and then a minutes rest and then the signal is repeated followed by a minute's rest and so on until help comes. The answer, by the way, is three blasts or flashes followed by a minute's rest.

Next you might like to consider carrying a polythene survival bag or Space blanket to shelter in if you or one of your party has an injury or suffers from hypothermia and has to lie out on the moor waiting for help.

You will need to take a small first-aid kit which you can either make up yourself or buy. It should contain bandages and dressings to deal with minor scrapes, cuts and blisters. On the subject of blisters it is far better to stop early on when the first slight burning soreness is noticed and put a plaster on. It is no good hoping it will go away. If you can feel it then the damage may have been done and blisters can ruin a days walk. If you then add antiseptic cream, a triangular bandage, a crêpe bandage and finally some pain killing tablets these will make an excellent and useful first-aid kit to take for a days walk.

Finally I know some people like to carry a short length of nylon climbing rope with them on Dartmoor. I think that you are unlikely to have to use it except as a last resort to cross a flooded stream or river or to pull someone out of a deep bog! However, if you do feel you need one, 30 metres of 9mm rope will be sufficient for Dartmoor though for more mountainous regions you will need 45 metres.

Maps and Compasses

For your safety and for you to get the maximum enjoyment from walking on Dartmoor it is wise to be proficient at understanding how to use your map and compass which are, of course, the last two and probably the most important bits of equipment you should have with you.

It does not take long to master elementary map reading but I hope you will want to take it all a step further, for maps can tell you a vast number of interesting and important things about an area. More than anything else you have to be aware of the limitations of maps because they represent the three-dimensional features of our earth on a flat sheet of paper but with practice this soon becomes no problem. I am fascinated by maps and spend hours just poring over them and imagining the countryside they portray.

First you need to consider the scale. The most popular map of Dartmoor used to be the one inch to the mile (1:63360) Tourist Map which contained the whole of the moor on one map. With the move to metric maps the ones that are now available are the Landranger Series of Great Britain which are a scale of 2cm to 1km (1:50,000) or about 1¼ inches to the mile. You will need two sheets for the whole of Dartmoor. Sheet 191, Okehampton and North Dartmoor and Sheet 202, Torbay and South Dartmoor.

The Ordnance Survey have produced a Dartmoor map in their Outdoor Leisure series Sheet 28. This is a marvellous map for detail as the scale is 4cm to 1km (1:25,000) or 2½ inches to the mile but as it covers the whole of Dartmoor it is a huge sheet and printed on both sides. The problems of folding and getting the relevant section, that you want to use, visible are enormous on windy, rainy days! Even if you prepare the map before you set off you are bound to want a section that is hidden.

You can of course buy smaller individual sheets of the 1:25,000 maps both First and Second Series but you will need quite a few of them to cover longer walks. However, this scale is ideal for Dartmoor as many more details are shown as well as walls and small differences in height, both important when navigating on the moor.

Finally Harvey Map Services Ltd. have produced a Dartmoor map in their Mountain Recreation Series with a scale of 2.5cm to 1km (1:40,000). They use an orienteering map style of presentation with different colours to indicate vegetation. The physical features of the moor are all important on this map and there are very few place names printed; the result is a very clear and uncluttered map. Unfortunately it does not cover the moorland to the east of Widecombe which includes such areas as Hay Tor and Hound Tor.

Next you will need to consider the conventional signs; the short-hand of maps. Most sheets have the conventional signs printed on them.

I was taught to repeat like a parrot that contours are imaginary lines joining all places of equal height. This may be so, but more important is to be able to read the contours so that you can see if you are going up or down or if it is a steep slope or a gentle slope and where there are valleys and gullies. It does not take long to get the feel of the land from them.

The parallel lines printed on all the maps that you are likely to use are the Grid Lines. Each line has a number to identify it. The numbers of the lines that run up and down the sheet increase as they move towards the right or east and the lines are called Eastings. The ones that run across the map increase as they move up the sheet or north. They are called Northings. Each of the squares created by the Grid Lines is 1km X 1km. The diagonal across the square from corner to corner is 1.5kms. Once you know this it is a very quick and easy way to estimate distance. Regardless of the scale of the map the Grid squares are always 1km X 1km. Obviously the larger the scale of the map the larger the square will be on the map.

The other more important use of the Grid Lines is to give Grid References and I shall by using these in the Guide to pinpoint places. You must always give the Eastings first and then the Northings. So to give the position of a large area such as a village you need only give a four figure reference which would indicate the square e.g. the village of Holne lies in the square 70 Eastings and 69 Northings in other words S.X.7069. However, it is usual to give six figure references and to do this you will have to subdivide each square into tenths. You give the main number of the Easting square followed by the tenths eastward followed by the main Northing square and the tenths northward e.g. the reference for Dartmeet would be 672 Eastings and 732 Northings, given as just S.X.672732. It must be remembered though that this actually represents a square 100 X .100 metres on the ground and if you want to become really accurate then eight figure references are better but to be honest it is almost impossible to work them out correctly. You should always prefix your Grid References with the Grid Letters as similar references recur at intervals of 100 kilometres. For Dartmoor these letters are SX, but as I am obviously only referring to Dartmoor I have not included them.

A lot of your navigation will be done visually and to do this you must orientate your map. I must assume that you know where you are when you start! So to orientate your map you identify some obvious features in the countryside such as a tor, a forest boundary or a building and you turn your map until the features are lined up with their representations on the map and everything else will fit into place.

But now you need to consider the compass. There are many different makes on the market ranging from simple ones costing £3 to £4 to the more sophisticated costing up to £20. You will need a proper navigating compass as the small button compasses you can buy are no use. They should have a clear plastic base like a protractor with a swivelling capsule and at least a luminous needle but other luminous points are useful for night navigation.

You can now orientate your map using the compass. The top of the map is always true north and for all intents and purposes the Easting Grid Lines point to true north.

First place your compass on the map with the rotating capsule turned so that the north arrow on the compass card or dial is in its correct position at 0 (or 360) degrees, and with the whole compass pointing to the top of the map (north). You can use the Grid Lines to help you do this. Slowly rotate the map, and yourself if needs be, keeping the compass firmly in place pointing to the top of the map (north) until the compass needle itself swings and points to magnetic north which is just 5 degrees, in 1986, to the west of true north, in other words 355 degrees. Your map is now set and you should be able to identify features.

This last operation mentioned that the compass needle points to what is called magnetic north located to the north of Hudson Bay in Canada rather than true north and this must always be taken into consideration when navigating and especially in the next stage of compass work.

There will be occasions where the moor is so featureless, or you are in thick mist, or even at night, when you will not be able to navigate visually either by lining up features or walking towards known points identified both on the map and on the ground. It is then that you will have to rely on your compass by taking and using compass bearings.

To do this place the edge of the clear protractor part of your compass along what is called the line or direction of travel; in other words from where you are to where you want to go. Now turn the capsule until N (north), usually shown by an arrow engraved in the bottom of the dial, points to the true north (the top of the map). Once again the parallel Grid Lines will help you do this. Pick up the compass and ADD by gently rotating the capsule, what is called the magnetic variation (the difference between magnetic north and true north) which as I mentioned is 5 degrees in 1986. However, it does decrease over the years and you should check with your map which will give the information. Now hold the compass in front of you and turn your body until the red (north) end of the swinging compass needle points to north on the compass dial: this is the arrow engraved on the bottom of the capsule. The larger direction of travel arrow on the front, longer end of the compass, will now point at where you wish to go. Choose a landmark or a feature on this line (not a sheep or a cow!) within the limits of the visibility and walk to it without looking at the compass except perhaps for a brief check. When you arrive choose another new landmark and repeat the procedure until you arrive at your destination.

With this brief information you should be able to find your way around on Dartmoor but navigation is a fascinating subject and well worth following up and it is just as well to have more than one person in your party who is competent with a map and compass.

One final bit of advice. I should get a good large waterproof map case or cover your map with a clear, plastic, self-adhesive sheet or spray it with one of the waterproofing fluids that are available. Wet, windy days on Dartmoor can quickly destroy a map!

Dartmoor Letterboxes

This unique curiosity, found in no other moorland or mountainous region, was more or less started in the last century by a man called James Perrott whose grave you will find in the churchyard at Chagford.

James Perrott was known as the Dartmoor Guide and he used to take his clients to the remote and barren areas known as Cranmere Pool in the heart of the north moor. (There is yet another Dartmoor legend about Binjie Gear by the way, associated with Cranmere Pool.) To record this achievement the walkers used to leave their visiting cards in a pickle jar that Perrott had left there in a small cairn that he built in 1854. When you consider the costumes of those Victorian times, especially for the ladies, and the fact that there was no military road from Oakhampton to within a mile of the Pool as there is today, the walk of over seven miles over difficult moorland was certainly something worth recording.

Fifty-one years later, in 1905, two keen moorland walkers placed a visitors' book there so that people could sign their names when they arrived at the desolate spot. By 1908 the numbers visiting Cranmere each year had risen to over 1700.

The most famous person to sign his name at Cranmere was perhaps the late Duke of Windsor who, when he was the Prince of Wales, visited the box in 1921.

The next letterbox to be established on Dartmoor was in 1894 at Belstone Tor.

After Cranmere the next best known box is at Duck's Pool on the south moor which was placed there in 1938 in memory of William Crossing the writer of many books about Dartmoor, the most outstanding of which is his *'Guide to Dartmoor'*.

By the 1970s there were some 15 boxes and the positions of some were even marked on the one inch maps of this period.

You are now probably wondering how the name letterbox arose. It developed from the idea that when you visited a box you left a letter already stamped and addressed ready for the next person who came there to collect and post in a conventional letterbox. The interesting thing was to see how long it was before your letter came back to you. In the early days of the 1950s when I walked on the moors it would often be weeks, especially in wintertime. As most of the boxes had their own specially made rubber stamp your letter would come back with a most unusual postmark! Sadly vandals and pilferers have been responsible for this custom no longer being a sensible or even a possible thing to do.

Since the 1970s some people would argue that the Dartmoor letter-boxes have got out of control. There is no law to stop anybody who wishes from establishing their own letterbox and while there are some excellent ones with beautifully made rubber stamps, there have been, at times, over 1000 boxes scattered around the moor but many of these new boxes only stay out for a few weeks.

As I mentioned earlier a great many of the popular, well-known boxes are visited by vandals and have their rubber stamps stolen and the books defaced. It is no wonder that there is an air of secrecy about the location of many of the new boxes, to be divulged only to genuine box hunters.

Taken by and large there are probably about 450 boxes now on Dartmoor and a club has been formed called the '100 Club' whose members are keen letterbox hunters who have found and recorded over a hundred boxes. There are two meets each year at the Forest Inn, Hexworthy, on the Sunday that the clocks go either forward or backward for British Summertime or Greenwich Meantime when over 200 enthusiastic box hunters get together to swop yarns but all moorland walkers are welcome.

Climbing on Dartmoor

Wherever there is a cliff or an outcrop of rock sooner or later man will want to climb it! Dartmoor is no exception and there is reference to climbing on the tors in a book called *'Climbing in the British Isles'* by the famous father of British climbing, Haskett Smith, published in 1894. In spite of this book there is no more recorded information about rock climbing routes on and around Dartmoor until 1935 and 1936 when climbers tackled the great granite cliff of the Dewerstone and put up what are still considered the classic routes of the area; 'Climbers Club Ordinary' and 'Climbers Club Direct' both over 160 feet.

It was not until after the war that there was an enormous increase in activity with climbers both on Dartmoor itself and at the Dewerstone. Mention must be made of one man, Admiral Keith Lawder, who pioneered a lot of the routes himself but more importantly with his infectious enthusiasm encouraged many young climbers to develop the area and then documented all the new routes in the first professionally produced guide-book.

Both in the 1960s and 1970s there was another surge in climbing on

the moors and many new routes were added and increasing numbers of people came to Devon to climb, not to mention a strong local climbing group and the instructors at what was then the Outward Bound School at Ashburton.

So as you will have gathered there is plenty of excellent climbing to be had on a great many tors from short 'bouldering' problems to longer routes of 100 feet and at all standards, while the Dewerstone offers a whole range of climbs in a magnificent setting high above the river Plym.

For those of you who are interested there is a guide-book entitled *South Devon and Dartmoor* published by Cordee which covers all the climbing in those areas and supercedes the previous guides published by the Royal Navy Ski Mountaineering Club.

Walking on Dartmoor

Unlike many upland areas it is, of course, possible to walk almost anywhere you like on Dartmoor because of the character of the country-side. You do not have to follow ridges or valleys as you do in mountainous regions. You can choose a point and then walk more or less straight there, avoiding the bogs of course!

There are tracks marked on the maps of Dartmoor but to be honest they are really not much use except a few like the Sandy Way and the early parts of the Abbots Way. The others are not always in the position marked and in any case they soon peter out and with the maze of animal tracks on the moor it is hard to decide which is the actual path. So on the whole it is better to ignore them because one always assumes that the paths are going to where you want them to go and very often they do not!

There is no reason why you should not plan your own walks to go to areas you wish to visit and places that interest you but I have outlined in this Guide some walks that I hope will take you to some of the exciting locations Dartmoor can offer you.

Both on my suggested walks and the ones you may plan yourself you might like to work on the formula known as Naismith's Rule for finding out how long it is going to take you. Naismith was a Scottish climber, who in 1892, suggested that people walk at 3 m.p.h. and that they had to add ½ an hour for every 1,000 feet they climbed. In these days of metric maps this becomes 5 k.p.h. plus ½ an hour for every 300m. of ascent. This really is only a starting point because in bad weather, or if you are unfit, or carrying a load, or if the terrain is difficult you must take all or some of these into consideration and it is important for you to work out your own rule accordingly.

Dartmoor is deceptive country for walking. Because it is not a true mountainous region and looks just a rolling, undulating landscape many people think that they will be able to keep up with Naismiths fastest timings. This is just not possible because much of the walking on Dartmoor will take you over tussocks of grass, heather, bracken in the summer months, peat hags, marshy areas, gorse bushes, rocky slopes all within a few miles of each other. It is almost impossible to get into that slow, rythmical, steady stride that will keep you going all day and that is so important for easy walking. All the same try to keep a steady pace and with luck you may be able to average 2 m.p.h. or just over 3 k.p.h.. You should allow at least ten minutes every hour to rest and look around and certainly more if you wish to stop and explore some of the points of interest I shall mention.

Obviously avoid the really swampy areas (they are well marked on the maps) and also avoid the large clitters unless you have to thread your way through to get to a tor.

The higher parts of the moor are not necessarily the driest but they may be better than the stream valleys.

So plan your route. Work out how long it is going to take you.

Check the weather, by telephoning for a forecast before you set out and then keep a weather eye out, as they say, while you are walking.

Check to see if there is any firing on the ranges, if you are going on the North Moor, by looking in the local papers, Post Offices or telephoning if you have any doubts. Watch out for the red flags flying during the day and the red lamps at night on several high points on the edge of the ranges. Remember that it is dangerous to pass the line of red and white posts marking the boundaries of the ranges when there is firing in progress.

Solo walking is a most exhilerating and worthwhile thing to do but obviously it has its dangers. Ideally your party should be three in number, from a safety point of view, so that in the event of an accident, one of you can go for help while the other stays with the injured person. I hope it will never happen to you, but if you do find yourself in trouble on Dartmoor with an injured person, or one of your party is suffering from hypothermia, or if somebody is lost you may have to call out the Dartmoor Rescue Group. To do this either ring 999 and ask to be put in touch with the Police or go to the nearest Police Station and they will call out the Rescue team. This is the normal proceedure in all mountainous areas when you need to mount a rescue operation.

Some advice I most certainly would not give for people walking in the mountains in other parts of Britain but on Dartmoor would be quite safe to use, would be to follow a stream or river down if you are really badly lost. It will take you off the moor to civilization and probably a telephone.

Finally always leave word with someone telling them where you are going and how long you reckon you will be. Better still, leave a written route card with details of your walk and estimated times. If you live or are staying away from the Dartmoor area and just drive here to walk for the day, it is a good idea to leave a note on the windscreen of your car, again with details of your route and the estimated time it will take you.

Using the Guide

In order, I hope, to make the using of this Guide as easy as possible I have grouped the walks into four large areas of Dartmoor.

1. The South Moor with the road from Ashburton to Tavistock being the northern boundary.
2. The triangular eastern section with the road from Ashburton to Two Bridges being the southern boundary and the road from Moretonhampstead to Two Bridges as the northern edge.
3. The north-eastern part of the North Moor with the Moretonhampstead to Two Bridges road as the southern limit and approximately the 60 Easting Grid line as the western edge.
4. The north-western part of the North Moor with the Two Bridges to Tavistock road as the southern boundary and again approximately the 60 Easting Grid line as the eastern limit.

Obviously some walks, especially on the North Moor, will just edge occasionally into the neighbouring area.

I shall call the areas;

          1. The South Moor.
          2. Widecombe Walks.
          3. The North East Moor.
          4. The North West Moor.

As I have explained there is little or no public transport for much of the year on Dartmoor, though it is possible sometimes to use the Pony Express and the Dartmoor Link. However, these services may not take you to the areas that I shall be suggesting as the starting places for some of the walks so I have assumed that most of you will be travelling by car. This means that most of the walks will be circular.

I have graded the walks firstly by length;

          Long;   12kms or more.
          Medium; 4kms to 12kms.
          Short;   under 4kms.

Secondly, I have classed the walks hard, moderate and easy, depending on the difficulty of the terrain, the climbing involved and the map reading and navigation skills involved. With the last, however, it is wise to remember that what may be easy on a clear day may become tricky if the mists come down.

I shall assume that you will be able to find your way to the starting points by car from the six figure map reference that I shall give, but I must admit that the maze of lanes, on the eastern edge of Dartmoor particularly, can be confusing!

I shall refer to lefts and rights as if you are following the correct direction of travel. But I shall refer to the true left and right banks of streams and rivers; i.e. as is you are looking downstream.

I think that you will find it a good idea to read up the walk and how to reach the starting point before you set out and refer to the map so that you have a good idea of where you will be going.

Do not forget to check the Firing Notices if you are setting off for a walk on the North Moor.

I shall not give the time that I think the walk will take, as each of you will need to work it out for yourself depending on the age and fitness of your party, and whether you want to wander gently exploring and looking as you go or put your head down and rush round as fast as you can go! I hope it will be the former!

Quite often you will be passing by places or objects to which I have referred in my Introductions to the Guide so you may need to check back to the relevant section, but I shall hope to add more information wherever possible and indeed introduce new topics of interest.

I need to say a word on the controversial subject of place names on Dartmoor. Sadly the Ordnance Survey have published many of them incorrectly on their maps of the area. However, even if it will incur the wrath of some erudite purists, I shall give the names as printed on the maps you will be using so as to avoid any confusion.

With nearly all the walks, I have made it possible to shorten them by cutting off corners and leading back onto the route at another place. Even if I have not indicated this in the description of the route, by studying the map you will be able to make your own cuts, I am sure, if you wish. Equally so you might well find that you can cut into a walk from a starting place of your own choice different to the one I have suggested. Also it is often quite possible to link into one walk from another and even end up at the starting place of that walk, if you can get someone to drive the car round! What I am really saying is that I hope that you will use this Guide as a basis for walks that you can work out for yourselves rather than following slavishly the exact routes I

Dartmoor Ponies near Hound Tor

have described, though obviously I hope you will follow some of my walks as they are all ones that I have enjoyed over the years.

I cannot begin to cover every inch of the moor and take you to every hidden corner. There are many interesting things to see that would not really make up a full worthwhile walk. I must leave you to find out about these other places yourselves and visit them when you have time.

Finally I hope that some of you who cannot walk or may not want to walk will also be able to use this Guide so that, with the aid of a map and what I have written, you will be able to come on some of the walks, in your imagination, and find out more about this extraordinary and fascinating place, Dartmoor.

All that remains now is for me to wish you safe, enjoyable, and interesting walking.

THE SOUTH MOOR

1. Bel Tor Corner, Dr. Blackall's Drive, New Bridge, Spitchwick, Leusdon. *(See map p.42)*

START. Large Car park. Bel Tor Corner. Map Ref. 695732, on the B3357 road from Ashburton to Two Bridges.
There is a Post Office and shop as well as the Tavistock Inn at Poundsgate or a snack bar and restaurant at Dartmeet both within a few kilometres of the start.
Medium; 6½ miles or 10.5kms. Easy.

The start at Bel Tor Corner is a fine though popular viewpoint and it is worth spending a few moments with your map identifying far away points. Now you should set off along the wall towards Mel Tor leaving Bel Tor on your left on the other side of the enclosure. A left turn between the walls will take you onto the start of Dr. Blackhall's Drive a track that was constructed over a hundred years ago so that this enterprising Doctor, who lived at Spitchwick Manor, could drive along it in his carriage and enjoy the view in all weathers.

As soon as the track emerges onto the open moorland again, it is worth diverting slightly right to climb Mel Tor. The view from here is superb and one of the most impressive on the edge of Dartmoor. Below you there is the deep, wooded, winding Double Dart Gorge. Look left and you will see the outskirts of Holne on the other side of the valley. Opposite, about 2kms away, there is the Venford reservoir and lower down and closer, the low, squat shape of Bench Tor or Benjy Tor to give it the old, correct name. Off to your right you can just make out the top of the rockface called Luckey Tor, which many people call Eagle Rock, almost down beside the river on its left bank nearly 200 metres below you.

If you can drag yourself away go back to the Drive and continue along it to Brake Corner below Aish Tor. Here the track swings left and you leave a quarry on your right. After the quarry you can either make towards the River Dart or better still continue along the Drive until you come to the main road and then turn right back along it for about 200 metres. In fact it is quite possible to cut this corner off and

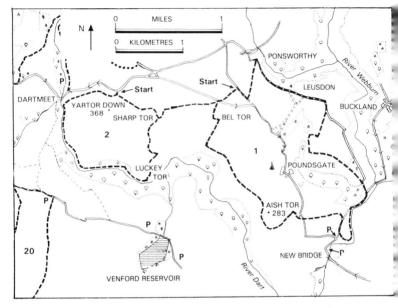

walk directly east from the Drive, across the road to Hannaford Manor and the main road, and onto the track that leads down to Leigh Tor. This is an interesting outcrop of rock and it will be obvious that you are off the true granite of Dartmoor. Here, at Leigh Tor, tourmaline has combined with quartz to produce a very hard rock called schorl. There are a few rock climbs here by the way. It is a good viewpoint and there is a fine feeling of height as you look down to the hairpin bends of the road and the great sweep of the river at Deeper Marsh.

Continue down the ridge via the path until you reach the road. It is worth turning right for 300 metres or so along the road until you are opposite the Car Parks before swinging left down to the river. You will arrive at a deep pool below some cliffs which is extremely popular in the summer as a swimming place and is often very crowded. Turn left now and follow the river downstream past several islands. Eventually the river and the road meet you and you should leave the bank and follow the road for some 300 metres to the fork where you must turn up left, signposted Lower Town. Soon there is a steep corner by some cottages and you now leave the road and follow the waymarked track through a conifer wood. You are now following The Two Moors Way

View from Bel Tor of the South Moor and Double Dart Gorge

for part of the route.

Both the 1:50,000 and particularly the 1:25,000 maps show the quite complicated rights of way where the path goes along three fields and meets the private road of Spitchwick House. By going right, along the road, to a gate into a field you will eventually find your way to Lower Town after going through another gate and following a hedge. At Lower Town turn left up the road past the 19th century Church of St.John Baptist. This is the only long part of the walk that is on a road but soon you will arrive at Leusdon Common where you will see, away to your left, what looks like a Bronze Age menhir; in fact it was put up in the 1977 Silver Jubilee year. You might like to divert to look at it but otherwise keep going along the road, leaving the old school on your left, towards Ponsworthy with the lovely, deep, wooded valley of the West Webbern below you on your right. On the bend turn left through Sweaton Farm and up a lane. Follow the directions on the signposts which will take you through a gate and over a stile to a small road. Turn right along this road until the open moor is reached and where you can walk along the wall. Aim at the corners of the walls, that you can see jutting out, cutting off the zig-zags, until you reach the main road at Bel Tor Corner where you started the walk.

2. **Sharp Tor, Rowbrook Farm, Double Dart Gorge, Dartmeet, Dartmeet Hill, The Coffin Stone.** *(See map p.42)*

START. Large Car Park. Bel Tor Corner. Map Ref.695732 or the large Car Park at the top of Dartmeet Hill Map Ref.681733, both on the B3357 road from Ashburton to Two Bridges.

There is a Post Office and shop as well as the Tavistock Inn at Poundsgate or a snack bar and restaurant at Dartmeet both within a few kilometres of the starts.

Medium; 4 miles or 6.5kms. Moderate.

Start 1. Follow the unfenced road west until it starts to turn south and then strike up to Sharp Tor ahead of you.

Start 2. Follow the path that leads towards Sharp Tor from the Car Park but do not go right to the bottom of Easdon Combe, instead contour round the head of the little valley, cross the stream and aim at the impressive Tor.

From the top of Sharp Tor you have magnificent views looking east and south-east right down to the coast across the South Hams. 200 metres below you the Double Dart Gorge can be seen with its interlocking spurs. On the opposite side of the wooded valley you can make out the low, squat shape of Bench Tor or Benjy Tor to give it the old, correct name.

To descend straight down to the road leading to Rowbrook Farm is an awkward, rocky route so you will find it easier to drop back down westwards to the Row Brook and then follow the stream down to the farm.

You will need to ask permission at the farm to pass through the gate marked 'Private. No right of way', but there is usually never any problem. Beyond this gate, after the barn wall, you will pass an intriguing number of old farm implements including an old binder for cutting corn and tying it into sheaves.

Walk straight down the field to another gate that leads out onto open land. Please do not forget to close it. The well defined path now descends to the right. Follow this steeply down to river level. To your left you will see the towering granite rockface of Luckey Tor. In fact this name is a corruption of Lookout Tor for it is said that smugglers used to pass this way and that the Tor made a good lookout for them to watch the Customs Men. It is also known as Eagle Rock from the days when eagles wheeled and soared over Dartmoor and, I presume, built their nests here. There are some hard rock climbs on the face.

It is worth going down to the river to look at the water roaring down

Dartmeet

through a narrow cleft and into Blackpool, a deep and mysterious basin.

Now turn right and follow the path up river on the true left bank. After a while the path becomes quite difficult where flood has washed sections of the bank away and exposed large platforms of granite. On the bend of the river and also the path, just before Combestone Island, keep a sharp lookout for a strange, stone-lined pit with long, low walls running from it. This is a type of vermin trap that drowned the predators caught in it unlike the other vermin traps (mentioned in the glossary) which used a trip catch to shut a slate gate so that the Warrener could kill the animals caught, himself.

Keep along the path until you reach the point where the East and the West Dart meet. Unless you are a gregarious person or are dying for a cup of tea you will probably wish to avoid this crowded, popular tourist spot! Keep then on the right side of the wall of the enclosure and at the far end do not go through the gate but turn right up the steep path on Yartor Down. The road swings away from the path but, as you climb, look away to your left and you will see a deep track between the road and where you are. This is one of the old ways across Dartmoor which crossed the rivers by the clapper bridges and linked important villages and towns.

Soon you should see a large, flat boulder beside the old track. This is the Coffin Stone and as the name suggests is where the bearers rested the coffins of people, who had died in the more remote parts of Dartmoor, as they carried them on their last journey to be buried in Widecombe churchyard. You will have experienced the steepness of the hill yourself so it will be easy for you to imagine the back-breaking task of carrying a coffin up here. They still had 6 kms to go! If you look closely you will see initials and crosses carved on this historic stone.

Continue up the path to the top of the hill to where your car will be waiting for you.

If you started at Bel Tor Corner, you can walk along the road to your car or follow the first part of this walk from the Car Park to Sharp Tor and then down directly to Bel Tor Corner.

3. Michelcombe, Sandy Way, Holne Ridge, Hapstead Ford, Chalk Ford. Scorriton. (Or back to Michelcombe.)

START. In the village of Michelcombe. Map Ref.696689. Please be careful to park without causing an obstruction or blocking gateways. There is a Post Office and shop at Holne and the Church House Inn where Archbishop Ramsey used to stay.
You will pass, or not as the case maybe, the Tradesman's Arms at Scorriton towards the end of the walk!
Medium. 6½ miles 10.5kms. Moderate.

This walk starts by heading west up the lane from the small village of Michelcombe. Just by a gate a track runs off north to Holne Moor by Great Combe. You go straight on. The lane now becomes a rocky track climbing quite steeply until you reach a gate called Lane Head. It is here that a path from the Mardle joins the track which is the alternative route for the return journey if you wish to miss out Scorriton. It is also at this gate that you move out from the enclosures onto the open moor.

A few hundred metres on you will pass over the dry bed of the leat of the Wheal Emma mine. If you look at the map you will see that it is a remarkable bit of engineering as it contours for miles round Holne Moor to above Venford Reservoir and beyond. However, away to your left the leat steepens to run down to the Mardle where the water was once used in the copper mines there.

From now on the track you are following is called the Sandy Way

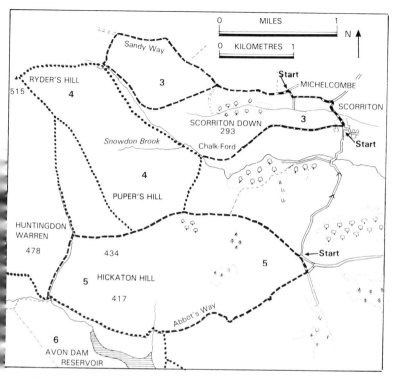

which is one of the ancient trackways of Dartmoor. It was probably used by early travellers going between towns as far distant as Ashburton and Tavistock. Certainly farmers and tinners used the track to move between Holne and Swincombe and on to Princetown. When French and American prisoners were held at the prison at Princetown many local people travelled there to barter with the prisoners and the Sandy Way was the easiest way to get there in the early 19th century from this south-east corner of the moor.

When you reach the disused tin mine workings with the deep gullies the Sandy Way peters out but in the old days it would have worked its way round Aune or Avon Head to Skir Hill, Ter Hill and then on; there are still traces of it.

You need now to aim towards Ryder's Hill, south-west, and drop down to Mardle Head and the tin workings there, just above Hapstead

Ford. The Ford is a river crossing again associated with ancient pathways on Dartmoor for travellers who wished to reach farms and villages further to the south. You should be able to get across the Mardle without difficulty here unless there has been heavy rain. There is, in fact, another ford about 1km downstream but if you have difficulties with Hapstead Ford, the lower one will also be tricky. If however, you wish to go back to Michelcombe you need to stay on the true left bank of the Mardle and, when you are more or less opposite Mardle Ring described in the next paragraph, the track begins to slant up the hill and crosses the dry Wheal Emma leat by a small bridge and reaches Lane Head where you can follow the lane back down to Michelcombe the way you came. This of course is a shorter walk by some 3kms.

If you stay with the longer walk the track now runs along the true right bank of the river until you reach Mardle Ring - marked as Homestead on the maps; this is a prehistoric enclosure with a hut circle in its upper part. From here the track stays high above the river until you cross Snowdon Brook and then on down to the bottom of the steep-sided valley of the Mardle.

Ignore the various other paths and make your way to Chalk Ford where there is a new footbridge. From here follow the obvious lane that climbs up through fields and then drops down to Scorriton.

All that remains now is to follow the small road past the Tradesman's Arms on your right, which is bound to be closed unless you have timed your walk very carefully, and after nearly 1km you will arrive back at Michelcombe.

The next three walks and Walk 3 have common ground so it would be possible to link some of them together and even end at the starting place of one of the others, if you have someone who would be willing to drive round and pick you up.

4. Scorriton, Chalk Ford, Hapstead Ford, Ryder's Hill, Snowdon, Pupers Hill, Lud Gate, Chalk Ford. *(See map p.47)*

START. In the village of Scorriton. Map Ref.704686. Please be careful to park without causing an obstruction or blocking gateways. There is a Post Office and shop at Holne and the Church House Inn. There is also the Trademan's Arms at Scorriton itself. Buckfastleigh is only 4 kms away with all the facilities offered by a small town.
Medium. 7½ miles. 12kms. Moderate

You start by setting off up the lane that runs west out of the village of Scorriton; it is the same lane that you might have come down if you completed Walk 3. It climbs quite rapidly to 256 metres below Scorriton Down. Do not take the track to the right through the gate but keep left down to Chalk Ford. You can cross the river here not by a ford but by the new footbridge. There used to be a clapper bridge here as this was an important route off the moor.

From the bottom of the steep valley of the Mardle you follow a track which runs westwards climbing up the hill. It is joined by various other paths but keep on until you cross Snowdon Brook flowing down from the tin workings higher up. The river Mardle is now well below you in the valley as you come, after a while, to Mardle Ring, marked Homestead on the maps, which is a prehistoric enclosure with a hut circle in its upper part.

Soon the path leads down to the river again and you will pass a ford and after 1km another one called Hapstead Ford. This is on one of the ancient pathways across Dartmoor for travellers who wished to cross the river to reach farms and villages to the south-east of the moor. Do not cross the river but follow on up through fairly marshy ground to the remains of the tin workings and the boundary stones to the cairn and Triangulation Point on Ryder's Hill which also has the name Petre's Bound Stone. Your height now is 515 metres.

Ryder's Hill has some other splendid names. In 1240 they carried out what was called The Perambulations of the Forest of Dartmoor which was to define and draw up the boundaries. In that they used the names Battyshull or Knattleburroughe for this important high point. Petre's Bound Stone and Petre-on-the-Mount refer to the stones marking the boundaries of the lands of Sir William Petre's Manor of Brent which ran up to Ryder's Hill. From here you get the most wonderful views across the South Hams down to the coast. On a clear day away to the east you will see Portland Bill and to the south-west it is said you can see the Lizard in Cornwall, though I have never been lucky enough to do this.

Now you must strike south-east to another boundary stone at the head of Wellabrook Girt and you have a choice of route.
1. You can follow down, through the maze of gullies and old tin workings, past Higher Huntingdon Corner and the end of Gibby Beam to just below the enclosures and ruins of the old Huntingdon Warren House and take the track that runs east towards Lud Gate.
2. You can aim slightly left to Snowdon. There are four cairns here in a line running north-south. The most northerly one is the smallest while the southerly one is the largest.

If you walk south now you will pass the head of Gibby Beam (an old tin working) and come soon to Pupers Hill. There are three masses of rock known as Pupers Rock, Inner Pupers and Outer Pupers. It appears that these are the remains of three pipers who were turned to stone for playing their pipes and dancing on the Sabbath! A legend that turns up in Cornwall though it is the Fiddlers and the Merry Maidens there.

If you look south-south-east you will see an ancient reave running down to Water Oak Corner marking the boundary of Buckfastleigh Moor. Follow the reave down to where it crosses the old Huntingdon track. Turn left or east down the track to Lud Gate, where one of the old routes came onto the moor. From here turn more or less north and keeping the walls on your right you will come back, after just over ½km, to Chalk Ford and then by the lane to Scorriton.

5. Cross Furzes, Water Oak Corner, Huntingdon Cross, Huntingdon Warren, Lud Gate. This is part of the Abbot's Way.
(See map p.47)

START.   Cross Furzes. Map Ref. 700666. It is possible to park off the road without causing an obstruction in this area.

Buckfastleigh is about 4kms away with all the facilities of a small town.

Medium.   6 miles.   9.5kms.   Moderate.

I shall return to the subject of the Abbot's Way later on in this Guide when I shall trace the whole route across Dartmoor. For now, however, you start this walk by setting off down the rocky lane that runs south-west, deep below the hedges from the cross roads, and which steepens as it reaches Dean Barn. I love these deep, dank lanes on the edge of Dartmoor that run through a tunnel of trees down to sparkling streams.

There is a fine clapper bridge over the Dean Burn with the dates 1705 and 1735 carved on it with various other initials. There is also a ford here for animals who might find the bridge too difficult.

You must now branch right through a gate and past an ancient mossy bank with gnarled beech trees growing on it. From here the track is marked and do not be tempted, a little later on, to take the lower path, though you can get through that way. Now climb quite steeply up to Lamb's Down where the path flattens out and you emerge into the large, grassy enclosures of what was Lamb's Down Farm with more beech trees and banks to your right. The path crosses a small stream by taking a wide bend and finally you climb on to reach Water Oak Corner by a few stunted pine trees. Go through a gate and you will emerge on the open moor.

To begin with the track is not clear but you need to walk slightly south of west and gain height and you should soon see the direction you need to go. Before you get too far over the hill it is worth pausing and having a look back at the view. You can just see Widecombe Church and of course down to the coast and the estuary of the Teign. Once over the shoulder of Gripper's Hill you will see the huge 50 acre expanse of the Avon Reservoir built in the 1950's more or less ahead of you. At the bottom of the gentle slope, about 400 metres away, you must look for Brookhill Ford over the stream of that name. From here on the track becomes obvious and wide again.

Immediately on the right of the track a few hundred metres after the ford and also away down beside the water of the reservoir itself are several most interesting late Bronze Age enclosures, pounds and hut circles. It is well worth pausing here to wander round and look at them. As so often happens when dams and reservoirs are built and forests are planted many exceptional archaeological sites disappear beneath the waters or are lost in thick forest. Luckily a lot of work was done before the Avon Dam was built and many artefacts were rescued. However, both Bronze Age and medieval buildings and enclosures are now under the waters of this reservoir.

From here on you will find the route easy to follow along the track but it has been eroded quite badly in places and is very rocky. After about 1 km you will see the Western Wella Brook flowing down from the north to join the River Avon. The area away to your left, by the Avon as it flows down to the reservoir, goes by the splendid name of Bishop's Meads; this could be a link with the monks of Buckfast Abbey who grazed animals and built farmsteads in this area in medieval times, but the old name for the area is Busshe Mead possibly a corruption of Bishop.

On the north side of the confluence stands Huntingdon Cross. It was put up in the 1550's to mark the boundaries of the Manor of Brent belonging to Sir William Petrie or to mark a route across the moor as many of the other crosses do. You can get across the Wella Brook here if you wish to look at the cross but it may result in wet feet! You would probably be better off staying on the true left bank of the Wella Brook and walking north but, if you can get across, it might be worth looking for the low banks of the artificial burrows for breeding rabbits, built by the warreners who lived at Huntingdon Warren; there are quite a number of them on the slope above the true right bank and are called

Artificial rabbit burrow or buries near Ditsworthy Warren

Pillow Mounds on the maps. Higher up still there are several little hut circles that are not Bronze Age. They could be some form of shelter either for the tinners who worked in this area or the Warreners.

If you keep on going up the left bank of the stream now you will soon come to a long, narrow building that contained a water-wheel that was used to work a pump to clear water from the New Huntingdon Tin Mines some way away. A little further on and nearer the stream, in a gully, there is another small, roofless building known as Keble Martin's Chapel. It was built in 1909 by a well known clergyman, Keble Martin, with the help of his brother when they used to camp in this area as boys and young men. Keble Martin later became famous as the author and illustrator of *The Concise British Flora.* The little chapel has seats at one end and a granite pillar at the other with a cross carved on it. It is said that as well as personal worship the chapel was apparently used once for baptising the child of the warrener who lived up the valley.

Across on the other side of the valley you can see the remains of the old Huntingdon Warren House with the enclosures and paddocks all round it and, of course, a great many of the artificial burrows for the rabbits. Just after the war I remember that the house was still standing and I had dreams of renovating it and living there! I think that I would have had just as hard a life as the farmers and warreners who were here from before the seventeenth century. It is a lovely but remote and lonely place that in the old days would have required a journey of several hours over the track to Lud Gate that runs east from here to get to shops and the markets.

It is this track that you must now follow uphill, first passing through the ancient reave from Pupers Hill to Water Oak Corner, and then on down to Lud Gate.

Until recently a relative of the last farmer and warrener to dwell at Huntingdon Warren House, called Michelmore, lived in the small house to the left just through Lud Gate, an old moorgate on one of the ancient trackways to Dartmoor.

From here you keep down the lane past the entrance to Hayford Hall and then follow the road back to the starting place at Cross Furzes.

6. Shipley Bridge, Avon Dam, Eastern White Barrow, Western White Barrow, Crossways, Red Lake China Clay Works, Broad Falls, Huntingdon Warren House, Gripper's Hill, Dockwell Ridge, Shipley Tor.

START. Shipley Bridge. Map Ref.681629. Large Car Park.
South Brent is 4 kms away with all the facilites of a small town.
Toilets at Shipley Bridge from spring to autumn and probably Ice Cream vans!
Medium. 11 miles. 17.7 kms. Hard.

The start of this walk is a beautiful but popular place, especially during the summer months when hundreds flock here to stroll and picnic by the river.

Those of you who are interested in industrial archaeology may be intrigued by the remains found around the car park of the nineteenth century naphtha distillery, which was later taken over and used by a china clay company. Naphtha is an oil produced from peat and there were several attempts to make its production a viable industry on Dartmoor; Rattlebrook Peat Works on the north moor is another example. When the naphtha buildings were taken over by the china clay industry large filters and settling pits were built which still remain.

The road striking north to the Avon Dam is the route you must take

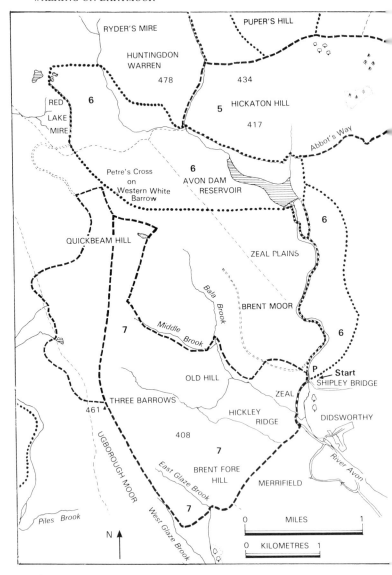

now. After a while you will see a small side road running off and back to the left which leads to the Avon Filtration Station. Just here there is a small granite block called the Hunters' Stone. If you look closely you will be able to make out the names Treby, Trelawny and Bulteel carved on the sides and Carew on the top. These apparently are the names of four local men who rode to hounds and were well-known huntsmen in Victorian times. The memorial was commissioned by the one-time owner of Brent Moor House, a Mr. Mohun-Harris, which is a little further up the road. The grounds of the house are still very beautiful with rhododendrons and it is worth coming here when they are in flower. On the left you may just see another memorial, this time of a small girl, the daughter of a Mr. Meynell who also lived at Brent Moor House at one time. Nothing remains of the house itself now except the foundations but earlier after private use it had been a Youth Hostel. When the dam was built it was no longer used for this and fell into decay. As this is such a popular valley it became a danger to visitors who used to explore the ruins and it had to be demolished by the Royal Marines.

From here the track emerges out into open country. You have steep slopes on either side going up to Black Tor on the left and Dockwell Ridge on the right. Soon the road crosses over a bridge to the other side of the river (the true left bank) and the slightly flatter area is known as Woolholes which was a good hiding ground for foxes.

The river is now running in a small canyon and on the map you will see that this section is called Long-a-Traw which must be a corruption of Long Trough.

There is another splendid local legend about a certain John Dill who was supposed to have jumped the river here on horseback hotly pursued by the farmer from whom he had stolen the horse! He was carrying at the time, it appears, smuggled goods for distribution in nearby villages!

Ahead now lies the wall of the Avon Dam which was built in the 1950's. The road takes another turn and crosses back over the river to the right bank. Follow the road to its end and take the path steeply up to the western end of the dam. From here you have to climb steeply up towards the west over open moorland and soon you will see, almost like a surfacing U-Boat, the huge shape of Eastern White Barrow rearing up out of the moor! It is an amazing example of a Bronze Age Burial Mound but it is doubtful if the unusual round 'conning tower' on the top was added by prehistoric man. The whole Barrow is about 76 metres long and 10 metres high and must contain thousands of tons of rock. The work involved in building such a tomb is astonishing and it must have been the last resting place of some important local warrior or chief. Eastern White Barrow was one of the boundaries used on the Perambulation of 1240 and later in this Guide I shall return to this subject as a possible much longer walk.

You must now strike out towards the north-west following a path for a while along the ridge for 1km to Western White Barrow. When you reach the cairn you will find not only the heap of rocks but the remains of a small building with also a stone post sticking up. This is what is known as Petre's Cross and accounts for why the 1:25,000 maps name the cairn 'Petre's Cross on Western White Barrow'. As you might expect, for this is Dartmoor, there is a story as to why there are the remains of a nineteenth century hut with a medieval cross sticking out of it, on a Bronze Age Barrow!

How the Bronze Age Burial Mound got there presents no problem except wonder at the work involved. Petre's Cross was put there in the sixteenth century for a good reason and that was to mark the boundary of Sir William Petre's Manor of Brent which came up onto the moor as far as here. The little hut then was the last addition for it was built in 1847 by men who worked at the peat works at Red Lake cutting peat for the naphtha distillery. Most of them lived at or near Brent and went home at weekends but during the week they needed a shelter near their work so they decided to construct a little hut, using the stones from the Barrow. When they reached the stage of requiring a long lintel to go above the fireplace they remembered Petre's Cross, knocked it down, smashed off the arms of the cross and used it as part of their hut. Accounts tells of how they slept on beds of dried bracken and heather under a slate roof and were not afraid to poach rabbits from Huntingdon Warren not far away. When the naphtha distillery closed down the men were out of work and no longer needed their hut which soon fell into decay. Much later the old cross was discovered in the ruins and was once again put up as a boundary marker, the only trouble being that it was placed upside down!

If you now walk west you will soon come to a shallow trench about six feet wide. This is all that remains of the Zeal Tor Tramway that carried the peat cut up here down to Shipley. All around this area you will see the rectangular peat ties as they were called. Turn right and follow the old tramway towards the north-west. Just down on your left you will see a large number of ruined relics from the china clay industry that flourished here in the nineteenth century and into this century. These are filter beds and settling traps that were used in the production of kaolin. You may want to wander down and have a look round them.

If not, keep on along the tramway past Crossways and after a while you will come to the much larger track of the Redlake Mineral Railway which runs southwards over 11kms to near the village of Bittaford, on the edge of the moor, where there was a drying plant. Obviously all the rails and sleepers have gone but the ballast remains in some sections and it is broad, firm track for a lot of its length. If you follow the track of this old railway northwards you will soon arrive at the large, conical spoil tip that has been visible for some time. This is the site of the Redlake China Clay Works. As well as the spoil tip there are three man-made lakes which are the flooded pits from which they dug the clay. The spoil tip by the way has proved for me, quite often, a most useful landmark when navigating in poor visibility in this area. I have been quite relieved to see it looming out of the mist! A good view can be had from the top of the tip if you have the energy to climb up there!

The china clay industry was established here in 1910 and was worked until 1932. Like the peat cutters on Western White Barrow the workers, nearly 100 of them, lived in this remote spot.

From the tip you now walk east and follow a small valley back down to the River Avon at Broad Falls where the river plunges down over many rocks. You should be able to get across the river without any difficulty and downstream, not far from the falls, you will see, on the true left bank, the remains of a tinner's blowing house. Although the actual building is in ruins you can make out the wheelpit, the leat which brought the water to power the wheel, the furnace and even a mortar for crushing the ore.

You have a choice of routes now. You can either continue on down the river through the area known as Stoney Girt and then past the little clapper bridge, said to have been built by the warreners, until you reach Huntingdon Cross. Or you can climb the hill eastwards for a short distance until you come to the dried-up course of an old leat which contours round the hill. If you follow this you see below you, to your right, two ancient enclosures and hut circles and also some other small, roofless, round huts. These are not prehistoric but it has been suggested that they were lookouts where the warrener could keep an eye out, in comparative comfort, for poachers coming down from the hut of Western White Barrow and even Redlake Clay Works to steal rabbits. Doubtless they crossed the Avon by the little clapper bridge that he had so conveniently built for them! Details of all this area of Huntingdon and points of interest to be seen can be found in the account of Walk 5.

If you wish you can now cut steeply down the hill to Huntingdon

Cross or go further to the north to the ruins of the old Warren House and off the moor at Lud Gate. However, if you want to make the circuit then you need to find a way across the Western Wella Brook. There are various fords marked on the map for both this stream and the Avon, but depending on the amount of water, I leave it to you to find the best way across!

On the true left bank of the Avon you will find the well-marked track of the Abbot's Way running south-east. Once you have passed over the ford on Brockhill Stream you can then contour round the slope, just above the reservoir, to the eastern end of the Avon Dam and then down a track through a settlement until you reach the road that you came up from Shipley Bridge at the start of this walk.

If you are feeling strong then you might like to slant up south-east and around Smallbrook Plains and over the flat area of the ridge known as Peathy's Path and Dockwell Ridge and then on down past Shipley Tor to the Car Park at Shipley Bridge to avoid retracing your outward route along the road.

7. Shipley Bridge, Zeal, Ball Gate, Glasscombe Corner, Three Barrows, Two Moors Way via Redlake Mineral Railway Track (or Quickbeam Hill), Western White Barrow, Petre's Pits, Bala Brook. *(See map p.54)*

START Shipley Bridge. Map Ref. 681629. Large Car Park.
South Brent is 4kms away with all the facilities of a small town. Toilets at Shipley Bridge from spring to autumn and probably ice cream vans!
Moderate. 8¾ miles. 14kms. via the Redlake Track. 7½ miles.
12kms via Quickbeam Hill. Hard.

The details for the area round the actual start of this walk can be found in Walk 6, but instead of setting off up the track north to the Avon Dam you must start by walking down the road that runs southwards. You will soon come to Zeal Bridge that crosses the Bala Brook and then a gate and a marked footpath. You must take this steep, rocky track, through the gate, which is called Diamond Lane. History relates that a coach and four were driven up here one day probably by a Devon version of Squire Mytton from Shropshire! After the steep climb the track flattens out a little and runs through enclosures and then finally onto the open moor.

Ahead you will soon see another wall and a large gateway. This is Ball Gate. Ball refers to Corringdon Ball and means a rounded hill.

This gate is on yet another of the ancient trackways of Dartmoor which connects the south-eastern part of the moor with further north and joins the Abbot's Way. The section here and indeed all along its length is often called the Jobbers' Path or, as the old moormen called it, the Joblers' Path. The name Jobbers comes from the woollen industry that flourished in this corner of Devon for centuries. A yarn jobber was a man who bought and sold wool and used the old trackways on Dartmoor for his packhorses carrying the sacks from the farmers down to the mills. The monks at Buckfast, Buckland and Tavistock Abbeys were Cistercians in medieval times and they were great traders and farmers and I am sure they also used this track that links with the Abbot's Way, for carrying wool.

Quite close to Ball Gate you will see to your right a long mound of earth called Long Barrow. It is claimed that this is a Neolithic burial chamber from before the Bronze Age but most archaeologists agree that while Neolithic man may well have come up onto the moor he left behind no evidence of his living and dying here.

You must now follow the wall on your left and as the land begins to drop down to the East Glaze Brook you will see, away to your right, a number of stones and stone rows that continue for quite a distance. These are from the Bronze Age. Once past the stone rows you descend a little again, this time to the West Glaze Brook and Glasscombe Corner.

There is a vast amount of evidence of the tinners in this area with their spoil tips and gullies and it might interest you to wander round looking at the remains. Away to the west is another 'Homestead' which is a Bronze Age enclosure and many other stone rows and cairns, all marked on the map. However, you should now turn north-west and aim towards Three Barrows. You should soon come across the long reave that runs N.N.W./S.S.E. and this will lead you to the summit.

Three Barrows has many different names. Threberis, Triborough even Tre Boroughs! As the name suggests there are, of course, three cairns or burial mounds here. Once again this is a marvellous viewpoint both over the moor itself and away over the South Hams.

From here you can either walk west for some 300 metres until you find the disused track of the old Redlake Mineral Railway or you can aim along the reave towards the north-north-west and then, when it peters out, turn further north and strike out towards Quickbeam Hill and Petre's Cross on Western White Barrows.

If you follow the disused track it is easier walking but a little bit further as the track twists and turns. You will be on the Two Moors

Way which links Dartmoor with Exmoor. This again is one of the old tracks used in the past and parts of it are called the Mariners' Way because it linked Dartmouth with Bideford and was used by sailors walking from one port to the other looking for another ship to join. On the track you will pass the remains and ruins of the old China Clay industry that was carried on up here in this remote spot until the 1930's. On your right you will see one of the man-made lakes which are the flooded pits from which they dug the china clay. There are also various ruins of buildings and settling tanks. If you want a few more details of this industry you will find them in Walk 6.

If you have come across the moor you should strike a shallow trough running north-west/south-east just before you reach Petre's Cross on Western White Barrow.

If you are following the disused railway track you will have to strike uphill to the east for just over 400 metres about 300 metres before you come to the large area of filter tanks and settling pits on your right - before the track swings gently further round to the west.

Again if you aim at Western White Barrow you should come to the trough first. (Details about this trough and indeed Petre's Cross and White Barrow are all found in Walk 6.)

You must follow this trough, which was part of the Zeal Tor Tramway for carrying peat down to Shipley for the naphtha works, south-east. Not much remains now but occasionally you will see the granite sleepers and milestones. Soon you will see to your right, not far from the track, a wide but fairly shallow valley, marked on the map as Petre's Pit. This is another area where China Clay was dug to be taken down to Shipley Bridge. Walk down to the head of the Pit and then strike south over a fairly flat area, leaving Knatta Barrow on your left. You should soon be able to see the beginnings of the little valley that has the source of the Middle Brook in it. Right at the head of this valley there is the ruin of a small building marked on the 1:25,000 maps. This is known as Uncle Ab's House and apparently this old building used to be the stables for the horses used in the Red Lake Peat Works. On a granite block lying near the ruin you will see carved the date 1809 and the initials C.B. (Obviously if you had wished to shorten this walk you could have come straight across here from the section where you were walking from Three Barrows to Quickbeam Hill.) This ruin is also known as Petre's Pits House and the valley of the Middle Brook below the house is called Petre's Pits Bottom and it is down this valley you must go.

You are now in another area that has a great many things to look at and look for and you may be just content to wander at will seeing what you can find. There are many Bronze Age enclosures and huts and you will also see a large number of the ruins and works left behind by the tinners. On the north or true left bank of Middle Brook you will see ruined buildings that were probably used for the water-wheel and the crushing mills for the tin ore. On the opposite side of the valley there is an enclosure with hut circles in it and, set into the wall, another small building which was probably constructed by the tinners using the stones from the prehistoric remains. These little huts are found all over Dartmoor and the tinners probably used them for storing their tools, even the ingots of tin. It has been suggested that there was quite a good 'black market' for tin and they may have used some of these remote little huts to hide ingots to avoid the tax! Another such bee-hive can be seen further downstream near the next enclosure which has its north wall missing.

If you follow the Middle Brook down you will come soon to Bala Brook flowing down from Petre's Pit. Cross the stream carefully; you may have to go upstream a little to look for a suitable place. Once across, walk down the true left bank and you soon find yourself in another area of Bronze Age enclosures and hut circles near a wire fence. Next to one of the groups of hut circles you will see more of the small bee-hive huts that have been constructed probably by the tinners, but they are much smaller than the early ones you saw on the Middle Brook. I can find no explanation as to why they were built.

From here you will have to walk towards the east and follow a wall uphill until you come back to the old Zeal Tor Tramway you left at Petre's Pit. Follow the tramway to the road that leads to the Avon Filtration Station. Cross over the road and drop steeply down back to the car park at Shipley Bridge.

8. New Waste, Erme Valley, Piles Copse, Downing's House, The Dancers, Erme Plains, Erme Head, Langcombe Hill, Yealm Head, Yealm Steps, Stalldown Barrow, Hillson's House.

START. New Waste. Map Ref. 6256ll. Park off the track inside the moor gate.
Cornwood is 1.5kms away with all the facilities of a small village.
Long. 12 miles. 18.3kms. Hard. (There are possibilities of shortening this walk by cutting off to the west at several points to link up with the last part of the complete walk.)

Set off along the concrete track towards the reservoir and Water

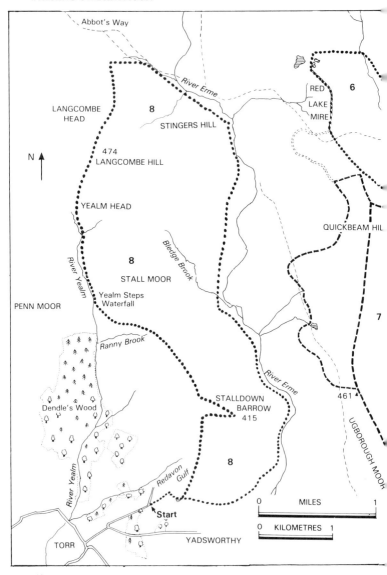

Treatment Works. There is no access through the Works so you must turn right along the railings to keep outside. It gets very wet below the little reservoir so keep well away from the fence. Beyond the boundary of the Works you will see the moorland wall with a gate that leads onto the open moor. Go through the gate and you will soon find the track which swings round the edge of the open moor with enclosures well below you called Yadsworthy Waste. Waste being the name on the south moor meaning a Newtake.

You could also start the walk by not going up as far as the Works but by cutting diagonally across the marshy land west-north-west to find the gate onto the open moor.

The track runs through an area of a great many Bronze Age enclosures and hut circles that are well worth exploring.

As you start to turn north you will soon see the River Erme below you in the steep-sided valley and on the opposite side of the valley, on the true left bank of the Erme, lies Piles Copse. This is one of the three ancient primeval oak woods on Dartmoor; the other two being Wistman's Wood and Black-a-Tor Copse which is the largest. There is information about these woods in the part of the Guide which deals with the flora. The river is quite wide here but, if you can find a way across without getting too wet, you might like to wander round in Piles Copse as these ancient woodlands are unique and well worth a visit.

Follow the track on now as it gently climbs up the valley above the river. Again on the far side, the left bank, you will see more enclosures and hut circles.

Where the fast flowing stream called Downing's Brook comes down from the left there is one of the best examples of a medieval tinners' beehive hut with its domed roof. It is called Downing's House on the map but it was also known as Smugglers' Hole and might well have been a hiding place for contraband.

You could, if you wished, cut the walk short here by turning west up Downing's Brook and later swinging south to Stalldown Barrow and completing just the last part of the walk by Hillson's House.

However, if you are feeling strong, keep going up the Erme because you will pass through some of the most interesting tin mining and prehistoric areas on Dartmoor. You will also be right in the remote heart of the South Moor and feel the real loneliness of true Dartmoor.

After a while, as you walk north, the track comes to an end by some ruins and now I will have to leave it to you to find your best route up the river. You will get quite a feeling of being in the bottom of a deep valley and therefore there are not many distant views at this stage;

they are to come later.

If you look at the map you will see that there are a great many remains of tinners' huts and blowing houses to be seen as well as numerous enclosures and hut circles, the latter particularly after crossing Bledge Brook. It is worth a steep climb of about 30 metres height up the hill ½km after Bledge Brook to a maze of enclosures and hut circles. Just beyond them, about 150 metres away to the north, you will find one of the most outstanding stone circles on Dartmoor. It is known as the Dancers and also Kiss-in-the-Ring and, as we find all over Britain, but particularly in the old Celtic regions, there are legends associated with such stone circles that tell of wicked maidens being turned to stone for dancing on the Sabbath and worse, if the other name is true!! There were 26 of them here apparently up to no good, ranging in height from 2½ feet to 5 feet. From this cairn circle, as it is called, which marked the burial place of some Bronze Age Chief you will see the start of the longest stone row in Britain and in the world. In fact it is probably the end of the row as they usually led to a burial site. From here it stretches more or less north, crosses the River Erme near Erme Pound and almost reaches Green Hill over 2½ miles or 4kms away. You can either drop back down to the river or follow the row to the river near Erme Pound.

I seem to be suggesting that you cross the river quite often but obviously it depends on the flow of water, and I am afraid that on winter walks it may well be impossible, but if you can get across, it is worth looking at Erme Pound. This was a Drift Pound where animals were driven during the gathering but there is evidence of this site being used both as a dwelling area and a pound for animals for many thousands of years. Grim's Pound, which I hope you will visit on another walk, was used more as a permanent settlement where the inhabitants drove their animals inside the surrounding walls at night for protection and where they also lived themselves. Both date from the Bronze Age. Even if you cannot get across the river you can clearly see the Pound.

You should continue on up the river now, past the area known as The Meadow. You will see to your right and on the other side of the river the very marshy and wet valley of Red Lake Mire. I have a friend who went into this mire on horseback and the horse sank in so deeply that he had to stand on the saddle and leap for safety! He had to walk many miles to get help and they only got the horse out by using a block and tackle. *This is one place where I shall not suggest that you cross the river to have a look!*

Here the river swings north-west by Dry Lake Ford to the north

Yealm Steps

Pile's Copse

and Hortonsford Bottom on your left, to the south. The name Horton comes from the fact that a local farmer of that name used to graze his cattle here. After 1km. Blacklane Brook comes in from the north where there is a ford. I keep on wanting to add extra sections to the walks as there are so many things that I think would interest you. As it stands, this is one of the longest walks I shall be including in the Guide but if I mention two other points of interest near here now, I can leave it to you to decide whether you have time to look for them and are feeling strong and fit enough to add another kilometre or so to the walk!

Another river then comes in from the north and is called Blacklane Brook. This corner has the name Wollake. You must now turn up this valley northwards. At this stage it is probably best to stay on the true right bank of the brook especially if you would like to try to find Grant's Pot. This is a strange pit with a short tunnel at the north end, probably the remains of some mining activity. It is about ½km. from the confluence of the brook with the Erme and is about 100 metres from and above the stream on level ground just before the bend. A well marked path leads to and from it. It is quite easy to enter the tunnel and there is a letter box set into the right hand wall. Map Ref. 629671. On the left bank of Blacklane Brook and another 200 metres

Mouldstone in Blowing House on Yealm

or so further north from Grant's Pot and about 150 metres from the little river there is Phillpotts' Cave. You will see the large, low slab of rock on the hillside and if you walk up there you will discover that you can get right under the huge boulder into quite a large cavity. A small wall has been built on the north side to give more shelter. There are two explanations for the name. One is that it is said that Eden Phillpotts the writer of so many books with Dartmoor background used to come here and even spend nights sleeping in the snug cave. The other is that a Tony Phillpotts, a hunt servant, used the cave to hide food and drink to be distributed when the local hunt met in this area.

Back to the main walk. You are now approaching one of the most intensely mined areas of Dartmoor. The whole valley is a fantastic mass of spoil heaps and gullies where the ancient tinners carried out their open workings and streamings. Erme Pits is a good name. There are the remains of two buildings also to be seen and you may have noticed a great slab of granite, as you came up the valley, called the Table Stone. In 1672 there was mention of Armed Pits which was well known for producing an ore called zill tin. This name comes from the fact that the Erme was often called the Arme and even Irm.

Just at the far end of Erme Pits the infant river rises at Erme Head but the whole area is very marshy and it is hard to pinpoint the exact

Stone row on Stalldown Barrow

source. You must now climb up the hill to the south for a height of some 40 metres to an ancient Mound and Boundary Stone. It is a fairly flat and undulating section of moorland here. Keep going south until you should see slightly west of south, after Langcombe Hill, the source of the Yealm, Yealm Head, nestling in the shallow valley. Soon though the sides of the valley steepen and you follow the river down, staying on the east or true left bank. After just over 1km, on the right bank of the Yealm, there are the ruins of a blowing house that has a granite mould stone nearby. Another river crossing is called for if you wish to see it! There is another blowing house further downstream however.

A few hundred metres after the hut the river flows down in a series of lovely waterfalls at Yealm Steps. The view from the top of the small cliff here is splendid. There is a steep path down the cliff on the east or left bank of the river.

Keep on down the valley until you come to the second tinners' blowing house which is quite difficult to find. It is worth hunting about as there are two mould stones here that were used for forming tin ingots.

If you wish to look at more enclosures and hut circles you can climb steeply up a height of 50 metres in a north-easterly direction but you

Downing's House (a tinner's beehive hut)

may prefer to contour round without losing height below the enclosures I have just mentioned to the head of Ranny Brook, a side stream flowing down from the north-east.

Once at the head of the shallow valley aim east until you come to the plateau with rising ground to the south. You must turn south now and climb towards what appears to be a large number of other walkers coming over the horizon from Stalldon Barrow. After about 1km. you will discover that the 'walkers' are in fact a very fine stone row with some of the stones or menhirs over two metres high and the whole row nearly ½km. long standing on the summit plateau. There are also quite a number of cairns hereabouts.

Further east and on the highest point at 415 metres there is another cairn and what appears to be a ruined building on it. It is marked as Hillson's House on the map. 'Son of the hill' seems an appropriate name, for the story goes that a baby boy was discovered lying out on Stall Moor and the little foundling was adopted by some local people and given the name Hillson. Later in life, the story goes on, he returned to Stall Moor, where he had been found, and built the little hut that you are looking at, where he dwelt and earned a living by making eight day clocks! A remarkable story but as I have said before this is Dartmoor!

It is all downhill now off Stalldown Barrow south-west to New Waste and the end of the walk.

9. Cadover Bridge, Trowlesworthy Warren House, Trowlesworthy Tors, Hen Tor, Shavercombe Head, Shell Top, Penn Beacon.

START. Near Cadover Bridge. Map Ref. 555646. There is plenty of space in this area to park off the road
Shaugh Prior is 2.5kms. away with all the facilities of a small village. Ice cream vans park at Cadover Bridge in the summer and at weekends.
Medium. 8¼ miles. 13.8kms. Moderate

The start at Cadover Bridge is a popular place as there is a large open area near the River Plym where people can picnic and swim. The name is interesting because you might assume that it meant that there was a way over a river called the Cad but the name Plym or Plymma had been known from before 1291. But apparently there had been a battle near here in Celtic times and cad is a Celtic word meaning a slaughter or conflict.

However, you must set off south-east along the track that runs on the true left bank of the Plym about 200 metres from Cadover Bridge. You are here right on the very edge of the boundary of the Dartmoor National Park. Soon you will come to a smaller stream that joins the Plym from your right. This is the Blacka Brook which you may follow down on your return at the end of the walk.

For now, cross the bridge over the brook and follow the track towards Trowlesworthy Warren House. There are old pounds and hut circles to your left. As you will read in the Glossary of the Dartmoor Terms a Warren House was a farm where they bred rabbits on a commercial basis. Usually near the Warren Houses on Dartmoor you can see the artificial burrows that were built for the rabbits. Trowlesworthy is one of the oldest on the moor; mention is made of it in medieval times when the deeds were owned by a Sampson de Traylesworthy.

You must follow the left-hand branch of the track round the end of the house and then it turns right towards the open moor and the tors. All this area and indeed Trowlesworthy Warren House itself is owned by the National Trust and there is a Nature Trail nearby. The high-walled yard that hides the house was where the warreners kept their

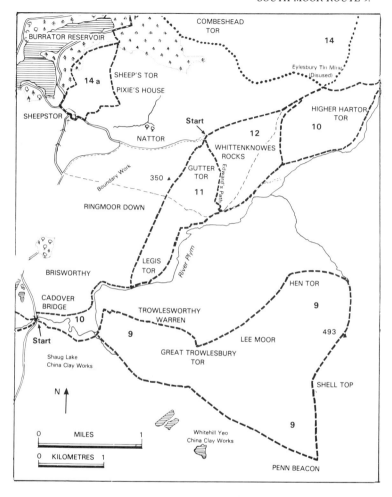

dogs and I shall write more about these yards when one of the walks visits Ditsworthy Warren House.

Climb gently up the track which soon crosses the Lee Moor Leat by a clapper bridge. This leat which provides water for the nearby china clay works has a great many small bridges over it. You must aim south east diagonally up the hill to Trowlesworthy Tors. If you wish you can contour round the hill a little and visit some of the enclosures and hut circles below the tors.

Back on route you will first pass Little Trowlesworthy Tor and then after a few hundred metres you will come to Great Trowlesworthy Tor.

All around here you will find signs of man's work. The granite is of a fine red colour in this stretch of moor and you can see many pits and dips where they quarried the stone. Also there are several blocks that were partly dressed but never finished. One such block is most interesting being circular and about 1.5 metres high. It was intended as a base for some monument but either it was never needed or nobody could work out a way to move it away!

From the tors you must walk north-east passing over the stream with the strange name of Spanish Lake. I cannot find out why it has this name. Your next point is Hen Tor, unusual in that it is on the side of the hill rather than on the top as most of the other tors are. A mass of clitter is found below.

Further down the hill from Hen Tor between four and five hundred metres away there are a great many enclosures and hut circles. But there was also a farm here in more recent times called Hen Tor Farm and there are ruins of the buildings to be seen mixed up with the prehistoric pounds and huts. In the last half of the eighteenth century this land was owned and cleared by a man called Nicolls and it is said that as many as ten oxen were used for ploughing and other work on this remote farm.

If you are feeling strong you can now climb south-east slowly and steadily straight towards the Triangulation Point at 492 metres. It gains a vertical height of 90 metres in about 1km. Or you may prefer to do it more gently and aim first just north of west to Shavercombe Head and then swing south to Point 492. It was here in this area that a bronze dagger was found in 1892 by a man cutting peat.

You must go gently down the ridge, more or less south-west to Shell Top where there are the remains of a cairn. There are huge vistas from here both looking back into the moor and south to the sea. Now keep south to Penn Beacon following the reave.

Being high on the very edge of Dartmoor Penn Beacon is a most marvellous viewpoint. Over 150 metres below, you can see the largest clay pit in the world of the Lee Moor China Clay Works. However much you might be against mining on the edge of a National Park, there is something very exciting and fascinating about the weird moonscape. Plymouth on the Sound and Devonport on the Tamar are all visible and, of course, the valley of the Tamar itself. Whilst beyond, away in Cornwall, you can see Bodmin Moor and St.Austell Moor and the other well-known china clay works in Britain. Today most of the tips there have been landscaped to look more like Iron Age forts but in the old days the conical tips were known as the Cornish Alps! There is another Triangulation Point here and also a small lookout hut and wall built from the stones of the prehistoric cairn.

If you can drag yourself away from the view you must now start a long descending traverse in roughly a north-westerly direction above the china clay works. There are various reaves and cairns you can look for but your main objective is the double stone row about 2.7kms from Penn Beacon which lies across the Lee Moor Leat crossed at the start of the walk. It is 130 metres long and has a stone circle at its northern end. There are no legends connected with this circle, as far as I know, but like many of the Bronze Age circles this was probably a burial site lying at the end of the row.

You can either follow the leat for a while to the clapper bridge crossed on the way up to Trowlesworthy Tors and then back past the Warren House, the way you came, or slant again down across the hill to the small bridge over the Blacka Brook where it joins the Plym and then back to the start.

10. Cadover Bridge, Trowlesworthy Warren House, Valley of the River Plym, Ditsworthy Warren House, Giants Basin, Plym Steps, Plym Ford, Eylesbarrow Mine, Scout Hut, Gutter Tor, Legis Tor. *(See map p.71)*

START. Near Cadover Bridge. Map Ref.555646. There is plenty of space in this area to park off the road. Shaugh Prior is 2.5kms away with all the facilities of a small village. Ice Cream vans park at Cadover Bridge in the summer and at weekends.

Medium. 10 miles. 16kms. Moderate (There are several possibilities of shortening this walk by cutting off corners and I shall indicate the places where you can do this in the description of the walk.

You might like to read the first two paragraphs of Walk 9 if you want to find out about the name Cadover.)

Just up the Meavy road from Cadover Bridge you will see a track that runs off towards the east. You must take this track for the start of the walk. However, if the river is low, you might prefer to start the walk by following the same route as Walk 9 and then try to find a way across the River Plym somewhere after Trowlesworthy Warren House. Whichever start you take you need to be, sooner or later, on the true right bank of the River Plym, where the track to Brisworthy Burrows turns into a rocky path and follows the river as the valley swings north and then east. You will pass below Legis Tor and close to many enclosures and hut circles that you might like to explore. Do not go up to Legis Tor itself yet as you will be coming back that way.

At Meavy Pool you will find a well marked path that leads up to Ditsworthy Warren House. This is yet another of the Warren Houses where rabbits were bred commercially and you can see many of the artificial burrows around the buildings. Though nobody lives here permanently the house is in quite good order with the windows and doors shuttered. It is used as a base for youth groups for adventure training at certain times of the year. The small, enclosed grass area in front of the house with the stream flowing through from the collecting well at the back of the building is a peaceful and quiet place when the youth groups are not there!

To the east of the house there is another walled yard or paddock such as the one at Trowlesworthy where the warreners kept the dogs used to drive out rabbits into the nets. It is known as a kennel court and you will see several kennels let into the granite walls. It is said that the dogs were so vicious that the warreners had to stand on the walls to throw them their food rather than entering the enclosure! Apparently this farm was used for warrening until the 1950's when the Rabbit Clearance Order was introduced and it became illegal to farm rabbits in this way.

You could now, if you wished, cut off a corner here and take Edward's Path which runs north for 1 km from Ditsworthy to near the Scout Hut and join the walk again just below Gutter Tor.

If, however, you want to keep on, take the track behind the Warren House towards the north-east. Soon ahead you will see several splendid stone rows in the area called Drizzle Combe, a corruption of Thrushelcombe, 1 km from Ditsworthy. On the maps you will also find the name Giants Basin which refers to the large cairn with a depression in the middle quite close to the barrow where the first row ends and down towards the river.

Hansford Worth, whose book is listed in the bibliography, mentioned in a paper which he read at a meeting of the Plymouth

Institution in 1889, that he had noticed several of the tallest and finest menhirs were lying on the ground in this area. As a result of this they were put up again in the summer of 1893 and these are the ones you see today. While they lay on the ground Worth had measured them and found that the three largest measured 17 feet 10 inches, 12 feet 6 inches and 9 feet 5 inches. Even with part of them buried in the earth, as they are now, the largest standing stone is still about 14 feet from ground to top and is the tallest on Dartmoor.

There are a great many other Bronze Age relics to be seen around here and, if you have time, it is worth wandering around. There are three kistvaens, one of which is an excellent example though it has obviously been plundered as the stone lid has been pushed aside. Up on the hill north-west from the rows near Whittenknowles Rocks there is a large enclosure with many hut circles where the stone row builders must have lived.

Keep on up the right bank of the Plym. There are various tracks and paths to follow but soon the valley narrows and steepens through quite a gorge until you come to what is called Plym Steps. Steps usually mean stepping stones but there are none even though one branch of the Abbot's Way was supposed to cross here.

Again you could cut a corner off and climb up steeply left to Lower and Higher Hartor but it is quite rough through a lot of heather. From the tors you would then have to aim directly towards the ruins of Eylesbarrow Mine.

If you have time to cross over there are two tinners' blowing houses on the true left bank of the river and another good example of a kistvaen near Calveslake Tor. Otherwise keep on up the river and you will pass Evil Combe on your left and then come to Plym Ford. This name is what it implies and it is where the Tavistock branch of the Abbot's Way crosses the Plym. There is a wheel pit to be found in the gully directly above the ford with various conduits around. This was all part of the workings of Eylesbarrow Mine which is where you are going now.

Turn up the track northwards and then very soon look for the path running back south of west, parallel with the river for a short way. It soon becomes a well defined track and drops down into a small side valley with many spoil tips and gullies of tinners' works and some ruined buildings with another wheel pit which was powered by water from Crane Lake. This large wheel worked two ore crushing mills.

The track now passes over a level area until you come to the ruins of Eylesbarrow Mine itself but all the remains you have been seeing were part of this extraordinary engineering and mining achievement of the eighteenth century connected with Eylesbarrow. There are a great many walls, banks, pits and ruins to explore here. It is hard to say what every building was but one was where they smelted the tin ore, another, on the south side, was a house for the mine captain. On the north side there were the 'barracks' which was the building where the miners lived. It was a thriving village with nearly 100 men working here and there would have been a smithy, various stores and an office called a count house. There are also several wheel pits for the great wheels which worked the stamping mills and pumping machinery and were powered by water brought by leats from the upper Plym. Near the track, if you walk north-east, and in other areas too, you will see pairs of stones every 20 metres or so with grooves cut in the tops for holding the iron axles that supported the flat rods which slid backwards and forwards transferring power from the great wheels to the pumps to keep the mines from being flooded. I would give a lot to have seen them in action; a crude but efficient way of transmitting power! What an extraordinary place this must have been, and there were many like this all over Dartmoor, in the seventeenth, eighteenth and nineteenth centuries. There were many more people living and working in remote desolate, lonely places on the moor than there are now. This also applies to prehistoric times too.

For you now it is a long, gentle, easy descent down the track towards the south-west past the pit for the largest wheel of all built in 1847, to the Scout Hut about 2kms away. Keep an eye open for the view as you go. After the hut follow the road for a while and then strike left up to Gutter Tor. A strange name that comes from the fact that goats grazed near here. There are quite a few Bronze Age remains on Gutter Tor and some Pillow Mounds which are the old burrows for rabbits.

A new fence has just been put up to enclose the whole of Ringmoor Down. There are stiles and gates in it at convenient intervals and you will have to use them. The first stile is just beyond Gutter Tor as you aim towards the Triangulation point 350. If you climb over it you will now be within the fenced area. Aim just west of south towards Legis Tor which you should see ahead, 1.5kms away. There are ways through the enclosures and you will find this the easiest walking surface you are likely to get on Dartmoor; dry, firm turf. When you reach the summit rocks of Legis Tor clamber over them or go round to the south side where you will see an excellent example of a vermin trap. There are many to be found in various states of preservation on Dartmoor usually near the Warren Houses. They were used to catch predators such as stoats, weasels and polecats. The one here has the funnel-shaped approach paths at each end clearly marked out by low walls of stones. This, by virtue of its shape, led the stoats to the main part of the trap which was a tunnel about 60cms long made of slabs of granite with a thick, stone lid. The lid has holes bored in it and the sides slits which allowed a slate to be suspended on wire as a shutter which was triggered by a pressure or tripping arrangement. The unsuspecting stoat, forced in by the narrowing walls of the funnel, entered the tunnel, trod on the pressure plate and soon found itself trapped inside, to be desposed of by the warrener!

By now you probably want to get back to the start, for this has been a long and interesting walk, but there are, of course, prehistoric remains and a stone row to be seen on Ringmoor Down if you have time! You will see the new fence again now just to the south of Legis Tor and to get over it you must either follow it down west to the little stream, Legis Lake, where you will find a stile or walk east about 200 metres along the fence and again you will see another stile. All you have to do now is to drop down to the River Plym and either cross the main river to Trowlesworthy Warren House and back that way or continue on the right bank to Cadover Bridge.

The next two walks cover the same ground as Walk 10 but by using two halves. Obviously they are shorter and can be followed when you may not have enough time to complete the whole of Walk 10

11. Gutter Tor, Legis Tor, Meavey Pool, Ditsworthy Warren House. *(See map p.71)*

START. Burcombe Ford on Sheepstor Brook. Map Ref.579673. There is plenty of space to park off the road here.
Meavy is the nearest village about 4kms away with a pub and a Post Office stores, otherwise you will have to use Dousland or Yelverton for other facilties.
Medium. 3¾ miles. 6 kms. Easy

Set off south-west towards Gutter Tor which can be seen on the sky-line. A strange name that comes from the fact that goats grazed near here. There are quite a few Bronze Age remains on Gutter Tor and some Pillow Mounds which are the old burrows built for rabbits.

A new fence has just been put up to enclose the whole of Ringmoor Down. There are stiles and gates in it at convenient intervals and you

Vermin trap - Legis Tor

will have to use them. The first stile is just beyond Gutter Tor as you aim towards the Triangulation point 350. If you climb over it you will now be within the fenced area.

Aim just west of south towards Legis Tor which you should see ahead, 1.5kms away. There are ways through the enclosures and you will find this the easiest walking surface you are likely to get on Dartmoor; dry, firm turf. When you reach the summit rocks of Legis Tor clamber over them or go round to the south side where you will see an excellent example of a vermin trap. There are many to be found in various states of preservation on Dartmoor usually near the Warren Houses and they were used to catch predators such as stoats, weasels and polecats which attacked the rabbits. The one here has the funnel-shaped approach paths at each end clearly marked out by low walls of stones. This, by virtue of its shape, led the stoats to the main part of the trap which was a tunnel about 60cms long made of slabs of granite with a thick, stone lid. This lid has holes bored in it and the sides have slits which allowed a slate to be suspended on wire as a shutter which was triggered by a pressure or tripping arrangement. The unsuspecting stoat forced in by the narrowing walls of the funnel, trod on the pressure plate and soon found itself trapped inside, to be disposed of by the warrener!

You will see the new fence again now just to the south of Legis Tor and to get over it you must either follow it down west to the little stream, Legis Lake, where you will find a stile or walk east about 200 metres along the fence and again you will see another stile. Having crossed one or other of the stiles, drop down to the River Plym; keep an eye open for the pillow mounds and enclosures. Then turn left up the true right bank of the river to Meavy Pool and from here you will find a well marked path that leads to Ditsworthy Warren House. This is yet another of the Warren Houses where rabbits were bred commercially and you can see many of the artificial burrows around the buildings. Though nobody lives here permanently the house is in quite good order with the windows and doors shuttered. It is used as a base for youth groups for adventure training at certain times of the year. The small, enclosed grass area in front of the house with the stream flowing through from the collecting well at the back of the building is a peaceful and quiet place when the youth groups are not there!

To the east of the house there is another walled yard or paddock such as the one at Trowlesworthy where the warreners kept the dogs used to drive the rabbits into the nets. It is known as a kennel court and you will see several kennels let into the granite walls. It is said that the dogs were so vicious that the warreners had to stand on the walls to throw them their food rather than entering the enclosure! Apparently this farm was used for warrening until the 1950's when the Rabbit Clearance Order was introduced and it became illegal to farm rabbits in this way.

From the Warren House you must walk a short way past many burrows until you turn north on to Edward's Path. Keep an eye out for the foundations of a longhouse and a little further on the remains of another vermin trap.

The path will bring you easily back to the start.

12. Ditsworthy Warren House, Giants Basin, (Plym Steps, Plym Ford) Eylesbarrow Mine, Scout Hut. *(See map p.71)*

START. Burcombe Ford on Sheepstor Brook. Map. Ref.579673. There is plenty of space to park off the road here.
Meavy is the nearest village about 4kms away with a pub and a Post Office stores, otherwise you will have to use Dousland or Yelverton for other facilities.
Medium. 5½ miles. 8.5kms via Plym Ford. Moderate

Medium. 4¼ miles. 6.7kms direct to Eylesbarrow from Giants Basin. Moderate

You will set off along the obvious track called Edward's Path below Gutter Tor. If you like, you can divert and climb up the tor itself at the start of the walk. It has its strange name because goats were supposed to have grazed here at one time. There are quite a few Bronze Age remains around the tor and Pillow Mounds. From the summit follow the slanting path down south-east towards Edward's Path. Wild cats were also said to have lived and hunted here.

Once on the path keep an eye out for a vermin trap and the remains of an old longhouse. Soon you will pass many of the artificial burrows of the Ditsworthy Warren House. This is yet another of the Warren Houses where rabbits were bred commercially and you can see many of the artificial burrows around the buildings. Though nobody lives here permanently the house is in quite good order with the windows and doors shuttered. It is used as a base for youth groups for adventure training at certain times of the year. The small, enclosed grass area in front of the house with the stream flowing through from the collecting well at the back of the building is a peaceful and quiet place when the youth groups are not there! To the east of the house there is another walled yard or paddock such as the one at Trowlesworthy where the warreners kept the dogs used to drive the rabbits into the nets. It is known as a kennel court and you will see several kennels let into the granite walls. It is said that the dogs were so vicious that the warreners had to stand on the walls to throw them their food rather than entering the enclosure! Apparently this farm was used for warrening until the 1950's when the Rabbit Clearance Order was introduced and it became illegal to farm rabbits in this way.

Take the track behind the Warren House towards the north-east. Soon ahead you will see several splendid stone rows in the area called Drizzle Combe a corruption of Thrushelcombe, 1km from Ditsworthy. On the maps you will also find the name Giants Basin which refers to the large cairn with a depression in the middle quite close to the barrow where the first row ends and down towards the river. Hanswood Worth, whose book is listed in the bibliography, mentioned in a paper which he read at a meeting of the Plymouth Institution in 1889, that he had noticed several of the tallest and finest menhirs were lying on the ground in this area. As a result of this they were put up again in the summer of 1893 and these are the ones you see today. While they lay on the ground Worth had measured them and found that the three largest measured 17 feet 10 inches, 12 feet 6

*The tallest menhir on Dartmoor
near Giant's Basin on River Plym*

inches and 9 feet 5 inches. Even with part of them buried in the earth, as they are now, the largest standing stone is still about 14 feet from ground to top and is the tallest on Dartmoor.

There are a great many other Bronze Age relics to be seen around here and, if you have time, it is worth wandering around. There are three kistvaens, one of which is an excellent example though it is has obviously been plundered as the stone lid has been pushed aside.

On the hill north-west from the rows near Whittenknowles Rocks there is a large enclosure with many huts circles where the stone row builders must have lived.

You have a choice here if you want to shorten the walk. If you do then you must walk towards a group of huts north-east from the end of the stone rows and then north past a fine kistvaen and into the valley of the stream running down to Drizzle Combe. Near the source of the stream there are some ruined buildings one of which is a blowing house dating not from medieval times but from the 1820's.

You will soon find the broad track leading on up to Eylesbarrow Mine. If you do not follow this route then keep on up the right bank of the Plym. There are various tracks and paths to follow but soon the valley narrows and steepens through quite a gorge until you come to what is called Plym Steps. Steps usually mean stepping stones but there are none even though one branch of the Abbot's Way was supposed to cross here.

Again you could cut off a corner and climb up steeply left to Lower and Higher Hartor but it is quite rough going through a lot of heather. From the tors you would have to aim directly towards the ruins of Eylesbarrow Mine. If you have time to cross over there are two tinners' blowing houses on the true left bank of the river and another good example of a kistvaen near Calveslake Tor.

Otherwise keep on up the river and you will pass Evil Combe on your left and then come to Plym Ford. This name is what it implies and it is where the Tavistock branch of the Abbot's Way crosses the Plym. There is a wheel pit to be found in the gully directly above the ford with various conduits around. This was all part of the workings of Eylesbarrow Mine which is where you are going now.

Turn up the track northwards and then very soon look for the path running back south or west, parallel with the river for a short way. It soon becomes a well defined track and drops down into a small side valley with many spoil tips and gullies of tinners' works and some ruined buildings with another wheel pit which was powered by water from Crane Lake. This large wheel worked two ore crushing mills.

The track now passes over a level area until you come to the ruins of

Eylesbarrow Mine itself. All the remains you have been seeing were part of this extraordinary engineering and mining achievement of the eighteenth century with Eylesbarrow. There are a great many walls, banks, pits and ruins to explore here. It is hard to say what every building was but one was where they smelted the tin ore, another, on the south side, was a house for the mine captain. On the north side there was the 'barracks' which was the building where the miners lived. It was a thriving village with nearly 100 men working here and there would have been a smithy, various stores and an office called a count house. There are also several wheel pits for the great wheels which worked the stamping mills and pumping machinery and were powered by water brought by leats from the upper Plym. Near the track, if you walk north-east, and in other areas too, you will see pairs of stones every 20 metres or so with grooves cut in the tops for holding the iron axles that supported the flat rods which slid backwards and forward providing power from the great wheels to the pumps to keep the mines from being flooded. I would give a lot to have seen them in action; a crude but efficient way of transmitting power! What an extraordinary place this must have been and there were many like this all over Dartmoor, in the seventeenth, eighteenth and nineteenth centuries. There were very many more people living and working in remote desolate, lonely places on the moor than there are now. This also applies to prehistoric times too.

For now it is a long, gentle, easy descent down the track towards the south-west past the pit for the largest wheel of all, built in 1847, to the Scout Hut about 2kms away. Keep an eye open for the view as you go.

Follow the track down to where you started this walk.

13. Shaugh Bridge, West Down, North Wood, Dunstone, Cadover Bridge, Wigford Down, Dewerstone Rock.

START. Shaugh Bridge. Map. Ref.533638. There are large parking places 50 metres or so from either side of the bridge.
Shaugh Prior is the nearest village just 1.5km up the road with a Post Office, a stores and a pub. Ice Cream vans in the summer at the bridge.
Medium. 4¼ miles. 7kms. Easy

If you start just east of the bridge in the obvious parking area you will see some old remains of what were probably settling tanks and loading bays for the local china clay industry. It only seems a few years

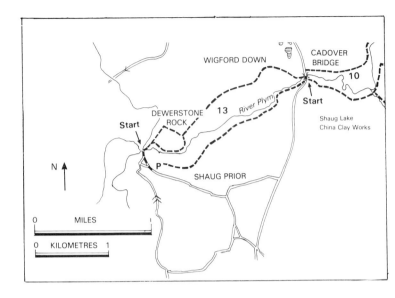

ago that the River Plym was a milky, white torrent running down from the china clay works at Shaugh Lake but, with conservation very much in mind, the China Clay Company has made sure that the river remains the sparkling, moorland stream you see today.

The whole area is very beautiful, by the confluence of the River Plym and River Meavy. The result is, of course, that it is very popular, being only a few kilometres from Plymouth and many people come out here to picnic, swim and wander in the woods. The National Trust owns the woodlands and the Dewerstone Rock by which you will return.

Just beyond the car parking area you will find some steps which lead onto a footpath. The path at the top will take you east to start with, towards Shaugh Prior, and runs through many spoil tips from the disused kaolin works that were once here. By some houses the path takes you to West Down and you can either follow it at first just inside or outside the woods as you wish. However, through a gate, you will soon be back in the woods and when there, if you keep an eye out, you will see a pipeline sometimes exposed, sometimes buried below the surface of the path which follows it. China clay suspended in water flowed down this pipe to the settling tanks you saw below, all the way from Shaugh Lake.

Soon the path swings north-east and runs along the top edge of the woods across West Down. Deep below you hear and occasionally see the River Plym running almost in a gorge and on the far side of the river The Dewerstone rears out of the thick cloak of oaks that fill the valley. There are three main buttresses and, as you will have read in the section on rock climbing, all the rockfaces offer some of the best climbing in the area, especially the main cliff which is over 120 feet high. The view across from this side of the valley of The Dewerstone is magnificent.

As is often the case amazing natural formations have legends associated with them and The Dewerstone is no exception. Dewer was supposed to be the Devil himself who as the demon hunter rode with his Wish or Whist hounds across Dartmoor. These hounds were coal black with burning red eyes and with the Dewer in full cry hunted their victim, driving him always closer and closer to The Dewerstone until finally in wild mounting terror he plunged over the edge to be smashed on the rocks below. It was said that if you ever set eyes on the hounds you would die within the year. Another legend related by the locals is that one winter night when snow lay deep around The Dewerstone they found the prints of a naked, human foot, footprints of dogs and a line of prints of a cloven hoof leading to the edge of the cliff. And one final story before you get on with the walk or perhaps you might prefer to get back as quickly as you can! The main sport of Dewer also seems to have been hunting the souls of unbaptized babies. One night a farmer returning from the White Thorn, the pub in Shaugh Prior, met Dewer and the Whist Hounds on his way home. Fortified by drink he boldly asked the Devil whether he had caught anything that night. Dewer turned towards him and said that he could certainly share the kill with him and threw him a bundle. On returning home the farmer and his wife undid the bundle and found the dead body of their own unbaptized child.

Soon the path goes through a gate into North Wood. After a stream you will come near a farm called Dunstone and the path now keeps close to the river so that you will arrive eventually at the flat, grassy area near Cadover Bridge. (On fine, summer's days you will find hundreds of people and ice cream vans!) Cross over the bridge itself by the road and then swing left onto the open moor of Wigford Down. You will soon see a granite cross probably medieval which is on one of the old tracks across the moor used by monks travelling from one Abbey or Priory to another.

Keep the enclosures on your left, unless you want to move onto the moor, and look for the various hut circles and cairns there. The small standing stones with L carved on them are boundary stones for the estate of a local family called Lopes. There are also quite a number of reaves to be seen here. You should now be aiming towards the high ground of Dewerstone Hill. Some 200 metres before you reach the summit rocks you will cross a great, double, semi-circular bank of rocks that sweep round in an arc. Further on there is another enclosure with a hut circle in it. The area is marked as Fort on the maps and this is clearly what it was. It must have been a fine defensive position with its back and right flank guarded by the rocks and the Dewerstone rock and the huge double wall lower down the hill protecting the dwelling and pound from frontal attack across the moorland. It is thought to be late Bronze Age or early Iron Age. There are quite a number of Iron Age Forts around the edges of Dartmoor.

On the summit itself of Dewerstone Hill you will see that some of the rocks have quite a number of carvings on them. One of them refers to Nicholas Carrington, the Dartmoor poet, and gives the month and the year of his death, 1830. Apparently he often used to sit up here to get inspiration for his poetry and what a lovely place it is. The view stretches away to Cornwall in the west.

You must walk now south-east and will soon come to the sheer cliff of the Dewerstone itself which you saw from the other side of the gorge. There are several very steep and quite tricky paths down between the buttresses to the river. If you feel happy to follow them down then it is worth going to the foot of the rockface to appreciate the height of the cliff and maybe watch some climbers in action. But I repeat that it is a steep descent, sometimes quite muddy and with rounded granite crystals lying loose on the path that act like ball bearings if you do not go carefully! If you do go down the cliff then at the bottom turn downstream to your right and follow the obvious path that keeps fairly high above the river until it joins a larger well made-up track that drops down almost like a staircase past a small mine adit and ruined buildings that might have been a paper mill, to a wooden bridge over the Plym that leads to the car parking area. If, however, you do not feel like making the steep descent, then if you go west from the summit of Dewerstone Hill you will find a path that will take you down right, past a quarry. The path was an old tram way for quarried granite blocks and soon runs to the top of an inclined plane, near some ruined buildings, leading down through the trees to the left. The loaded trucks were lowered down the incline by cables and winding gear and you can still see the remains of the machinery in the ruins.

Burrator Reservoir

You can follow the inclined plane down, still with some of the granite sleepers for the rails in position, until you come to a track that, if you turn left, will take you down, by a series of zig-zags, to the wooden bridge over the River Plym. Cross the bridge to the car parking area.

If you would still like to stand below the great rock of the Dewerstone you could wander along the track that runs quite high above the true right bank of the Plym for about ¾km to the cliff.

14. Norsworthy Bridge, Burrator Reservoir, Deancombe, Cuckoo Rock, Potato Cave, Eylesbarrow Tin Mine, Nun's Cross Farm, Siward's Cross, Stone Row, Down Tor.

START. Near Norsworthy Bridge, Burrator Reservoir. Map Ref.568693. There are plenty of places to park your car off the road in this area. Dousland is about 4kms away with all the facilities of a small village. Meavy is also quite close with a pleasant pub. There are Ice Cream Vans parked near the dam of the reservoir at weekends and during the summer.

Medium.   5¾ miles.   9.3kms.   Moderate.

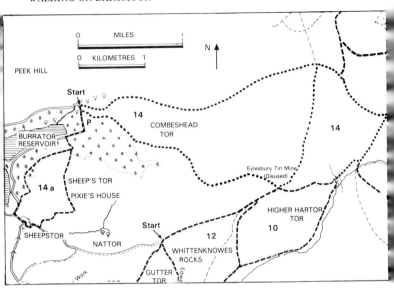

Once again the start for this walk is a popular and crowded place during the summer and at fine weekends. There are places to picnic by the rivers and streams on the edge of the woods and forest.

Walk 14A. Before you start the main walk, or maybe when you get back, you might be interested in driving round to the little hamlet of Sheepstor which is only 2kms away along a pleasant road through the pine forests on the south-east side of the reservoir. Or if you are feeling strong then there is a track marked on the maps that enters Narrator Plantation 1km from the start of Walk 14 and skirts the forest below Sheepstor for a while then cuts through a section before dropping down to Joey's Lane, and ancient packhorse route. Turn left at the bottom of the lane and you are almost in Sheepstor. The name obviously comes from the tor standing high above the hamlet but nobody is really clear what it means except that it is nothing to do with sheep! It could be a corruption of 'schittes' a medieval word meaning a steep slope or 'scyttel' meaning a bar but in 1168 it was called Sitelestorra. So your guess is as good as mine!

The main feature of Sheepstor is obviously the lovely little sixteenth century church but, as is so often the case, it was built on the site of a

Sheepstor village with Sharp Tor behind

much earlier Saxon or Norman church. To enter the churchyard you can pass through a lychgate near the village cross. There is another cross at the top of some steep stone steps where there is a stile. The most interesting tombs are probably those of the four members of the Brookes family three of whom were known as the White Rajahs of Sarawak. It is a fascinating story of the days of the British Empire and how James Brooke and his successors became the Rajahs of Sarawak in Borneo. When they returned to Britain the small village of Sheepstor became their home and they lived and died here. In the outer wall of the churchyard opposite a cottage you will find St. Leonard's Well with a carved canopy obviously taken from the church some time.

Reference is made to a bull ring near the Vicarage and in 1908 an iron ring was found buried to which they must have tethered the bulls.

If you came here on foot you might like to make a circuit now by way of Sheepstor itself.

Leave the churchyard behind you and follow the little lane set in deep walls towards the south-east until you come to the first turning left. Take this lane and follow it up past the farm until you find the open moor on your left. There is one obvious track that runs up towards the rocks of the tor and if you came by car and just want to

Sheepstor Church

wander up Sheepstor there is room to park here. On the way up, to your left, if you search around, you might find the entrance to the small chamber formed by rocks called The Pixies Cave or Piskies House. Over the years the shifting rocks have made it much smaller for, at the time of the Civil War, the Elford family, who were lords of the Manor of Sheepstor, were supposed to have hidden in the cave when being hunted by the Roundheads.

The south-east rockface of the tor has quite a number of climbs on it while at the foot you might be able to make out the relics of a vermin trap. If you clamber round to the summit, where there is another vermin trap, you will see one of the finest views on Dartmoor. Below is Burrator Reservoir which, in spite of what the critics of man-made lakes say, is one of the most beautiful settings in Britain. To the west and north-west you can look away to Cornwall.

You will notice if you have the 1:25,000 map that the word Feather Bed is printed on the area of Sheepstor. This refers not to a quaking bog but to flat pavements of exposed granite found usually on summits but in other places such as Joey's Lane which you might have used to get to Sheepstor hamlet as well.

From the top of the tor you can either walk west down to Maiden Tor a low outcrop on the flank where there are some Pillow Mounds, the old burrows for rabbits and rejoin the path north-east back to the start of Walk 14 or you can aim north, straight down to Narrator Plantation and the ruins of Narrator Farm, to reach the road where you turn right to get to the start of Walk 14.

If you brought your car then obviously you must retrace your steps to where you left it.

Walk 14

Just where the road round the reservoir begins to swing south there is an obvious track that runs along the edge of the forestry plantations in a south-easterly direction. This is the track you must follow. It is easy walking with pleasant glimpses to your right into the forest of mature trees, mainly conifers of course. However, there are quite a number of gnarled beeches growing on the mossy banks to your left.

You will pass some old, ruined mine buildings set in a dell on your right and then ahead, up a rocky lane, you will see the ruins of Dean Combe Farm. Being a romantic at heart I always feel sad at the sight of these old moorland farms that in our hard world of economic farming were just not possible to run. Until a few years ago the whole pattern of the buildings and the house were easy to see and you could make out how the farm must have looked. There was one building with the granite mushroom-shaped supports for the floor to keep vermin out, still in position.

Go through the farmyard and ahead you will see Cuckoo Rock standing up ahead of you. Walk through the fields and onto the open moor. There is a muddy corner by a stream to hop across. An obvious path climbs quite steeply up to Cuckoo Rock. I suppose it might look a little like a young, gaping cuckoo waiting to be fed by its foster parents! Or maybe this corner is a favourite haunt of cuckoos.

There used to be a Dartmoor Letter Box on the summit of the rock but as the climb up and particularly the descent were dangerous it has been removed. There is sometimes a box hidden nearby but as this is a popular and easy place to reach it is often vandalized.

You now aim diagonally down across the hill following the obvious path towards the clump of trees in the valley. If you follow it right down you will discover the ruins of another farm; Combeshead Farm, a place of more ghosts.

Having had a look round the ruins now face north and you will see a path that runs uphill for 200 metres past some walls on the bracken covered slope. Follow this path and in a low, walled bank you will find a small entrance to what is called the Potato Cave. It is quite snug and dry inside and a possible place to bivouac if you get caught out. There

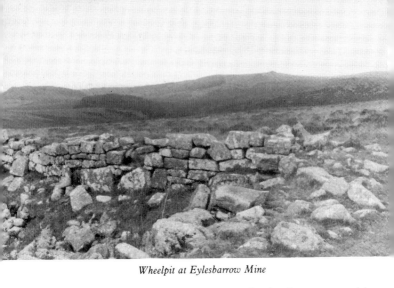

Wheelpit at Eylesbarrow Mine

is sometimes a Letter Box here. The name is what it suggests and is where the farmer probably kept his crop of potatoes dry and at an even temperature, though it might have been made by the tinners from the workings above. There is also a suggestion that this and the other cache you can visit in a minute were made for illicit stills!

You must now walk back to the ruined Combeshead Farm and on down to the river by the hut built by South-west Water. You should be able to cross the stream easily here at the ford. Follow the path as it strikes uphill and slightly left until you see a trench or gully on your right, part of the tinners' workings. Leave the path and follow the trench in for a few metres and you will see a low entrance in the hillside. It is usually a little wet but if you duck down you can get into the chamber and once in you are able to stand up. The walls are well constructed in stone and it has a beehive roof. This must have been a tinners' cache for tools, ingots and possibly a still!

You can either climb on up the rest of the hill ahead of you for a few metres and turn left or east along the top of the stream valley or go back down to the Narrator Brook itself and follow that in an easterly direction. Whichever you do you will soon find yourself in what was an area of intensive tin streaming and digging from medieval times and then you will find evidence of the workings connected with the complex Eylesbarrow Mines of the eighteenth and nineteenth centuries. There is an adit marked on the 1:25,000 maps and you will find a low entrance at the head of a gully with a stream running out of it. The walls and roof are extremely well built with stone.

Higher up at the head of a marshy area by a wheel pit and at the end of the line of the twin stones that held the flat rods that I shall be mentioning later, there is the low, wet entrance to another tunnel, the Two Brothers Adit. While it is possible to explore this old mine working, it is extremely dangerous with the possibility of collapse trapping you inside and I would not recommend entering more than a few feet. You must now walk east towards Eylesbarrow Mine. If the visibility is poor you could use a navigation trick pioneered by Sir Francis Chichester - aiming off and using an attack point. You will notice on the map a well defined track running from Eylesbarrow Mine towards the south-west. If you now aim south of east, sooner or later you will hit the track. Because you made the deliberate error of aiming south of east rather than due east, you will know that the mine lies to your left or north-east. Turn left along the track and after a level area you will come to the ruins of Eylesbarrow Mine itself but all the remains you have been seeing were part of this extraordinary engineering and mining achievement of the eighteenth century connected with Eylesbarrow.

There are a great many walls, banks, pits and ruins to explore here. It is hard to say what every building was but one was where they smelted the tin ore, another, on the south side, was a house for the mine captain, on the north side there was the 'barracks' which was the building where the miners lived. It was a thriving village with nearly 100 men working here and there would have been a smithy, various stores and an office called a count house. There are also several wheel pits for the great wheels which worked the stamping mills and pumping machinery powered by water brought by leats from the upper Plym. The wheel pit for the great wheel built in 1847 is back down the track westwards.

Near the track, if you walk north-east, and in other areas too, you will see pairs of stones every 20 metres or so with grooves cut out in the tops for holding the iron axles wich supported the flat rods which slid backwards and forwards providing power from the great wheels to the pumps to keep the mines from being flooded. I should give a lot to have seen them in action; a crude but efficient way of transmitting power! What an extraordinary place this must have been, and there were many like this all over Dartmoor, in the seventeenth, eighteenth and nineteenth centuries. There were many more people living and working in remote desolate, lonely places on the moor than there are now. This also applies to prehistoric times too.

If you follow the track that runs north-east you will pass several mineshafts and more of the flat-rod stones. It shows how far they had to transmit the power from the great wheel.

Once you have passed the workings, aim almost north from the mine to the actual summit of Eylesbarrow with its two burial cairns and you will also see the most splendid panoramic views of large areas of Dartmoor.

Find the northward descending track which will take you gently down to Nun's Cross Farm about 1½kms away. Again there are marvellous views. This empty farm is a typical example of a fairly modern newtake and you can see the fields around the building that were enclosed by a John Hooper in 1870. The building seen now replaced the original little, thatched croft which he first built on his land. There was a tradition that if you could build a dwelling and have a fire burning in a hearth within 24 hours you could claim the land around. How true this is I should not like to say.

A few years ago Nun's Cross Farm was derelict and had been badly vandalized but it is Duchy of Cornwall property and I am glad to see that it has been repaired and is to be used again as a youth training base.

If you went straight to the farm you walked over the tunnel of the Devonport Leat and obviously you would not have seen it. It is worth wandering back down towards the south-east from the farm, following the track along the line of a wall, to where the leat flows into the entrance of the tunnel. Look closely and you may see small brown trout flitting along in the peaty water. It is an amazing feat of engineering for the whole leat, which starts on the Cowsic River north of Princetown, and this tunnel, were built in the 1790's. It contours round the hillsides so that the flow is controlled. Before Burrator Reservoir was built it took water to Devonport, part of Plymouth. Lower, disused sections of this leat and a much earlier one called Drake's Leat, built in the 1580's, can still be seen running almost to the outskirts of Plymouth on Roborough Down.

Devonport Leat now flows eventually into Burrator Reservoir so, up to a point, it still helps to provide Plymouth with water as Drake's Leat did earlier for nearly three centuries.

Walk back to the farm now and go diagonally across the field north-west to the tall cross you can see standing by the broken wall. This is Nun's Cross or Siward's Cross. It is one of the earliest crosses on Dartmoor as it was mentioned in 1240 as a boundary mark of the

Nun's Cross or Siward's Cross

Dartmoor Forest on the Perambulation of that year. So it looks as if this cross could have been put up in the time of Edward the Confessor when Siward, Earl of Northumberland held the manors of Tavei and Wifleurde. If you look carefully you will just make out his name carved on the east side of the cross and on the other, the words Boc Lond which must refer to Buckland and was carved by the monks of Buckland Abbey whose lands reached as far as here.

To bring you more up to date you will see that the cross has been broken and mended by two metal clamps. Apparently two local lads whilst out looking for cattle in 1846 knocked it down and it broke. A local stone mason called John Newcombe repaired it after quite an outcry. One final word about the name. Nun could well be a corruption of a celtic word 'nans' meaning a valley or dale. It was named Nannecross in early records, dated 1699. From the cross walk west and you will find the place where the Devonport Leat flows out of the tunnel. There is a little ruin which was probably a tinners' shelter with a good fireplace just north-west of the exit. Keep on the true left bank of the leat and aim out across the hillside; it is quite awkward going with a lot of heather and grass tussocks to wade through. If you keep quite close to the leat and the stream you will come across some enclosures and hut circles.

You should now walk towards the south-west to a cairn and you will soon see one of Dartmoor's finest stone rows with a stone circle at its west end. Another pre-historic Dartmoor burial and worshipping place.

Down Tor just north of west is where you should aim now and from the tor an obvious, well-worn path, through the ruined walls of some enclosures of an old farm, leads you back down to the start near Norsworthy Bridge.

15. Norsworthy Bridge, Track. (Newleycombe Lake), Older Bridge, Devonport Leat, Crazy Well Pool, Raddick Lane, Leather Tor Bridge, (Lowery Cross).

START. Near Norsworthy Bridge, Burrator Reservoir. Map. Ref.568693. There are plenty of places to park your car off the road in this area.
Dousland is about 4kms away with all the facilities of a small village. Meavy is also quite close with a pleasant pub. There are Ice Cream Vans parked near the dam of the reservoir and other places at weekends and during the summer.
Medium. 5 miles. 8kms. Easy.

The start for this walk is a beautiful and therefore popular and crowded place during the summer and at fine weekends. There are places to picnic by the rivers and streams on the edge of the woods and forests. On the north side of the bridge in a very beautiful wooded area a track runs off towards the north-east, near the site of the old Norsworthy Farm. This, I suppose, is one of the reasons against the forestry industry. The old farm area and the surrounding fields are now buried in the new plantations but, of course, there would have been problems of possible pollution with the farm so near to the reservoir.

Follow Norsworthy Lane, as it is called, as it works its way along the edge of the forest until, after a while, you come to an old gateway on your right that leads down to the ruins of Kingset Farm standing below Down Tor. It is here that you can drop down to the ruins, if you wish, and then follow the valley of the Newleycombe Lake up past a great many remains of tinners' huts and workings until you come to the spring just below Older Bridge. If, however, you would prefer to keep to the track then keep going and eventually pass through Cockles

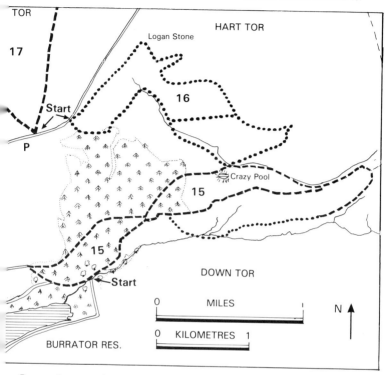

Gate and across the open moor leaving the forest behind.

You will soon see a deep tinners' gully called a gert on your left. Again a decision can be made here. You can strike up the hill directly to Crazy Well Cross and Crazy Well Pool, if you wish, cutting the walk short by nearly 2 miles or 3kms. However, if you keep on, it is an easy, striding walk along the track. You will see on your right, below the track, Newleycombe Cross one of the granite Dartmoor crosses usually put up on the old routes used by the monks to cross the moor.

At Older Bridge you will come to the Devonport Leat, an amazing feat of engineering, which starts on the Cowsic River north of Princetown and was built in the 1790's. It contours round the hillsides so that the flow is controlled. Before Burrator Reservoir was built it took water to Devonport, part of Plymouth. Lower, disused sections of the leat and a much earlier one called Drake's Leat, built in the

1580's, can still be seen running almost to the outskirts of Plymouth on Roborough Down.

Devonport Leat now flows eventually into Burrator Reservoir so, up to a point, it still helps to provide Plymouth with water as Drake's Leat did for nearly three centuries previously.

It is time for you to turn back now and follow the leat above and parallel to the track. You will pass quite a number of footbridges for animal access to the common on the other side. Soon the leat pulls away from the track and after a marshy corner with several gerts and close to the fourth footbridge you must turn down left to Crazy Well Pool which lies just over 100 metres from the leat and is not really visible until you reach it. However you might like to go and have a look at the Crazy Well Cross first which stands about 100 metres from the eastern end of the pool. It is yet another of the crosses on the routes between Buckfast, Buckland and Tavistock Abbeys. It stands about 1.5 metres high and has been restored; the shaft looks newer than the arms.

Crazy Well Pool itself is a fascinating if slightly sinister place. Nearly all the small lakes and pools on Dartmoor are man-made, usually by the tinners and clay workers who probably, in the first instance, were responsible for draining all the natural pools and tarns! This pool must have been a reservoir for the tinners who had many workings around here and the area of water covers about an acre.

There are several legends and stories connected with Crazy Well. The first one concerns its depth. It was said to be bottomless for, as the story goes, the local villagers took the bellropes of Walkhampton Church tied them together and with a bell on the end lowered them into the pool. It was paid out for its whole length and it did not touch the bottom and they could hear the bell ringing under water! The Pool, in fact, is 20 feet deep. Another legend tells of how the water level goes up and down with the tides in Plymouth Sound! This is probably an attempt to account for sudden changes in level that occur after heavy rain but as Crossing says in his Guide it was *'yeers agone'!*

In a romantic poem written by a Rev. John Johns called 'Gaveston on Dartmoor', the knight of that name, who indeed did have rights on the Forest of Dartmoor under Edward II, slept by the pool one night and woke to meet the Witch of Sheepstor! I think you might consider this to be fiction!

From Crazy Well Pool aim more or less west at the straight edge of the plantation ahead and the gateway to Raddick Lane. This pleasant lane runs down through the trees until you come to the river and quite soon a bridge over it. This is Leather Tor Bridge and is basically a

Devonport leat near Burrator

clapper bridge but with parapets. The present bridge was built in 1833 but it lies on the path the monks used to take between Buckfast and Buckland Abbeys which is marked by the crosses on the open moor seen earlier. There was probably an older bridge here and, as you can see, a ford.

To get back to the start you must take the left hand branch of the track back down to Norsworthy Bridge, but you might be interested to walk for a slightly longer circuit on the track that continues west and then south-west to have a look at a large cache that was said to be used by smugglers; yet another smugglers tale connected with Dartmoor. Beyond the cache, on the right, you will find the ruins of yet another old farm; Leather Tor Farm which with the bridge take their name from the huge tor towering above. Continue on along this track, cross over the Devonport Leat and soon you will reach the road by the old and rather battered Lowery Cross. Here turn left down the small road until it joins the road that runs round the reservoir and follow that back to Norsworth Bridge. This would add about 1 mile or nearly 2kms to your walk.

If you took the left fork at Leather Tor Bridge you would come down through marvellous woods until there is a bank above the river on your right, a hundred metres or so above the site of Norsworthy

Farm. There is a blowing house to be found by the river with some mortar stones nearby. Follow the track and river until you reach the place where you started this walk.

16. Stanlake, Devonport Leat and Aqueduct, Raddick Hill, Cramber Tor, Cramber Pool, Hart Tor, Prehistoric and Tinners' Remains on River Meavy, Black Tor. *(See map p.97)*

START. On the road that runs across Walkhampton Common. There is a quarry at Map Ref.566711 on the north side of the road but it is on a dangerous, blind corner and parking there needs care. However there are plenty of places to park on the verge of the road that runs towards Princetown. There is also a good parking place marked on the 1:25,000 maps at Map Ref.561709

Princetown is about 3kms away, depending on where you park, with all the facilities you would expect in a small town with a large, summer tourist trade. I need hardly mention that this is the town where Dartmoor Prison is sited. However, the history of the building of the prison is not widely known.

Sir Thomas Tyrwhitt, Secretary to the Council of the Prince of Wales and later Lord Warden of the Stannaries, had always had a dream of creating a town in this high, bleak spot, which he would call Princetown in honour of the Duke of Cornwall, Prince of Wales who later became George IV. He planned to turn it into a 'garden city' growing vegetables to sell in Plymouth and to develop quarry industries. I feel that he had not done his research into Dartmoor weather! It is ironic that it was he who laid the foundation stone of a prison here on 20th March, 1806, having suggested this as a possible location for a settlement. It was therefore a prison, for French prisoners captured in the war against Napolean, not a 'garden city' that brought a sort of fame and certainly a notoriety to Princetown. By 1812 there were over 9,000 prisoners here; an astonishing number, who lived under appalling conditions with no heating or even glass in the barred windows. There were also Americans held at the prison together with the French. The Latin inscription over the gate takes on a poignant meaning. *'Parcere subjectis*, 'Pity the conquered'.

After Waterloo, in 1815, the prisoners were repatriated and the prison, even though it was used as a naphtha factory for a while, was empty for many years and slowly started to fall in decay, as did the houses in the town. In 1850 it was decided to use the prison for our own convicts who would normally have been deported to the colonies

Tunnel on Devonport Leat near Nun's Cross Farm

and so the village and the prison of Princetown were revitalised. Once again the hardships for the convicts are difficult to imagine. They spent many hours working in the nearby granite quarries, chained together, and wore clothing marked with the broad arrows that I thought was seen only in the old, silent, comedy films of Charlie Chaplin!

The prison is still in use today but the life of the inmates is very different from that of those early prisoners and attitudes have changed radically over the years. But in spite of that, the massive, crouching group of grey, granite buildings with all its associations has a sinister aspect, especially on bleak winter's days when Princetown is wreathed in mist.

I must now get back to the walk before I bring in any more red herrings! From whichever of the suggested parking places you have chosen you must get to the bend in the road near the spot height 352, Map Ref.566710. From here look for a track that runs down south-east towards the wall of an old enclosure, where there is a gap to get through. There are some cairns on your right if you want to divert to look at them. However, keep down the track towards the Devonport Leat with the forest to your right and you will enter an area of ancient enclosures of another old, ruined farm called Stanlake. You can see

101

where it stood on the edge of the forest on the far side of the leat. If you have not already been on Walks 14 and 15 you might take a quick look at them if you would like more information about the Devonport Leat.

There is another possible start to this walk further along the road towards Princetown on Walkhampton Common where the road drops down into a slight dip and there are several lay-bys for parking. Map Ref.567715. There is a marshy area here with a stream running round to the enclosures. If you walk south-east across the open moor from this point, towards the enclosures, you should find a way down to a point where the leat swings south towards the forest and enters it next to a stile. Whichever start you use you must walk eventually along the true right bank of the Devonport Leat, north-east, with a muddle of hut circles and more recent enclosures on your left. Set into the far wall, the true left side of the Leat, just above the water, is the porcelain face of a small doll. It is said to have been placed there by French prisoners working on the Leat. It is about 100 metres from the aqueduct towards which you are heading and hard to see; sadly vandals have smashed it.

Ahead now you will soon see a large iron pipe from which water is gushing and to your right an aqueduct for the Devonport Leat, known locally as Iron Bridge, taking it over the River Meavy. Beyond the aqueduct the leat cascades down in an amazing torrent on the steep slope of Raddick Hill.

You could now cut this walk short and continue straight up the right bank of the River Meavy, which has been running parallel to the leat, to Black Tor Pool. This would reduce the walk by some 2¾ miles, 4.5kms.

If you wish to complete the whole walk then keep on the true right bank of the leat and climb steeply up beside the rushing, roaring water. Once on the top it is an easy walk along the leat to the first footbridge near Crazy Well Pool. You could, if you wished, wander down to the Pool and if you wanted information, both true and fictional, about it then you will find it in Walk 15!

But here you must cross over the bridge to the north side of the leat and then strike north-east towards the highest point of Cramber Hill which has a Triangulation Point on it. You should soon find a tinners' gully called a gert running up just east of north which you follow until you reach Cramber Pool.

This is one of the most beautiful secluded spots of Dartmoor, not often visited, with the most marvellous views to Bodmin Moor in Cornwall, Plymouth Sound and the great expanses of the North Moor beyond Princetown Church. As you walk due west, along the ridge towards Cramber Tor, you will have the views with you all the way. The tor is unusual, as is Hen Tor that you may have visited on a previous walk, in that it is more on the side of the hill rather than the highest point and is very broken up.

Just west of north and about 1km away you will see Hart Tor. It will mean a loss of height and a climb up if you want to reach the Tor by crossing Hart Tor Brook but again the views are good and, on the far side - north, there are the remains of the target area of a disused Rifle Range. If, however, you want to give the Tor a miss then walk down Hart Tor Brook until you come to the obvious crossing place in the shallow valley, where there are stepping stones across the brook before the valley steepens. In fact, you can probably get across almost anywhere if you cannot find the ford, as long as the brook is not in flood.

You might though prefer to stay on the left bank to have a look downstream at the good, if overgrown, example of a Bronze Age village. The entrance into the pound still has its pavement stones in place and some of the huts have the angled entrance passages visible. They were built in this way to keep the weather out of the huts by protecting the door from the wind and rain. Standing within the pound are two small stunted iron posts and many others are to be seen scattered around this area. They may have been something to do with a project to build a dam in this area rather than lower down at Burrator.

If you went to Hart Tor you must now walk down south-west towards the stone rows standing a 100 metres or so from the River Meavy. There are in fact three rows here; one single and one double and a burial mound or cairn at the north-east end of each row. The cairn of the double row has a ring of standing stones round it. The medieval tinners had no respect for ancient monuments and they drove one of their gerts right through the stone rows!

If you visited the Bronze Age village you can now cross Hart Tor Brook and go to the stone rows if you wish.

There is a lot to see in this valley and in some ways it is better for you to work your way round them in any order you wish depending a little on the state of the brooks and rivers. You may have to walk back down to the aqueduct to cross the Meavy in times of heavy rain if Black Tor Ford just above Black Tor Pool is impassable.

So far then there is the Bronze Age village on the south side of Hart Tor Brook and the stone rows on the north side.

Upstream from the confluence of the Meavy and Hart Tor Brook

Black Tor Hole or fall with blowing houses

you will find an idyllic spot known as Black Tor Hole and Black Tor Falls. The river Meavy sparkles over a winding waterfall to form a deep pool with mountain ash growing all round. On either side of the pool there are the ruins of two tinners' blowing houses that were working until the seventeenth century producing tin for the nearby stannary town of Tavistock. In the one on the true left bank or east side there are two mortar stones for crushing the tin ore. Also at this same blowing house, which is the better preserved of the two, you can see that the door-lintel, which is still in position, has the Roman numerals XIII carved on it. I assume that it was probably a stannary registration number. It was a splendid place to build these little smelting huts where there was a steep fall of water to power the bellows to fan the fire to produce the intense heat needed to smelt the tin ore and also to drive the stamps to crush the ore. The remains of the leats that brought the water to the wheels and the wheel pits, though overgrown, can still be found in and near these two blowing houses.

Obviously as well as the ruined buildings in this little valley you will see a large number of pits, mounds and gerts left behind after the workings by the medieval tinners.

If you can draw yourself away from this fascinating spot you must follow the steep zig-zag path towards the north-north-west and Black Tor, the last point of call before the end. Black Tor is in two masses. The smaller of these has what is called a logan stone. This is the name given to huge rocks and stones pivoted in such a way that they rock if pushed gently. Obviously they have reached that state after thousands of years of erosion by ice and water. I am afraid that I cannot get this one to move - probably the delicate balance has been upset possibly by more erosion or more likely by man! The most famous logan stone pushed off balance by man was the one at Treen near Porthcurno in Cornwall.

It is worth wandering around Black Tor as there are many extraordinary cracks and chimneys.

From the tor aim back to the road westwards and the place where you started this walk.

17. Routrundle, Disused Railway Track, Ingra Tor, Swelltor Quarries, King's Tor, Merrivale Prehistoric Remains, Yellowmeade Farm, Foggintor Quarries, Leeden Tor.

(See map p.106)

START. Car Park. Map Ref.561709 on north side of Princetown to Yelverton road. B3212. Princetown is 4.2kms away with all the facilities of a popular tourist village. See notes for Walk 16.

Long; 7½ miles. 12kms. Easy.

As with many of the other walks it is possible to shorten this one by cutting off corners and leaving out some of the places of interest to be visited later maybe. It is also possible to start this walk at the other end by leaving your car in the quarry at the start of the track that leads past Yellowmeade Farm to Foggintor Quarries. Map Ref.567750. If you use the start on Walkhampton Common then you must set off over the open moor in a north-westerly direction down to the disused railway track near Routrundle Farm.

What an incredible railway this was and what a shame it was closed under the Beeching axe in 1956. If it was still open today it would be an amazing tourist attraction, especially if some enterprising company could run steam trains on the winding, twisting track that contours round the moorland gradually gaining height to Princetown at 427 metres or nearly 1,400 feet. The views from the railway were superb as I remember when I rode on it a few months before it closed, looking out over the lowlands to the west of Dartmoor and across the moorland itself.

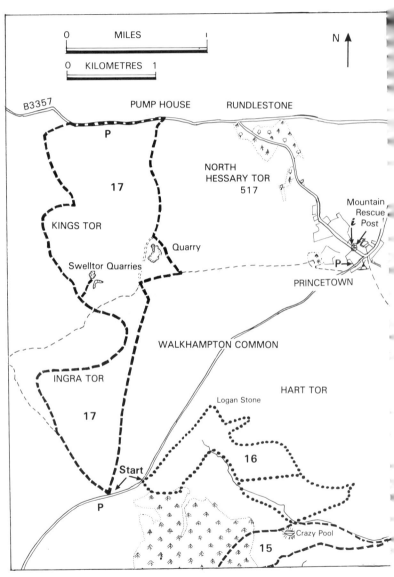

It started life in 1823 as the Plymouth and Dartmoor Railway which in fact used horse-drawn trucks to take granite from the quarries opened by Sir Thomas Tyrwhitt as part of his scheme to establish Princetown as a thriving community. See the notes at the start of Walk 16 again. The trucks ran down as far as the Plym estuary some 25 miles, 40kms away, to ship the granite to other parts of the country. This track was eventually taken over by the G.W.R. and it shows how well the early engineers must have laid it for the steam trains more or less followed the same route.

It is easy, fairly level, walking along the old railway track with quite a lot of the ballast remaining. Soon you will swing round Ingra Tor and back along the hillside in an easterly direction. You will pass a few sidings and quarry entrances. The old track goes through a cutting with a bridge over it and then along an embankment and over a bridge with a stream flowing underneath. To your right you will see the horseshoe curve of what was the track for the old 1823 horse-drawn trucks which also passes over an ancient bridge before joining our track again. You will now be in an area of enclosures and soon you will notice, on your right, a muddy well-defined track coming down the hill towards you. This is the track you must follow back down to here on the return leg of the walk.

After a ruined building on your left you will see, to the right, a long green incline leading up towards some quarries and some tower-shaped rocks which form the summit tors of this end of the ridge. This incline, down which they lowered the great blocks of granite to the trucks below, is the first part of the Swelltor Quarries. It is worth wandering up and spending quite a bit of time exploring this area. To your right at the top of the incline is a deep quarry with water in it, though you can walk into this large pit by following the gully on the right below the incline.

You can now scramble and explore where you will but take care, there are some fearful drops! There are a great number of levels and tracks with many ruined buildings but at this end of the quarries there is one hut where if the weather is poor, you can shelter since it is still roofed. Work your way north-west along the various levels and you come to several more huge pits all with openings towards the south-west and the railway sidings and inclines below.

In the early nineteenth century a lot of this Dartmoor granite was used for buildings in London including Nelson's Column and the old London Bridge. The quarries were working until the 1930s.

Again facing out towards the south-west there are the long peninsulas of waste tips like jetties sticking out into a sea.

Corbels for London Bridge at Swelltor Quarries

The views here are marvellous looking away to Cornwall. You will just make out a corner of the Tamar where it is joined by the Tavy and the railway bridge that goes across to Gunnislake.

At a lower level, if you climb carefully down, you will see the siding or incline that ran north-west towards the main line with many sleepers still in position and beside it several ruined buildings.

There are quite a number of half-finished blocks of dressed granite lying around here where the stone masons had been hard at work but never completed their tasks for one reason or another. A few hundred metres north-west of the old quarry buildings, on the right of the track, there are some even more remarkable stone objects that were, in fact, completed. They are the large corbels that were cut in 1903 for the widening of London Bridge and never used and have lain here ever since. They look like the supports for some gigantic bookshelf and are over 2½ metres long and 1 metre high. It is odd to think of Dartmoor granite ending up in the United States of America but it is to Arizona that the old London Bridge was taken, bit by bit, in the 1960s when it was demolished. So stone from Swelltor Quarries and Hay Tor Quarries now stands in the desert; London Bridge no longer falling down!

If you wanted to cut the walk short you could now retrace your steps

Stone rows at Merrivale Antiquities

back along the main track south-east to the bend where there was the obvious bridge over the cutting. Clamber up the steep bank here and head for Leedon Tor almost due south up a long gentle slope and then back to the start. If you want to go on then your route now runs gently down the incline to the main line which has been below you all the time by the fence. The rocks on your right are King's Tor and soon you will see another siding and inclined plane.

The track of the old Plymouth and Dartmoor Railway and that of the G.W.R. part company, deviate and join again eventually where there are cuttings, embankments and a bridge. The siding is, in fact, part of the old tramway track.

If you follow the track of the Plymouth and Dartmoor Railway out onto the spur, on the bend, you will find three iron clamps for the rails still in position from 1823.

The views down the valley of the Walkham are fine here and you can look across to Longash Common where you are going now but again, if time is short, you could continue on round the bend on the disused railway track to Foggintor Quarries and cut the walk short by about ¾ mile or 2kms.

However, the prehistoric remains on Longash Common are worth looking at and if you wish to go on then strike north, after getting

Kistvaen at Merrivale Antiquities

King's Tor dead behind you. You will see a wall of an enclosure ahead which you will soon reach. Follow it round to the right and cross the stream by the tinners' workings.

North-west are the prehistoric remains known as the Merrivale antiquities. The first one that you will notice, quite close to the wall that you were following before but which has now turned north-west, is the standing stone nearly ½ metres high called the Longstone. Then, further on, there is a stone circle and 200 metres beyond that the famous double stone rows. The southern row has the burial cairn in the middle marked by a stone circle and you can just make out the remains of the kistvaen in the middle of that. If you have already been on some of the previous walks you will remember that in most stone rows the burial cairns or mounds are at the end and not in the middle. You will also find nearby another excellent example of a large kistvaen with a defaced coverstone still in position. These are all relics of the Bronze Age and, as is often the case, there is a hut circle village north-north-east from the rows.

In the middle of the huts there is yet another strange unfinished granite object that could not be prehistoric. It is remarkable how many of these abandoned, half-finished stones can be found on the moor. This was probably a grindstone or some part of an apple crusher used for making cider.

Unfinished mill stone or apple crusher, Merrivale

Follow the road towards the east, past the remains of what was once a school for the quarry workers' children. This was a remarkable school said to be the highest in England with very high standards. I remember seeing it derelict but still standing in the 1950's.

Opposite a Pump House, you will see the disused quarry where you could park if you wanted to start the walk at this end.

From the quarry a rough track runs south which you must now follow. On the right you will see the ruins of what was once a row of cottages called Red Cottages where the quarrymen lived. The track has stones embedded in it with grooves and holes in them, which you can see here and there, they were the sleepers for the rails on which ran the horse-drawn trucks that carried the granite out to the main road which you have just left.

On the right you will soon see Yellowdale Farm lying within its enclosures. On the hill to the left near the farm you will also find an ancient signpost with T carved on one face and A on the other. It has been said that this is seventeenth century and T stands for Tavistock and A for Ashburton which seems likely.

Soon you will arrive at Foggintor Quarries, in some ways almost more remarkable than Swelltor. On the right there are a great many ruined buildings, all that remains of what must have been a busy,

111

thriving community but living a hard, punishing life in this bleak remote spot. Also on the right are the long piers of the spoil tips for the waste material leading out into a tumble of rocks and boulders.

You can get into the quarries on the left by following a narrow cutting and you will be in an astonishing area of huge rock walls and deep lakes. The granite was first quarried here for Sir Thomas Trywhitt when he started his plans for Princetown and eventually for the prison which was built there. See Walk 16.

As with Swelltor quarries I find this a fascinating and even beautiful place with its secret pools. I am always astonished how man can create such havoc and destruction by eating away the moorland but how nature takes over when man has gone and turns a stark, ugly industrial place once again into something quite magical and fine.

Walk on now leaving this exciting place behind until you come, beyond the last bank of waste materials, to the railway track that you left at King's Tor. Running off down to the right there is the track I mentioned just before Swelltor Quarries and you must now follow that down to the track below.

Retrace your route back the way you first came over the bridge across the stream until you come to the cutting with the bridge over it.

Climb steeply up to the left and then take the long gentle slope up to Leedon Tor with its wierd shaped summit rocks. You will pass a reave near the top which is said to stretch as far as Chagford. It is a long walk to find out if this is true!

A slight rise now, south and then down past some hut circles to the start. It is a long walk but a superb one with a great many interesting things to see but, as I explained, you can cut it short and do small sections of it one at a time.

18. Vixen Tor. Heckwood Tor. Pew Tor. Feather Tor. Windypost Cross.

START. Near the entrance into the Merrivale Granite Quarries. Map Ref.545751. There are places to park on the verge off the road. There is a pub just below the Quarries on the old road and Princetown is about 4kms away with all the facilities of a popular, tourist village. *Medium 3¾ miles. 6kms. Easy*

The walk more or less follows the public footpaths shown on the 1:25,000 maps and does not require much description from me except perhaps to mention some of the points of interest to be seen.

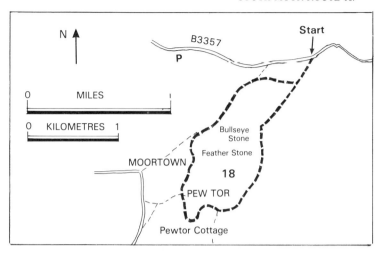

Set off then by the wall towards Vixen Tor which is obvious to see towards the south. From this angle it is said to look like an old man wearing a cap with his back to his wife but from a position further west it is supposed to resemble the Egyptian Sphinx. Whatever you think it looks like, it is a most spectacular tor standing, as it does, completely isolated and so tall. Away to your right you can make out the return route by Windypost Cross and to your left the stone rows you might have visited on Walk 17. You can cross the Grimstone and Sortridge Leat by a sturdy bridge. By a corner of the wall you will see a notice asking you to use the stile to reach Vixen Tor. You will also see a boundary stone for the Whitchurch-Sampford parish. After the second notice and round the corner you will find a stile that takes you over the wall into the newtake and onto the path to the tor. It is also requested that dogs are not allowed into the newtake which in fact is private land.

When you are close to Vixen Tor you appreciate what a fantastic rock it is, over 28 metres on the lower side and 16 metres on the higher, the highest single tor on Dartmoor. There are some good rock climbs on it and if you are a climber you will find three rock basins on the summit worn away by weathering. There is also a small cave on the south side. How the name came about I do not know but I can only suppose that foxes lived in the area. Legend has it that there was a witch of Vixen Tor who lured travellers across the moor into the

113

Vixen Tor with Hessary Tor TV mast behind

quaking mires nearby!

Return to the stile and climb back over it to the open moor and follow the wall down to the stream and go across at the ford with the stepping stones. Keep on, up the hill, by another boundary stone and then follow the track off to the left to Heckwood Quarry. The large granite block you will find there was said to have been prepared for the building of Plymouth Breakwater in 1812 but was never used; yet another of the huge, granite, dressed stones that you will keep finding on these walks, almost completed and then abandoned. There are quite a few to be found on this walk if you keep your eyes open. From the quarry you must leave the track and climb up right to Heckwood Tor with its fine views down the lovely, wooded valley of the River Walkham below you to the east. There is a path to follow for a while now, which crosses a leat as you climb up to Pew Tor.

Not all the tors you will visit on this walk are on the highest parts of moor but they all have interesting features and good views. Pew Tor is shaped almost like a castle with a central grassy courtyard with four towers in each corner. There are several rock basins. Once again the views from here are tremendous as Pew Tor stands on the edge of the moor and you can see down to Mount Edgecumbe on the other side of Plymouth, the Channel and to where the Tavy joins the Tamar just

Windy Cross, Vixen Tor behind

above Saltash.

Your route now lies more or less north as you aim towards the low lying rocks of Feather Tor. You may have to cross and recross the leat a few times unless you walk along it. Feather Tor shows all the evidence of frost and water erosion over millions of years by the large area of clitter lying around it.

You will now see Windypost Cross ahead of you. This 2 metre cross has an apt name as this is indeed a bleak, windswept col. The Abbots' Way and Jobbers' Path or Joblers' Path as the old moormen called it came this way. The name Jobbers comes from the woollen industry that flourished in Devon for centuries. A yarn jobber was a man who bought and sold wool and used the old trackways on Dartmoor for his packhorses carrying the sacks from the farmers down to the mills.

There is another interesting object to be seen near here. As granite was all around and easy to come by and even though difficult to cut and dress, all kinds of unlikely and unusual objects were made from Dartmoor's rock. On a future walk you will see rails for trucks made of granite and here a sort of sluice gate called a Bullseye Stone. As you will see this stone with a hole cut through the middle was used to control the flow of water in this leat and was a traditional Dartmoor use of granite.

The Bullseye on Grimstone and Sortridge leat

You can, if you wish, climb up gently to Barn Hill for the views over the western edge of Dartmoor to Brent Tor or keep along the leat.

Whichever route you follow you should visit a small ruin by the leat called 'The Blacksmith's Shop' that did work for the local quarries. Yet another granite object lies outside the ruins and is said to be a wheelwright's stone.

Drop down to the pretty little ford by two more boundary stones of Sampford Spiney. Finally climb up to the Grimstone and Sortridge Leat and follow it back to the start.

19. Nun's Cross Farm, Abbot's Way, Plym Ford, Great Gnats Head, Erme Pits, Grant's Pot, Phillpott's Cave, Ducks' Pool, Black Lane, Fox Tor, Childe's Tomb, Whiteworks.

START. Park in the disused quarry by the bridge over the Devonport Leat near Whiteworks, south of Princetown. Map Ref.609708. Princetown is 4kms away with all the facilities of a popular, tourist village.

Long. 7½ miles. 12.3kms. Hard. (This walk takes you into the heart of the South Moor and in poor visibility could produce navigation

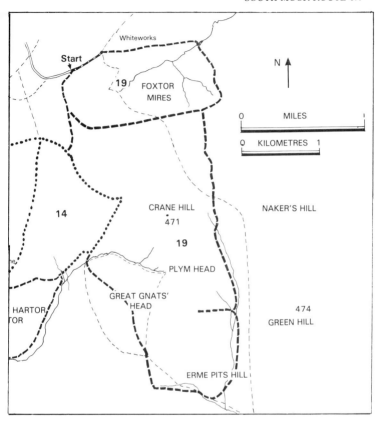

problems. It links up with Walk 8 if you would like to traverse the South Moor.)

Set off along the left or south bank of the Devonport Leat. Details of this extraordinary engineering feat can be found in Walk 14. You will see below and to your left Fox Tor Mires and there will be more about them towards the end of the walk.

Below Nun's Cross Farm you will come to the tunnel that takes the leat for some 500 metres through the hill to the valley of Newlycombe Lake. If you would like to divert here to take a look at the old farm

117

Ducks' Pool

and the newtake surrounding it and also Siward's Cross then turn right after the tunnel and approach the farm up a lane. Again details about Nun's Cross Farm and Siward's Cross can be found in Walk 14.

To continue the walk aim for Nun's Cross Ford and cross the marshy area in a south-easterly direction. To begin with there is a fairly obvious track which is part of the Abbot's Way but, as I mentioned in my introduction, many of the Dartmoor tracks and paths that are marked are a snare and a delusion! Either they are not where they are marked or there are so many sheep and cattle tracks that it is hard to say which one is the path you want. The Abbot's Way is a bit like that here. If you have the 1:25,000 map you will see that it climbs up south-east towards Crane Hill and then takes a right angled bend south-west to Plym Ford. The name Crane Hill is odd. Obviously it cannot refer to the birds unless crane was another name for a heron but more likely it is a corruption of the celtic word 'aun' meaning water.

Plym Ford is the Abbot's Way crossing for the Tavistock branch of the track; the one that went to Buckland crossed by way of Plym Steps. These are both places you may have to come to on Walk 10.

Your next point after the ford is Great Gnats Head and, as the summit cairn is not really visible until you are quite close to it, you

Tinner's blowing house near Ducks' Pool

may need to go on a compass bearing. The actual Abbot's Way does not go to the summit but contours round and it is quite easy to do this by mistake if you are trying to reach the cairn. You may prefer to follow this route anyhow but if you do go to the top of Great Gnats Head it might amuse you to look for the letter-box hidden in a low peat bank which is 100 metres on a compass bearing of 100 degrees magnetic from the cairn. This is also the way you must go if you want to cut the walk short and go straight to Ducks' Pool. Again it might be a good idea to use the compass to reach this shallow valley which runs east/west and has the letter-box on its southern edge. Do not try to cut straight across the marshy pool area if you find yourself on the north edge of the valley. It is very wet and large areas are real quakers. It is far better to retrace your steps back to the head of the little valley, the west end, and walk out along the southern edge to the rock that marks the spot where you will find the box. More about this later.

If you are following the whole walk then either try to follow the Abbot's Way round the flank of Great Gnats Head or, if you have gone to the cairn, walk just east of south. You should now be aiming at Broad Rock which is very hard to find, being only 1 metre high, 3.5 metres long and 2.5 metres wide! Crossing talks about a pole standing near it with B.B. Broad Rock carved on it which must have made things easier. Now the rock has the same letters and name on it. It marks the boundary of the Forest of Dartmoor, the Parish of Cornwood and the Manor of Blatchford. Anyway there is no problem now with navigation because the valley will lead you down past Erme Head Ford. The whole area is pretty marshy so you may have to hop about a bit! If there are difficulties keep left.

You are now approaching one of the most intensely mined areas of Dartmoor. The whole valley is a fantastic mass of spoil heaps and gullies where the ancient tinners carried out their open workings and streamings. Erme Pits is a good name.

In 1672 there was mention in records of Armed Pits which was well known for producing ore called zill tin. The name Armed Pits comes from the fact that the Erme was often called the Arme or even Irm. There are the remains of two buildings to be seen and lower down a great slab of granite, called the Table Stone.

This really is one of the most remote and lonely spots on the South Moor and you will be unlucky to meet anyone else. I love these empty places. Empty that is from a human point of view but full of a sense of History and indeed wonder at the herculean tasks undertaken by the tinners in their search for wealth. Now all is quiet and gentle as time and nature have softened the once raw spoil tips.

Just after Erme Pits Ford another river comes in from the north called Blacklane Brook and this corner has the name Wollake. You must now turn up this valley northwards. At this stage it is probably best to stay on the true right bank of the brook especially if you would like to try to find Grant's Pot. This is a strange pit with a short tunnel at the north end, probably the remains of some mining activity. It is about ½km from the confluence of the brook with the Erme and is about 100 metres from and above the stream on level ground just before the bend. A well marked path leads to and from it. It is quite easy to enter the tunnel and there is a letter-box set into the right hand wall. Map Ref. 629671.

On the left bank of Blacklane Brook and another 200 metres or so further north from Grant's Pot and about 150 metres from the little river there is Phillpotts' Cave. You will see the large, low slab of rock on the hillside and if you walk up there you will discover that you can get right under the huge boulder into quite a large cavity. A small wall has been built on the north side to give more shelter. There are two explanations for the name. One is that it is said the Eden Phillpotts the writer of so many books with a Dartmoor background used to come here and even spend nights sleeping in the snug cave. The other is that a Tony Phillpotts, a hunt servant, used the cave to hide food and drink

Phillpott's cave

to be distributed when the local hunt met in this area.

The best path is on the true right bank of the river so I should cross back to that side after Phillpotts' Cave and, if you keep quite close to the brook, you will come to another amazing area of tinners mounds and low walls. I have seen adders here basking on the rocks in the hot summer sun.

A small stream comes in from the left and between this and the main brook there are the remains of a blowing house.

Follow the shallow valley round to the left, or west, still with many tinners mounds in it. Away to your right you can see another small ruined hut with a fine fireplace still visible.

The path is now very obvious and after going over a few mounds will lead you to the pointed rock by the Ducks' Pool letter-box. If you had come here directly from Great Gnats' Head the actual mire to the north of the box is very treacherous and you could well sink into it. Like many of the so called pools on Dartmoor there is no expanse of water only quaking bog, the tinners having drained the area using the water for their workings. When the pool was there it must have been quite a size, almost filling this valley, and could well have been the haunt of wild ducks and herons.

On the pointed rock you will see a bronze plaque that tells you that it was put in this remote spot in the 1930's in memory of William

Crossing, the author of *The Guide to Dartmoor*, first published in 1909. William Crossing was born in Plymouth in 1847 and died in 1928. He lies buried in Mary Tavy churchyard overlooking the moors that he loved and knew so well. Lower down in a specially constructed cache there is a copper box which contains the book for signing your name and the rubber stamp and ink pad to frank your letter or some other piece of paper. The box is maintained by a group known as Dobson's Moormen. You will find more about the Dartmoor letter-boxes in the Introduction to this Guide.

You must now retrace your steps back to the Blacklane Brook. If you have just come down from Great Gnats' Head then you will be able to look out for the little hut with the fireplace, the tinners' spoil heaps and the blowing house mentioned earlier. You may have to do quite a lot of clambering up and down the gullies and mounds to reach the brook but when you do, swing north and follow the true right or west bank again. I know the path is marked on the maps as being on the east side but I have always found it better to stay this side. The valley is very marshy with many reeds and indeed is called the Black-lane Mire. Away on the other side of the stream you will see a post sticking up out of the bog.

It is a slow, gentle climb and after a while where the peat banks on either side seem to crowd in, the track crosses over to the east or true left bank of the trickling brook and follows the shallow valley that branches slightly east. Suddenly you will see another post standing at the col. It is, in fact, a railway sleeper and has the words 'Cater's Beam' carved on it. This, in fact, is not Cater's Beam but Blacklane from which the brook gets its name, and is one of the old peat passes used by moormen driving cattle from one area to another and also used by tinners and other moorland travellers. The name comes from the fact that the peat hags and the peat cuttings or ties around here are a rich, black colour. I must say that seeing the post looming out of the mist on several occasions has been a great comfort when the trust in my navigation has been stretched a little!

You must follow Blacklane down to the north now until you come to the edge of the deep gully and later the huge pit of Fox Tor Grit. If you search around on the west side you should find the remains of Fox Tor House a medieval tinners' hut some 7 metres long and 4 metres wide. You will see the low squat shape of Fox Tor to the north and you will aim for that now. It is best to skirt well to the left or west of the girt as the bottom is very wet and marshy. Fox Tor standing as it does on the edge of the slope overlooking Fox Tor Mires has impressive views to the north over the fen. You can make out Whiteworks on the far side and probably the quarry where you left your vehicle. Beyond, both north and east a large area of central Dartmoor can be seen.

The Mires have a sinister look to them especially on grey, misty day. It is said that Conan Doyle described them when he was writing about Great Grimpen Mire in *The Hound of the Baskervilles.*

Without doubt Fox Tor Mires can be dangerous especially in the middle, and several animals become trapped there each year. It is said that an escaped prisoner from Dartmoor Prison at Princetown was sucked down into the depths and died a terrible death.

There is a way across the Mires at the western end that used to be marked by posts with orange paint on them but the north end of the route leading to Whiteworks is very wet and unless you are in a great hurry and have good boots and gaiters I should not try it.

Below you from Fox Tor and down on the edge of the Mire to the north you will see a granite cross standing on a platform of granite blocks that actually are part of a Bronze Age kistvaen. This is Childe's Tomb and you can read a short version of the legend in the Introduction to this Guide.

There are two ways that you can finish the walk and get back to the start:

i) If you have walked down from the Tor to Childe's Tomb you can now go north-east towards the ruins of Fox Tor Farm, a desolate place mentioned in Eden Phillpott's book *The American Prisoner.* You can get across the little River Swincombe without any difficulty. From the farm there is a sort of path that will lead you north-west to Stream Hill Ford where you should be able to get across the combined waters of Swincombe, Fox Tor Mires and Strane River but it might be tricky in flood and you may have to take some big leaps! There is a concrete platform here that could be useful to help you across. It was part of the sluice gates which controlled the water in the Wheal Emma leat built in 1859 and you can see the dried up course of the leat running north-east. You may have seen the other end of this leat on Walk 3.

Once across, walk up to the newtake wall and then follow this west to Whiteworks. Strane River may also be difficult to cross but there are several possible places including Strane Ford upstream.

Once over you will be in an area of mounds and pits from the old china clay workings. As with Eylesbarrow Mine this was a busy, thriving community with workers cottages, tramways, two large waterwheels and a smithy which was at full production in the 1820's. If you wander around you will see the ruins of many of the buildings but up the hill, along the road towards Princetown, the mine captain's house is still in good repair and is lived in. Past this house then and up the hill and you soon will be back at the start.

ii) The other return route will take you to Childe's Tomb, if you wish, but then you just come back to the newtake wall passed through by the hunting gate previously and follow it westwards.

If you do not go down to the tomb strike diagonally north-west down the hill after following the path for a while from Fox Tor that goes west. This direction will also bring you down to the newtake wall and you should see another hunting gate to go through. Beyond and almost on the edge of the Mire you will see a small granite cross standing on a rock. This is known as Goldsmith's Cross after Lieut. M.Lennon Goldsmith R.N. who discovered the cross lying on the ground in 1903 and had it cemented back in place on top of the rock; yet another of the medieval monks' trackway markers.

You should now continue west taking care to avoid the really marshy ground. You might be better off back near the newtake wall again. However, if you find, on the hillside, the dry leat that once carried water to Whiteworks you can follow that for some of the way as it contours round the hill.

In the corner leap over Nun's Cross Brook and then climb diagonally up in a northerly direction to find the Devonport Leat and the path that you followed at the beginning of the walk that will now get you back to the start.

20. Saddle Bridge, Horse Ford, O Brook, Hooten Wheals, The Henroost, Skir Ford, Skir Gut or Girt, Skir Hill, Horn's Cross, Combestone Tor.

START. Saddle Bridge on the O Brook. Map Ref.664719. There is a lay-by where you can park on the Hexworthy side of the bridge. The Forest Inn Hexworthy is 1.5kms away. Holne is 4½ miles away with all the facilities of a small, moorland village.
Medium. 5 miles. 8kms. Moderate

You start by walking up the very lovely little valley of the O Brook with a few small oaks and rowans growing by the deep pools. The stream is sometimes known as the Wo Brook and both these names could be derived from oak as they may have been plentiful in the valley; Oak Brook. But it could also come from a Saxon word 'wog' that means crooked or twisting which is more likely. Crossing says that it was here on the O Brook that the Prince Consort caught his first

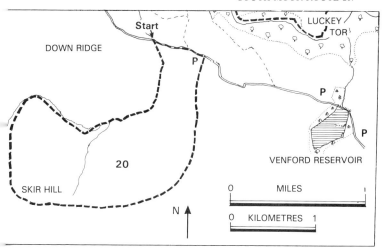

brown trout. If you are lucky you may see the descendants of this noble fish lurking in the pool!

Follow the true right bank where there is quite a good path. High on both sides of the valley you could find, if you looked, the dry course of the extraordinary Wheal Emma Leat which starts at Stream Hill Ford near Fox Tor Mires and contours for miles round all these hills to the other side of Holne Moor to provide water for the copper mines that were on the River Mardle.

You will soon come to Horse Ford and it was here that the leat crossed the O Brook on an aqueduct which has long since disappeared, but the leat remains and often makes a good path to follow on walks. Quite close to the dry Wheal Emma Leat on the east side there is also another leat full of water for Ventford Reservoir. This is the Holne Moor Leat.

From the ford strike steeply up the hill towards the north-east and an ancient cross, standing beside a broad, good track. As always this is another of the Dartmoor crosses on one of the old tracks running from Buckfast Abbey to Tavistock or Buckland used by the monks. You will return to the start by another cross such as this. They are both on an ancient track that is not so easy to see these days.

Anyway the track that you are on now is easy to see and follow so you must set off left towards the south-west to the mine workings and ruins that you can make out on the hill ahead. You will pass on your right some ruins that were the houses where the mine workers lived until the beginning of this century for these mines were worked until then. Cross the brook by the little clapper bridge which is clearly not a medieval packhorse bridge, to the mine workings.

If you have time there are many things to see in the area of the two mines, Hooten Wheals and The Henroost. What marvellous names these are. I can find no explanation of what they mean and why they were so called except, of course, that Wheal is a word meaning a mine in Cornwall and comes from the Cornish 'huel'. You will find wheel pits, various areas for washing and dressing the ore and quite a few pits, shafts and blocked adits.

You could now cut this walk short by contouring round to the east until you come to Holne Ridge which you can follow down to Horn's Cross.

If you want to continue the walk then follow the O Brook north-west to Skir Ford sometimes called Henroost Gully (you will see why) and then on a wide sweep round to Skir Gut or Girt an amazing tinners' gully which runs north/south. Continue on over a broad plateau at the top of the Girt. You will not be on a watershed, for just below and down to the south is Aune or Avon Head and Fishlake Mire. Be careful not to wander too far south or you will find yourself on the wrong side of the hill and having to climb back north to get home. In mist this is confusing country!

You should now walk east and see if you can find Wellaby Gulf. Keep contouring round until you can see Holne Ridge running north and start to follow this down. You will be in an area of prehistoric remains and you might feel like diverting to look at some of them but they are not outstanding. However, you will soon come to Horn's Cross which like the cross you saw earlier is on the monks' track across the moor. Keep on down the ridge and over a reave, one of the ancient boundary banks, until you come to the road and a large Car Park near Combestone Tor.

It is worth wandering over to the tor and looking at the view down onto the wooded valley of the Dart where you might have been on Walks 1 and 2.

A short, sharp descent either on the road or on the moorland beside it, will take you down west to the start by Saddle Bridge.

WIDECOMBE WALKS

This is one of the most densely populated corners of Dartmoor with quite a number of lanes and roads cutting across it. There are several steep-sided valleys and a great number of farms with enclosed land round them. In the Introduction I said that all enclosed fields are private property and must not be entered unless there are marked and acknowledged rights of way. All this makes planning circular walks difficult - trying to avoid too many miles on roads and keeping out of private land but yet visiting the many places of interest to be found in this part of Dartmoor. Where it has been possible I have made the walks circular but for some of them you might prefer to go to one of the further points and then retrace your route back to the start.

On a few occasions I have mentioned things that are worth looking at which are not on any of the walks and can be visited just on their own.

21. Saddle Tor, Low Man, Hay Tor, Hay Tor Quarries, The Granite Railway, Holwell Quarries, (Grea Tor), Smallacombe Rocks, Grea Tor Rocks, Medieval Village, Hound Tor, (Chinkwell Tor, Bell Tor), Bonehill Rocks, Top Tor, Foale's Arrishes. *(See map p.128)*

START. Car Park near Saddle Tor. Map Ref.749762. This is a far less crowded and popular Car Park than the one at Hay Tor.

Widecombe-in-the-Moor is 3.5kms away with all the facilities of a busy, popular, tourist village. If you want a quieter, less busy general stores and Post Office I suggest you go on through Widecombe to Ponsworthy, a pretty little hamlet with a water-splash. There is usually room to park almost outside the shop. Bovey Tracey is 8kms away and is a small town with all the facilities you might require. There are Ice Cream and Snack Vans situated at the Hay Tor Car Parks most of the summer and fine weekends in winter.

Long. 7¾ miles. 12.5kms. Moderate. (A long walk but this is certainly one that can be cut short or even done in separate sections,

127

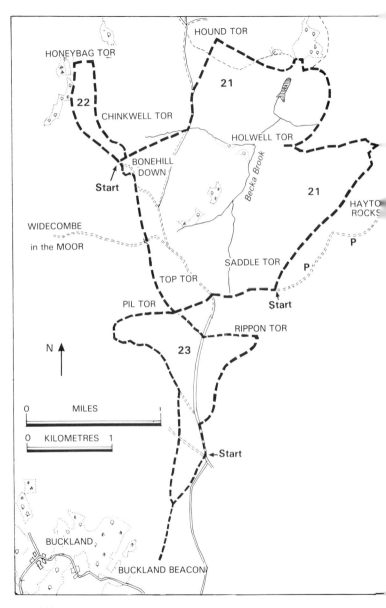

HOUND TOR

HONEYBAG TOR

22   CHINKWELL TOR

21

HOLWELL TOR

Becka Brook

BONEHILL DOWN

Start

21

HAYTOR ROCKS

WIDECOMBE

in the MOOR

P

SADDLE TOR   **P**

TOP TOR

Start

PIL TOR

RIPPON TOR

N ↑

23

0   MILES   1

0   KILOMETRES   1

←**Start**

BUCKLAND

BUCKLAND BEACON

Hay Tor

such as just including The Hay Tor Quarries from the Saddle Tor start or the Hound Tor, Saxon Village part of the walk as a short out and return from the Car Park at Hound Tor. Map Ref.739792.)

From the Car Park at Saddle Tor set off up the path north-east that leads to the col between the two summits. From there you will see the huge rockface of Low Man across a stretch of moorland about 1km away. When you reach it you will appreciate its size for it is the largest rockface on Dartmoor. There are some excellent and extremely difficult rock climbs on it, some of them 150 feet, but one of the less hair-raising ones, called Raven's Gully, goes up the obvious gully on the left of the face.

Walk round left below Low Man and then, if you wish to go easily to the top, scramble further round and you will find some steps cut with an iron hand rail and some rungs on the south-east side of the tor overlooking the Car Park.

Across the little grassy bay you will see Hay Tor itself. Again there are many good climbs on this rock too but if you wish to get to the top there is a flight of steps cut into the granite that start on the east side. Standing as they do on the south-eastern edge of Dartmoor, the views from both these tors are magnificent looking south to the coast with

Low Man - Hay Tor

Torbay and Lyme Bay and you can just see part of the Teign Estuary. Below you there are the flat areas of the Bovey Beds where there is a thriving clay industry utilizing decomposed granite eroded and washed off Dartmoor to collect in this basin. East you can see to Haldon Hill outside Exeter with its folly tower. Northwards you look over the eastern edge of the moor and up to Cawsands Beacon or Cosdon Hill on the northern limits of Dartmoor. All around to the north-west, west and south-west you can see the rolling moor stretching far away. It is no wonder that this is a popular place and if you prefer quiet and solitude do not come here at peak holiday times or fine weekends!

From the east side of Hay Tor you will see a path running down the hill towards the north-east to some granite spoil tips. When you get closer to the mounds of waste you can make out a wire fence round a quarry. There is a gate at the far, eastern, end where a track comes up from the south-east. Go into the quarry by the gate and you will find yourself in another of those unexpected, magical places where man has destroyed large areas of his environment but where nature has taken over again, when man has gone, returning it to something beautiful and unusual. Heather and gorse grow in profusion on the once harsh rockfaces whilst in summer dragonflies and butterflies flit over the man-made pools where water lilies grow. Trees and reeds have seeded themselves on the edges of the deep pits.

Not so huge and impressive as Foggintor and Swelltor Quarries but more beautiful, these are the Haytor Quarries that were operating in the 1820's. As with these two other quarries, Haytor granite from Dartmoor was used in the construction of many buildings in London such as the British Museum. In 1825 granite from here was used for the foundation stone of London Bridge and you still walk on bits of Dartmoor when you are in London for many of the old paving stones came from this quarry. Between the two pools at the west end lies an old wooden beam and iron winch, remnants of a crane for hoisting the blocks of granite on to trucks. How then did they get the granite out and away to London and other places? The answer to that will be found outside the quarry and to the east side. Go out through the gate again and work your way through the vast mounds of waste towards the east. The grassy area you will see was the site of quite a small village for the quarry workers with houses, a pub and even a school. You will soon also come to the remarkable granite rails of the tramway used for transporting the granite to the Stover Canal near Teigngrace and then on to Teignmouth for shipment all over Britain.

Both the quarries and the tramway were the work and brain child of a local landowner called George Templer. The rails are quite extraordinary when you consider the work involved in cutting the grooves for the wheel to run in and the distance that the track went; there is an exposed section of the rails still to be seen running beside a lane at Brimley near Bovey Tracey. There are points and sidings just as if the rails were made of iron but, of course, the granite was all around just for the quarrying, and cheap. Yet another example of this hard Dartmoor rock being used for the most extraordinary and unlikely objects. The blocks of granite were carried on huge, flat, wooden trucks pulled by as many as nineteen horses. Gravity looked after the downhill journey which must have been fairly hazardous as the trucks only had primitive wooden lever brakes.

Follow the granite rails now as they begin to swing west until you come to some points and here take the right hand track down hill. You will see ahead of you a jumble of waste mounds below Holwell Tor and soon you will be by the Holwell Quarries.

Again quite a few interesting things are to be seen here. An amazing sheer, smooth rockface is hidden just round a corner in the quarry. You can make out several small ruined buildings where stone masons and blacksmiths would have worked. There are several sections of the granite rail running at right angles to and across the main track that

Quarrymen's huts, Holwell Quarries

took the trucks out onto the jetties of rock facing north for dumping the waste material.

If you keep walking past the main quarries, where the track begins to swing round left, look down to a platform fifteen feet or so below on your right and you will see a small, stone, beehive hut with a low entrance. It has been suggested that this was built as a shelter for the quarrymen to use when they were blasting. It is still in remarkable condition but sadly over the last year it has begun to deteriorate, helped I am sure by vandals. Sadly this brave enterprise for the quarries and the transport of the granite was a victim of the arrival of the railways and the boom only lasted 30 years or so. By the 1860's the quarries and tramway were abandoned and deserted and gradually nature has claimed it back.

You must now retrace your steps back past the quarries and start to climb up the hill the way you came down the track. After 150 metres or so you will see a path on your left that contours round the head of the marshy valley of a side stream of the Becka Brook. Follow this path that will be deep in bracken in summer to what is called Grea Tor on the 1:50,000 Maps and Smallacombe Rocks on the 1:25,000 Maps. There are some hut circles on the flank of the tor, on your right, if you would like to find them. .

Go down north-west from the rocks to the edge of the woods below and you should find a path that will lead you to the right of way that crosses the Becka Brook after it has flowed out of the lakes made by damming the stream. This is a delightful valley owned by the Leighon Estate which is private land.

Over the stone bridge and then a steep climb up which will take you past Grea Tor Rocks which you will have seen from the opposite side of the valley. They form a long and impressive rockface seen from the east though, surprisingly, there are not many climbs here. If you are feeling agile you might like to traverse the ridge of Grea Tor Rocks. The views are splendid to the east, with the valley, clothed with bluebells in June, falling away to the lakes below and with Holwell Tor, Hay Tor and Low Man lining the hill opposite. You could almost imagine that you were in the high mountains here; Crib Goch, Striding Edge, the Alps even!

Follow one of the tracks to the ruins you will see on your right with Hound Tor, which now dominates the skyline, beyond to the north-west.

As you walk towards the low ruins you will see that the whole area of the wide flat valley of Houndtor Down has a great many banks and walls of ancient field systems. A corn ditch has been identified. You are now on the site of a medieval village mentioned in the Domesday Book as the Manor of Hundatora linked with the Abbey at Tavistock. It was the subject of intense archaeological excavations and digs in the 1960's and a great many interesting insights into how people lived and worked from the tenth to the fourteenth century were discovered with often a new dwelling being built on the foundations of an earlier one. The whole area, as was often the case, had been lived in earlier by Bronze Age people and it is interesting to note that this medieval period is when man changed from building round huts to rectangular houses but rather surprisingly out of wattle and turf. Why they rejected the granite lying all around nobody is quite sure. What you are seeing are probably the main foundations and low walls. The archaeologists discovered houses and barns, some with fireplaces and ovens, which can now be seen, used for drying the corn grown in the wet Dartmoor fields surrounding the village. There is also one building that has an entrance passage with the remains of an alcove in it facing north-east to avoid the sun and keep food cool. These were the beginnings of the longhouses that were to become the traditional style for Dartmoor farmhouses for centuries. It has been put forward that it was the Black Death in 1348 that caused such villages to be abandoned and to return into the soil. It is a fascinating place in a most beautiful

Fireplace - medieval village Hound Tor

setting.

Strike up the hill now towards Hound Tor. This, I think, is my favourite tor with its two wide grassy avenues running through, towering granite walls on either side. Great blocks of rock, pillars, cracks, small caves all covering a large area where you could spend a long time scrambling and exploring. From some angles it looks like a ruined castle or some great creature crouching on the hill. The name comes from the fact that one rock is said to be like a Hound's Head while others say that the tor looks like The Bowerman's pack of hounds turned to stone by the witches! Finally there are some fine rock climbs here.

The views looking back to Greator Rocks and Hay Tor are impressive while, away to the north, from the top of the highest point you will look along the eastern edge of Dartmoor, past Chagford to Cawsand Beacon or Cosdon Hill as it is called on some maps.

Walk south now from Hound Tor and divert if you wish to look for the Cairn Circle and kistvean on the open land opposite the drive to Hedge Barton. Bits of the kist are missing having been taken apparently by the road-makers some time ago.

Aim south now to the edge of the open moor where the wall will lead you down to the road.

Hound Tor with Hay Tor behind

A short section to walk now along the road and you will soon come to the cattle grid, after which you strike out right, across a rather wet and marshy area along the wall so it is best to keep away on the moorland to your left.

You will be going up Bell Tor and Chinkwell Top on another walk so unless you are feeling strong I should aim straight at Bonehill Rocks. These rocks are also worth exploring and the views from them over the Widcombe valley are superb.

Aim south from here across the open moorland to the top of Widecombe Hill where you will cross over the road and then walk on the Top Tor. From here you will see the low banks and walls of your next point which is Foale's Arrishes, south-east below Pil Tor.

This is an interesting settlement for it is late Bronze Age or even early Iron Age. There are not many of this period to be found on Dartmoor. There are a few hut circles standing within the 'Celtic' field system enclosed by banks and reaves.

You must walk east to the road junction at Hemsworthy gate to the area called Seven Lords Lands. Just north, along the road to Widecombe, and quite close to the wall on the left there is a fine large stone circle which is said to be the boundmark of seven manors hence the name Seven Lords Lands. A short walk along the road east, after the cattle grid, or on the verge on either side, passing several gullies or small gerts from a disused mine, will take you back to the Car Park below Saddle Tor.

22. Bonehill Rocks, Bell Tor, Chinkwell Tor, Honeybag Tor, Thornhill Lane *(See map p.128)*

START. Bonehill Rocks. Map Ref. 731776. There is plenty of room to park off the road near the rocks.

Widecombe is 1.6 kms away with all the facilities of a busy, tourist village. If you prefer a quieter village shop and Post Office I suggest that you go on through Widecombe to Ponsworthy, a pleasant little hamlet with a water splash. The shop there sells everything from bootlaces to brandy and there is nearly always parking space almost outside by the telephone kiosk.

Short. 2½ miles. 4 kms. Moderate.

Whenever friends come to stay with us and want a short walk I nearly always take them on this one. It has the most incredible views down the vale of Widecombe and a feeling of being on a high mountain ridge, if you keep looking left!

You can explore and clamber about on Bonehill Rocks either before you set off or when you get back. The views of Widecombe are good but they will be better still from Bell Tor. The tor is a favourite haunt of climbers who use it for 'bouldering'; a sort of rock gymnasium!

Follow the path northwards to Bell Tor with its extraordinary shapes, clefts and huge chock stone wedged in a wide chimney. As I said the view from here is breath-taking. You will see the vale of Widecombe-in-the-Moor stretching away with its pattern of fields running up to the edge of the open moor.

On the opposite side of the valley there is Kingshead Farm, one of the really high moorland farms owned by Ned Northmore, a delightful character, who used to take the part of Uncle Tom Cobley at Widecombe Fair, held each year on the second Tuesday in September.

Widecombe church, often called the cathedral of the moor, with its tall tower, was built by tinners and on one of the bosses in the roof you will find their symbol of three rabbits also seen in Chagford and other moorland churches probably built by them. With the Old Inn and the Elizabethan Church House standing round the square and some other

Bell Tor from Bonehill Rocks

pleasant houses the village is worth a visit but probably better out of the main holiday season.

There is another splendid pub in Widecombe called the Rugglestone Inn which lies about ½ km down the road that leaves the square towards the south-east. It is very small and you drink your beer, for it has no spirits licence, in the front parlour or, in summer, outside by the small brook that runs down from the rock from which the pub gets its name. The largest rock of the Rugglestone was estimated to weigh over 115 tons and was a logan stone which means that it was so balanced on a small pivot that it was possible to rock it but only by using the Widecombe Church key!

Enough of Widecombe, for the view extends to the great whaleback of Hamel Down on the opposite side of the valley and away to Princetown with the television mast on Hessary Tor visible ten miles away.

You must climb on now to Chinkwell Tor and it is here that you feel as if you are on a great mountain ridge.

Drop down a little and climb the last summit of Honeybags threading your way in and out of the great rock piles.

Beyond this last tor you will start to descend a little and then, when you can, turn left and make for the edge of the small wood where you will see a gate and a lane going through to the road in the valley. You will find a rough track now running back under the tors you have just walked over. This is the ancient Thornhill Lane that ran from old Saxon settlements up the valley down to the stannary town of Ashburton. It is easy walking along the track below the clitter and the stark tors above. Away on the horizon you can see the South Moor almost blocking the end of the Widecombe valley. Towards the end of the track high up to your left, on the flanks of Chinkwell Tor, you can make out a huge almost square tower of rock. On this there is an extremely difficult climb called Widecombe Wall.

A gentle stroll will bring you back to the start.

23. Cold East Cross, Rippon Tor, Newhouse, Foale's Arrishes, Tunhill Rocks, Blakslade Ford, Buckland Beacon. *(See map p.128)*

START. Cold East Cross. Map Ref. 741742. There is a large Car Park here.

Ashburton is 5.5 kms away with all the facilities of a small town. Widecombe is 5 kms away. Ponsworthy stores and Post Office is 5.5 kms.

Medium. 5 miles. 8 kms. Moderate.

Cold East Cross is a splendidly apt name. This is a bitter corner and whenever there is mist or snow or just bad weather you can be sure that you will find some of these or all three at this cross roads!

Walk about 300 metres north, parallel to the road, and enter the newtake by the gate on the east side which is set back in a recess. You will see a long track leading up towards the summit of Rippon Tor. As you walk you will see away to your right a large, squat, brick construction further east and down the hill. These are the butts of what were once the Rippon Tor Ranges. When I first came to live at Widecombe we could often hear the crackle of rifle and machine gun fire blowing on the wind. Thankfully the ranges were closed quite a number of years ago. On the way to the top you will see, to your left, a mass of rocks. Amongst these there used to be a logan stone called the Nutcracker Rock. Local people were supposed to bring their nuts up here to crack them at the festive season but really the tale does seem a little far fetched! It is hard to believe but it was blown up by mindless vandals so that the huge stone, over 3 metres long, no longer rocked on its pivot as it had done for thousands of years.

There are many things to look at on the summit of Rippon Tor

Summit burial cairns or barrows on Rippon Tor

which is 432 metres. To begin with, standing as it does on the eastern edge of the moor, the views looking out over the lowlands to Torbay, Lyme Bay and the Teign estuary as well as the South Hams are marvellous. But also turn and look back into the moorland and with your map try to identify the distant tors, hills and valleys both on the North and South Moors and away down the edge of Dartmoor to Brent Tor.

The huge mounds of rock are Bronze Age burial cairns for the chieftains of the people who lived in the various settlements around.

About 30 metres north-west from the summit you will discover one of the most curious stone crosses on Dartmoor. It is cut in relief in the living rock and is about 2 metres long and in a reclining position. It has been suggested that this holy symbol was cut here to drive away the evil, heathen spirits that might haunt this place of Bronze Age tombs.

Another 30 metres from the cross there is an unfinished mill-stone or possibly the base of a cheese-press; you will notice that there is a cross carved on it which could have been channels for the whey to run down, if it had been finished. There are two more half-finished stones nearby. It seems strange for the stone mason to work on them up here with all the difficulties of transporting them when they were completed.

From the summit now walk west with the wall on your left with the remains of the Nutcracker Rock on the other side. Below you will see a gate in the lower enclosure wall that will let you out onto the road to Ashburton. Turn left along it to where the wall that you followed down meets the roadside wall and you will see a flat rock with A carved on it and the date 1793. This is one of the boundary stones of the parish of Ashburton.

Walk on down to the ruins on the other, west, side of the road. All you will see now are low walls, some thorn trees and a pleasant grassy yard. This was Newhouse, a pub that was burnt down a great many years ago. It stood at quite an important crossing place with roads going off to Ashburton, Widecombe, Moretonhampstead, Bovey Tracey and Chagford. It was used by travellers using the bleak moorland road who were probably in the tin trade (both Ashburton and Chagford were stannary towns) but especially by the men who drove the wagons carrying wool to the woollen industry at Chagford and lime for the fields in that area, from Ashburton. Apparently they would drive like mad to get to the kilns early to avoid waiting. They would get rid of their loads of lime, wool and tin as quickly as possible and then spend the rest of the day in the pub on their return journey! A large number of carts with the patiently waiting horses could be seen lining the road near this lonely inn while gallons of cider and ale went down the throats of the drivers. Happy days! The last landlord of Newhouse was a man called Foale and it is to his arrishes that you are going next. 'Arrish' is Devon slang for field.

I should not try to walk straight to Foale's Arrishes as you might end up in Blackslade Mire but go north, along the verge of the road, until you can see an easy way across to the low walls of this ancient field system to the west of you. On the way you might notice some more boundary stones one of which has the odd name of Grey Goose's Nest. Within the 'Celtic' field system of this late Bronze Age or early Iron Age settlement there are several hut circles but all is rather overgrown. However it is interesting in that there is not much evidence of Iron Age Man on Dartmoor except here and Kes Tor. Obviously Foale, the landlord, did not make the fields but he may have used them for his own stock and it is his name that has remained.

There is another strange story told of how a local man boasted that he would build a house and farm within these ancient banks, or reaves, and hut circles and spend the rest of his days there. However he suddenly disappeared and was never seen again. Was it the pixies or the ghosts of the Iron Age people? Well this is Dartmoor!

Climb up now to Pil Tor, if you wish, or contour round to Tunhill

Rocks. There are good views into the Widecombe valley here but not so good as Bonehill Rocks, Walk 22.

If you strike south you will soon come to the ancient track that linked the farms of Blackslade and Tunhill with the Ashburton road.

Turn left along the track and follow it down past a Cairn and Cist marked on the maps. You can divert left a little and look at the kistvaen, if you wish. It is typical of many of the Bronze Age stone burial boxes that you can find on the moor. Sadly, typical also, quite a number of the stones are missing.

You must keep on down the track now to Blackslade Ford where you can get across the stream. You can now follow the stream, Blackslade Water, down on the true right bank, but this can be quite wet, to the pleasant little pine wood at Ruddycleave. This route would mean a short stretch on the road as you climbed back up the hill to the east to rejoin the route.

However, if you stick to the track you should soon find one of the paths made by the many pony trekking groups that pass this way, which will take you off the main track, south to a point halfway between the start at Cold East Cross and the road bridge back down at Ruddycleave.

Keep walking now across Buckland Common; be careful not to veer too far right. Soon you will come to a wall running parallel to your direction of travel with a well defined path beside it. Follow now the path to Buckland Beacon which you will see ahead.

This was probably one of the sites for the beacons lit to pass news quickly from one end of the country to another in Elizabethan times. The story of the sighting of the Spanish Armada is well known and how the news was flashed all over the country by the chain of beacons lit on high hills such as this one. The chain runs across Dartmoor. Ugborough Beacon, Buckland Beacon, Hameldown Beacon, Cosdon Beacon which could well have been seen from Dunkery Beacon on Exmoor. It is obvious why Buckland was chosen as one of these points for it is high, 390 metres, and looks out over a wide sweep of both moor and lowland. It is also quite close to farms and buildings. The view looking down onto the lovely wooded valley of Holne Chase is magnificent and such views down wooded valleys are only repeated from such places as Leigh Tor and Mel Tor on earlier walks.

The little village of Buckland-in-the-Moor is also below with its delightful church with its fine screen and Norman font. It has the words 'My Dear Mother' round the clock face instead of the numbers of the hours.

If you walk to the southern side of the Beacon you will find the two large rocks with the Ten Commandments carved on them by Mr. W.Arthur Clement, a sculptor, in 1928 on the instructions of Mr. W.Whitley who lived at Welstor, and was Lord of the Manor of Buckland. Mr. Clement lived in a small hut near the Beacon while he completed the work. It is said that Mr. Whitley had the carving done because of the decision by Parliament not to issue a revised Prayer Book.

If you climb up higher you will see another carving that tells you that it was not only in Tudor times that beacons were lit for they had one here in 1935 to celebrate the Silver Jubilee of King George V as you will read. With an eye to tradition local people also built a fire here for the Silver Jubilee of our Queen Elizabeth.

You must now retrace your steps back along the wall northwards and then find your way to the start either by walking along the road from the cattle grid and trees at Deadman's Corner or cutting across the open moor.

24. Bennett's Cross, Birch Tor, Headland Warren, Stone Row, Headland Warren Farm, Hookney Tor, King's Barrow, Grimspound, (Hameldown Tor), Headland Warren, Mines.

(See map p.144)

START. Bennett's Cross on the Moretonhampstead to Two Bridge road, B3212. Map Ref.681817. There is a Car Park close to the cross.

Postbridge is 4.5kms away with a Post Office and stores, petrol pumps and large Car Parks and Toilets. There are several small hotels and a pub. The Dartmoor National Park has an Information building here open from spring to late summer. The whole area is popular and busy in the summer months.

The Warren House Inn is just over ½km from the cross. This is said to be the third highest pub in Britain and obviously as its name suggests a place where the landlords also used to breed rabbits on a commercial basis using artificial burrows to keep them in. In fact, like the ruins of the pub on the Ashburton to Chagford road, Walk 22, the Warren House Inn was also known as Newhouse and was on the opposite side of the road where you can still see the foundations. It was a popular drinking haunt of the miners who worked in the various mines you will visit in these next walks. It is said that the fire, which used to burn peat, has not been out for 100 years. I leave it to you to believe that yarn or not. The other story told about the Warren House Inn also needs some believing but as the same tale occurs in various other parts of Dartmoor and indeed was recounted by Henry

The Ten Commandments Stone, Buckland Beacon

Williamson, the author of Tarka the Otter, in one of his short stories I am inclined to believe this one.

One stormy night the snow drifts were so deep around the Warren House Inn that a traveller going across the moor was forced to ask for bed and lodging there. He was received with great hospitality and after a good meal was shown to the bedroom. In the corner was a great chest and overcome with curiosity he peeped inside. You can imagine his horror when he saw, laid out in it, the body of an old man. He spent a sleepless night thinking that the owners were murderers who killed their guests for their money and then disposed of their bodies claiming that they had got lost on the moors. However, in the morning, pale and weary, he plucked up enough courage to ask about the body in the chest. 'Why bless you, 'said the landlady, 'That's father. He died a few months back and, what with the weather being so bad and the ground frozen so hard, we have not been able to bury him, so we salted him down as we do with the bacon! When the weather improves we shall take him to Widecombe to bury him'.

Back at Bennett's Cross there is one final Dartmoor legend that I should tell you. On the slope of the far side of the valley, looking across east to Birch Tor, where you will be going as soon as I can stop recounting Dartmoor tall stories, you will see several enclosures.

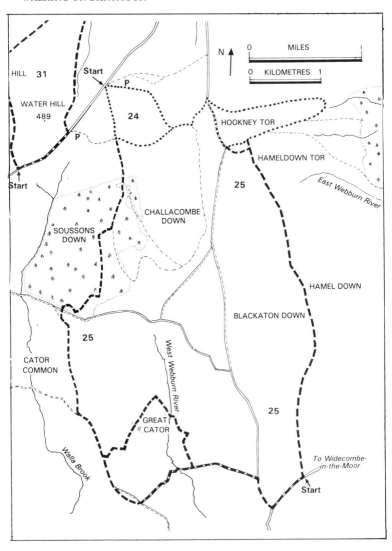

These, if your imagination is good, are said to look like the aces from a pack of cards and were supposed to have been dropped by the wicked tinner Jan Reynolds as he was carried on his last ride over the area by the Devil. See the full story in the section on Dartmoor Legends! *Medium. 5½ miles. 8.75kms. Moderate*

This is a walk that you most certainly can do in two short halves. One with the start as suggested here at Bennett's Cross, the other starting at the small lay-by below Grimspound. Map Ref.697809.

Bennett's Cross was put here probably to mark the track across the moor from Moretonhampstead. It also serves as a boundary marker for the parishes of Chagford and North Bovey. As well as this it was the bondmark for Headland Warren and has the letters WB cut into it to represent Warren Bounds. It might well also have connections with the tin trade for a William Benet from the stannary of Chagford was a juror in the Tinner's Parliament held on Crockern Tor in the reign of Henry VIII. An important cross you will see.

You will notice several paths leading off from the Car Park. Follow the one on the left that runs more easterly and towards Birch Tor seen on the skyline ahead. You pass near an enclosure and then round the head of two deep gerts, the disused mining gullies, part of the Birch Tor and Vitifer Mines. Keep following the path that will bring you to the Tor. The views from the top are good looking over the north-east edge of Dartmoor and also west to Princetown and the T.V. Mast on Hessary Tor.

You must walk just east of south now until you come to the miners track running over the col to Headland Warren Farm where you will be going in a minute. Cross the track and work your way round the head of two gerts at the east end, still moving south. You will soon see the Challacombe Down triple stone row with its burial circle at one end.

Walk back to the miners track after looking at the rows which in fact have been re-erected, the stones having been discovered lying on the ground last century. It is here that you can cut this walk short and go back down west to the mines by following the track and reading the description of what to see given at the end of the walk.

However, if you are going on, then swing to your right and walk east down the track to Headland Warren Farm. It is a remote and lonely place dating from the thirteenth century. I am always intrigued by the monkey puzzle trees growing beside the thatched buildings. This also was a pub frequented by the thirsty miners from the Headland Mine and the Birch Tor and Vitifer Mines. It was known as Birch Tor Inn at one time. A sign used to hang outside that said, 'Jan Roberts lives here, Sells cider and beer, Your hearts for to cheer; And if you want meat To make up a treat Here be rabbits to eat.' What more do you want?!

Another owner of Headland was a James Hannaford who, returning one dark night from the Warren House Inn to his home, fell down one of the many mine shafts in the area. Somehow his fall was stopped by a wooded platform but he was too far down to climb out. His faithful collie remained by the shaft all night whimpering and whining. Daylight came and search parties set out to look for James, the word having got round that he had not returned. After a considerable time, attracted and guided by the collie's barks, they arrived at the shaft and were able to haul the old man out. As you would expect James Hannaford never forgot that he owed his life to his faithful dog. When he eventually died James was buried in Widecombe, his coffin having been carried along the great ridge of Hamel Down to the churchyard.

There are several tracks that will lead you up to the road. Keep to the left hand one that will take you near to a quarry on the east side of the road. The path that skirts the hill from the quarry will take you round to Grimspound but, I should aim up towards Hookney Tor. Perched high on the slopes above the valley as it is there are some fine views south.

The strange parallel terraces running along the slopes of Challacombe Down, on the right hand side of the valley, that you can see are called lynchets. They are banks formed by contour ploughing with oxen in medieval times to prevent soil erosion and to enable the steep hillside to be cultivated. From the tor, if you aim just south of east, you will drop down to a fairly flat area but one that is covered in heather and, unless you can find the paths, it makes for tiring walking. Just to the right of the path, that you should meet, there is an interesting kistvaen. It stands in its retaining circle and has two stone lids one of which is still in position.

Return to the path and follow it for a while. This eventually leads on to the old miners track from Natsworthy to Headland. However, you will see a boundary stone to your left with a B carved on it which marks the outer limits of the parishes of North Bovey and Manaton so leave the path. Ahead is the large mound of King's Barrow. I am sure that this was the burial place of one of the chieftains who lived at Grimspound. Like so many of the barrows it has been badly disturbed, partly by treasure seekers and also, I am sure, to obtain stones and rocks for buildings and walls nearby. King's Tor is lower down to the north if you want to wander down to it. The view from the barrow is very fine looking towards Teignmouth and the south coast.

Turn back south-west and try to find the path that lies to the left or south side of the wet, marshy land called Grimslake, which will take you down to Grimspound.

This, of course, is the most famous and the nearest to the road and therefore the most frequently visited of the Bronze Age Pounds. It covers an area of about four acres and the impressive outer wall is over 500 metres in circumference. It is, in fact, a double wall with the gap between the two probably filled with rubble and earth. When first built it has been estimated that it was at least 2 metres high.

Inside the pound there are the remains of 24 huts, some with excellent angled protected entrances to keep the rain and wind out of the doorway. There is a massive gateway on the south side with its paving stones still in position. It would have been closed with great baulks of timber. It is quite easy to visualise in your imagination life going on here with these Bronze Age people.

The Pound was probably on the edge of the forest which clothed the lower slopes and valleys and which was the haunt of wolves and bears. The inhabitants of Grimspound would have grazed their animals on the slopes of Hameldown and Hookney Tors on either side. At night they would have driven their sheep, goats and cattle into the Pound for protection against not only the wild animals but other marauding tribes. Their water supply still flows from Grimslake on the north side of the wall.

Walk on down the track that runs west from Grimspound if you want to reach the lay-by where you might have left your car if you decided to do just this section of the walk.

If you have to get back to Bennett's Cross then cross over the stepping-stones in the little stream on the north side of the Pound and look for the lower contouring path which will take you back to the quarry on the road that you came to after Headland Warren. Then retrace your steps back down to the Farm and up the other side to the col and then on down the hill following the track. You pass, on your left, a huge 15 metre deep gert called Chaw Gully - Chaw being a corruption of Chough, the rare Cornish bird associated with the spirit of King Arthur that must have bred and flown here. This is just one of the amazingly deep gashes hacked and blasted out of the hillsides by the miners.

Soon you will come to the valley floor and a delightful grassy area with quite a number of ruins around. A small stream, the Redwater Brook that joins the West Webburn River, flows under a stone bridge.

Tinners' Pits near Headland Warren

Red I suspect because of the minerals in it.

You are now standing where there was a thriving tin mining industry, parts of which survived until the 1930's, that provided work for many people of Dartmoor from the nearby villages and farms. Thus ended a Dartmoor industry that had been in existence from before the twelfth century.

The mines at Vitifer went to over seventy-seven fathoms (all mine depths were recorded in fathoms) and the miners worked drenched to the skin in a constant downpour of water from upper levels. Power for the pumps and crushing mills came from water wheels and Vitifer had a leat of over eight miles to gather enough water for its huge wheel.

You follow the track north and then leave it for the path still going north. You will pass, on your left, the large flooded wheel pit that is quite dangerous; it would be hard to get out if you fell in and you may not have a collie with you!

You can either follow the path up steeply left or go on into the gert ahead. Whichever you choose you will soon emerge onto the heather covered open moor and a good path will bring you back to the Car Park at Bennett's Cross.

25. Hameldown Beacon, Hameldown Tor, Grimspound, Headland Warren Farm, Mines, Soussons Forest, Cator Common. *(See map p.144)*

START. Two Ways, Dunstone Down, Widecombe. Map Ref.708763. There is an area on the crest of the hill on the north side of the road where you can park.

Widecombe is just down the hill 1.3kms away with all the facilities of a busy, tourist village. Ponsworthy Post Office is less crowded. For more details of Widecombe and the facilities see Walk 22.

Long. 10 miles. 16kms. Moderate.

This is a long all day walk that takes place in a pleasant mixture of open moor, forest and lanes.

Set off north on the obvious track which in fact will lead you all the way to Grimspound. It takes you on a gentle climb with ever increasing splendid views down into the vale of Widecombe and across to Bonehill, Bell Tor, Chinkwell and Honeybags where you may have been on Walk 22.

On your right you will soon come to the upper enclosure wall of the fine, remote, moorland farm of Kingshead, owned by Ned Northmore, one of the last few true Dartmoor farmers who used to take the part of Uncle Tom Cobley on Widecombe Fair Day, the second Tuesday in September. You will see the farm tucked into a small hollow with windbreak trees around. A few years ago there was the most extraordinary landslide quite close to the farm buildings. A huge amount of water, after heavy rain, must have found a way underground from the moor above to collect like an enormous blister under the surface turf on the side of a steep field. When it could be contained no more it burst, with a roar, and sent hundreds of tons of mud and rubble sweeping down the valley, knocking down walls and fences. It left behind a huge scar on the hillside like a bomb crater 20 metres across which is still there today.

You will see to your left a track going north-west. This is part of the old Church Way or Widecombe Way. It linked the farms and other dwellings of the interior, such as Pizwell and Babeny, with the village of Widecombe so that the inhabitants of these ancient tenements could pay their tithes to the parson there rather than Lydford to which parish in those days they belonged. It leads down to the village by way of Church Head Lane to your right.

Your track goes on north, badly eroded by pony trekking and rain water, until you come to the summit cairn and carved stone on

Hameldown Beacon. There are fine views from here.

On the slope before the summit and indeed further on along the path you may have noticed some wooden poles now grey with age. These were put here during the Second World War to prevent German gliders landing. Marvellous 'Dad's Army' type escapades of the local Home Guard during the war are now almost becoming a new generation of Dartmoor legends and tall stories! The path follows the wall, on your left, of the newtakes of Blackadon Manor and will take you by Two Barrows and then Single Barrow and finally Broad Barrow, all Bronze Age burial sites.

All these graves yielded interesting finds in the form of burnt human bones, charcoal and, unexpectedly, a flint flake for there is no flint to be found on Dartmoor. But most exciting find of all was a bronze blade of a dagger with its amber pommel inlaid with small pins of gold.

The whale-back ridge allows you to stride along at a steady rhythm with a splendid feeling of being on top of the world.

Next on the route is Hamel Down Cross which was probably put up as a boundary stone. DS on it stand for the Duke of Somerset who once owned Natsworthy Manor down to the east.

Hameldown Tor with its Triangulation pillar is another fine viewpoint, especially looking down towards Grimspound as you descend. From here you can see to the north Yes Tor and High Willhays, the highest peaks of Dartmoor at just over 2000 feet or, rather less dramatic, 619 and 621 metres! North-east you can just make out Castle Drogo the last castle to be built in England and designed by Lutyens. It is now owned by the National Trust. To the east the low ridges are the Haldon Hills near Exeter with the folly Haldon Belvedere on them. Further away on fine days you can make out the Blackdown Hills in Somerset. South there is Hay Tor and Rippon Tor and then all away to the south-west, west and north-west you will see the whole expanse of Dartmoor. It is worth setting your map and trying to identify the distant hills.

Drop down steeply now to Grimspond. All the details of this Bronze Age settlement and the next section of this walk (Headland Warren Farm. Chaw Gully. Vitifer Tin Mines) will be found in Walk 24.

This is where you now leave the previous walk. You could, if you wish, walk on up the track from the ruined mine buildings to the Warren House Inn. Again you will find details of this pub in Walk 24 but unless you have timed things very carefully they are bound to be shut!

Follow the track south down towards the edge of the forest which

Main gate at Grimspound

you enter by the gate. Almost immediately you will find yourself in an area of ruined mine buildings and remains. These were once the Golden Dagger Mine and you will notice a large gert or gully on your right. If you have time you can scramble up along the edge and you will come to quite a number of open shafts that are fenced in. This is a dangerous area so go with great caution and care.

Back on the main track at the bottom you will see quite a number of footpath signs directing you to various places by following different rights of way. You will need to follow the right hand footpath and not go to Challacombe Down or even Soussons Farm.

I enjoy walking in these forestry planations. I love the deep, dark, secret glades and the smell of warm conifers or damp earth and pine needles in autumn when I come here looking for edible fungi!

If all goes well you should emerge on one of the larger rides where you turn right where the footpath sign points to a narrow track straight on back into the forest towards Soussons Farm. This large made-up track will lead you to the road quite close to Ephraim's Pinch. How it got this odd name is yet another Dartmoor story. It appears that there was a man called Ephraim who laid a wager that he could carry a sack of corn from Widecombe to Postbridge without dropping it. He set off going well until he reached this incline or pinch about 5½kms out from Widecombe. It proved too much for him and he was forced to drop the sack and from that day this little hill has been known as Ephraim's Pinch!

It might interest you to turn right, along the road, for a short while and have a look at Runnage Circle standing back in its own grassy bay. It is an almost perfect Bronze Age retaining Circle with the remains of a kistvaen. From the Circle walk across the heather land southwards and you will cross a stony track. This is the ancient Church Way crossed previously on your way to Hameldown Beacon which links Pizwell and other farms with Widecombe.

Go through the gate with the sign showing that it is a Bridle Way that leads out over Cator Common.

The path runs along the edge of a mire where in the dusk, if you are lucky, you will hear snipe thrumming.

There is another fine retaining circle to be seen which has been revealed after the removal of most of the rest of the cairn, on the right of the path if you wish to divert to it. Further on still, off to the right, there is Cator Pound another ancient enclosure.

You will have been walking parallel to a fine double line of beeches and pines planted as a windbreak that runs away on either side of the road that you will soon come to.

Pass through the gate and turn left along this road which links Poundsgate and Ponsworthy with Bellever and Postbridge. There is a wide enough verge for you to walk on grass for much of the way and the views off to your right are fine, looking towards Bellever and Laughter Tors beyond Riddon Ridge.

At the first turning left you can decide if you would like to go via Cator Court, a slightly longer route along pleasant country lanes, or go a little further along to the end of Corndon Down and take the next turning left through Lower Cator. Both will take you along unfrequented lanes over the West Webbern River to Rowden Cross.

When you reach this T junction you will see why it is called a crossroads. Ahead there is an overgrown lane that runs up past a little bungalow on the hill. This was the old road to Widecombe though it is impassable now. Turn right along the main road for 200 metres until you come to quarries both on your right and left. Strike up left now by the walls of the enclosed fields and onto the open moor. A long, gentle diagonal climb across short turf and gorse bushes will get you back to the brow of the hill and the start of the walk.

26. Prehistoric Remains, Bellever Tor, Laughter Tor, Huccaby, Brimpts, Babeny, (Dartmeet), Snaily House, Bellever.

(See map p.154)

START. Postbridge. Map. Ref.646787. I have given the map reference of the Car Park just inside the gate and cattle grid of the forestry plantations on the little side road to Bellever. However, there is a larger Car Park on the north side of the main Moretonhampstead to Two Bridges road B3212 that you could use. There is a National Park Information building there and Toilets.

Postbridge has a Post Office and stores with petrol pumps. There is a pleasant pub and several small hotels and guest houses.

The whole area is usually very crowded in the summer and at fine weekends. The well-known clapper bridge spans the river just south of the main road bridge. This route across the moor is very ancient and the clapper bridge was built for the packhorses and, of course, for the post-road hence the name Postbridge.

The Clapper Bridge is a fine sight with its immense slabs of granite forming the arches standing on piers and buttresses. However, round about the 1820's the northernmost slab was pushed into the river by a local farmer. His idea was that eventually he would lever all of them off and with luck they would lie on their edges leaning against the piers to form a dam across the river. The reason for this I would hasten to add was not pure vandalism, as might be the case today, but so that the ducks belonging to the man responsible for this would not swim off down the river! The plan, however, did not work, for the first slab fell flat into the river bed and the whole idea was abandoned. In 1880, on the insistence of the Duchy, it was put back in place but as one local inhabitant remarked it was placed, 'upside down and inside out.'!

Long. 9¼ miles. 15kms. Moderate. (It is very easy to cut this walk down to 5¾ miles. 9.5kms by leaving out Huccaby, Brimpts and Babeny. I shall explain where you can take this alternative route.)

The other problem is that if there has been a lot of rain and the River Dart is up, it is unlikely that you will be able to get across the stepping-stones between Brimpts and Babeny. Pessimistic people will tell you that this will be for eight months in the year! If you feel that there may be problems then you must go on down to the road to Dartmeet and follow the true left bank of the East Dart up to Babeny and leave out Brimpts.

Set off from the Car Park in the corner of the forest in a south-westerly direction down one of the ridges. Be careful not to take the left-hand southerly track; this is one you will return on. Soon you will emerge from the forest at Knaps Circle a Bronze Age settlement with hut circles.

You will see a broad corridor leading south between the trees and you will be aware that the forest has been planted in two sections, east

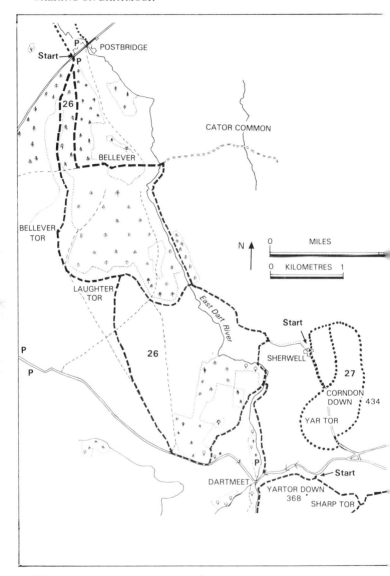

East Dart at Bellever Forest

and west. This is because the whole area to the south of you is rich in prehistoric remains and the Forestry Commission wisely did not wish to destroy them. However, a lot of damage had already been done by a local farmer when clearing the land many years ago.

You must work your way down looking at those remains that interest you and catch your eye, but you should not miss one of the best kistvaens on Dartmoor about ½km after Knaps Circle. It stands in a small clearing in the forest, to your left, surrounded by the usual retaining circle of stones and with a small stone row running off eastwards. The stone box is quite big enough to take a large body and is in fine condition. The whole site was, in fact, restored quite a number of years ago.

Keep on down the corridor and after another ½km you will find a well-defined track running east/west across your direction of travel which disappears into the forest. This is the Lich Way or Path of Death and you can trace its route east right across the North Moor to emerge near Lynch Tor on its way to Lydford. To the west the track runs to Widecombe which was partly the reason for the track being made. Like the Church Way it was used by the inhabitants of the farms and Ancient Tenements in the interior of Dartmoor to pray at the church in Widecombe which was much nearer than their parish church at Lydford. Walter Bronescombe, Bishop of Exeter, gave permission for them to do this in 1260. He also gave permission for the people of these tenements to carry their dead along the path for burial also in Widecombe churchyard hence the name The Path of the Dead. What a sight it must have been, these processions carrying the coffins of the dead along the ancient paths across the mysterious and unrelenting moor.

Ahead of you lies Bellever Tor and you will soon reach the summit after a gentle climb. It is a most marvellous viewpoint being the highest point for quite a few miles around at 443 metres standing in the heart of the moor. The old name for the tor and indeed the farm in this area, one of the Ancient Tenements, was Bellaford. The tor was a famous meeting place at the end of the last century and into the beginning of this. There was a kind of hunting festival that ended on the first Friday in May with a gathering known as 'Bellever Day' when hundreds of local people met for picnics, after hunt and pony and even foot races. In 1901 it was reckoned that over one thousand people were here, with at least five hundred of them on horseback while many others had come by carts, pony and traps and wagonettes. The meeting was said to be as popular as the Tavistock Goosie Fair. It is a sad reflection on our times that simple, naive even, but happy country gatherings such as these are gone forever and do not really have a place in our cynical, flashy world. The tor itself has been eroded in wierd and fantastic shapes with very pronounced layers called 'false bedding plains'; false because bedding plains, in fact, only occur with sedimentary rocks and this is granite. There are clefts, cracks and chimneys and if you look hard you will see sharp little faces peering out at you sculpted in the rock.

You must now walk on south and by the corner of the forest swing south-east towards Laughter Tor across more ancient field systems.

Again another name problem. This is really Lough Tor and is not so impressive as Bellever Tor but if you are here in late July or August bring a bag to gather wortleberries for this is a good area for them. Just south of the tor there is a large, rectangular enclosure with high walls known as Lough Tor Pound. Local moormen used to talk of it as a 'sheep measure'. The splendid idea was that because they knew its capacity, when it was full they did not have to count the sheep herded into it!

It is here that you can now make the decision whether to cut the walk short or not, but as I mentioned earlier about the stepping-stones below Brimpts there could well be a problem of the same sort here if you wish to cross the East Dart on another set of stepping-stones below Laughter Hole House to get to Snaily House.

If you have any doubts about the river then walk east from the sheep measure to the corner of the forest where you will see a gate and waymark leading into a forest track. This is the right of way that will take you through Laughter Hole Farm and on to Bellever hamlet.

If you wish to try to cross the river then follow the edge of the forest down past Laughter Hole House, on your left, to the stepping-stones I have already mentioned. Once on the far bank then follow the path north beside the river.

If you want to complete the walk then walk south from Lough Tor Pound towards the tall standing stone called Laughter Man near a double stone row. After these two Bronze Age remains still keep south beyond the wall and you may come across an area of gullies and shafts from the old Brimpts Mine. Like most of the Dartmoor mines this was closed over a century ago. In 1866 it produced 3½ tons of black tin. The track you will also cross is called The Postman's Road and was used by the local postmen riding on horseback to deliver the mail to remote farms in this area.

Something else that might interest you is off to your right and that is Outer Huccaby Ring, a prehistoric enclosure.

You walk downhill now past the low lying Huccaby Tor and down to Huccaby Ring, another but smaller enclosure. Below you is a gate that will lead you onto the Ashburton to Two Bridges Road, the B3357.

Turn left and there is a short walk along the road or on the verges past Huccaby Cottage for ½km to the entrance to Brimpts. Turn in left and follow the drive past the farm, that is if you do not want a cream tea! The path is waymarked.

(If you have any doubts about the state of the river then I am afraid that you must continue on down the road to Dartmeet and go through the huge

Car Park area past Badgers Holt and find the busy but delightful path that runs up the East Dart below Yar Tor to join our route just before Babeny.)

Brimpts is one of the thirty-five Ancient Tenements on Dartmoor; farms of great antiquity that were probably in existence even before the bounds of the forest were drawn up. They were not owned originally by the Duchy but in quite a few cases they have now been bought by the Duchy. The owners had several privileges, one of which was, until 1796, a right of enclosing eight acres of new land if the father and grandfather of the tenant had held the farm successively.

The path drops down diagonally across fields towards the river which you hear and see glinting below in its tree filled valley. There are gaps or gates in the walls of the fields to get you through and the actual path is not obvious. Please do not forget to shut any gates. You will pass, on your left, an old ruin of which one wall is still standing with a massive granite lintel in position over the fireplace and an upper fireplace half way up. This is Dolly's Cot.

It is told how, in the time of Sir Thomas Tyrwhitt, there was a cantankerous and moody local man who brought his beautiful young wife, whom he had recently married, to live in this remote house to keep her away from the large number of ardent male admirers who had been flocking around her! Apparently some of these were the guests at the bachelor house-parties of Sir Thomas Tyrwhitt who had built and lived at Tor Royal near Princetown. (See Walk 16.) It was even rumoured that one of these admirers was the then Prince of Wales who became Prince Regent and later George IV who was, of course, a friend of Sir Thomas; who knows!

You will soon be on a delightful wooded path beside the East Dart a most marvellous contrast with the open moor, one of the things that make this walk so fine. The path will lead you to the stepping-stones across the river. Watch out for some are pretty small and wobbly and all can be slippery when wet. Once across follow the true right bank of the Walla Brook, straight ahead, which has its source near the Warren House Inn and enters the Dart just here by the stepping-stones.

You will soon come to an interesting three span clapper bridge over the Walla Brook. Cross over and dive through the thorn trees and you will find yourself in a wide, grassy glade lying in a bowl surrounded by the steep hills of the Brimpts Plantations and Yar Tor. Another delightful spot; one of the most beautiful and secluded on Dartmoor.

Follow the path round until you come to the road opposite a very pleasant small camp site. Turn left and walk up the hill through the farm gate to Babeny. Once again the path is well waymarked here so please follow it as you are well within the farmyard and its buildings.

Babeny is yet another of the Ancient Tenements who obtained permission to pay their tithes, worship and bury their dead at Widecombe from Bishop Bronescombe in 1260. In 1302 the people of Babeny built their own mill here, the king supplying the timber which came from his nearby forests. In return they had to supply the labour to work the mill when required.

Follow the waymarked path until you will emerge from the enclosed land once again onto the open moor.

You will soon drop diagonally down the hill to the edge of the forest and the stepping-stones below Laughter Hole House which you could have come across if you had taken the shorter alternative.

You walk along the path between the pine forest and the river for about ½km and you will notice an overgrown ruin set back on the edge of the trees. This is Whiteslade or Snaily House.

Yes, I am afraid you have guessed it, there is another Dartmoor story coming up!

Two spinster sisters lived at this remote farm, long before, of course, the forests were here. In spite of the fact that it was a very poor farm with little or no livestock the sisters always seemed plump and well fed. One night, overcome with curiosity at how they managed to survive so well, their neighbours crept down and peeped through the window at the two old ladies sitting down to their evening meal. You can imagine their astonishment and maybe disgust when they saw that the two spinsters were tucking into a large bowl of black slugs! The secret was out! It is said that the two sisters were so ashamed that they soon faded away and died.

The ruins have a strange, ghostly air about them and you can still see the ancient fireplace where the two old ladies would have brewed up their slug stew!

Keep on along the river and out of the forest. The thickly planted trees continue on the steep hillside opposite. It is easy, pleasant walking here on short turf and it is a popular place in summer for picnics and swimming in the river.

You will soon come to the two Bellever Bridges. One is the fairly modern road bridge while the other is a fine clapper bridge. Sadly, however, the central span of the clapper bridge is missing but there is no sign of it lying in the river. It could have been removed or it is just possible that the gap did not originally have a stone but baulks of timber instead. The crossing point is important and ancient as it is on the Lich Way to Widecombe crossed earlier so could well date from before the thirteenth century.

Turn left and walk up the road. There is an entrance into the forest, left, with large Car Parks and Toilets open in summer. There are Picnic Sites, Nature Trails and Forest Walks here, arranged and organised by the Forestry Commission so you might enjoy coming back here another day.

Bellever hamlet is mainly owned by the Forestry Commission who have a large works and headquarters here as well as the line of houses and there is also, of course, the Youth Hostel.

You can decide now to walk back to the start either in the forest or out of it.

If you want to follow the road or the footpath just to the right or east of it, then walk up round the corner by the houses leaving the Youth Hostel on your left and continue up the hill towards Postbridge.

If you would prefer the forest then walk up the track to the west leaving the Youth Hostel on your right. This is the Lich Way. Soon turn right along the fields and then after a while left. It is quite a climb up to 405 metres. At the crossroads nearly 1km after the Youth Hostel turn right and walk north along the forest ride, passing another kistvaen and circle in the woods on your right. In 1.4kms you will be back at the start after a splendid striding walk through the sweet smelling pines.

27. Corndon Down and Tor, Sherwell, Yar Tor. *(See map p.154)*

START. Near memorial cross on Sherwell Road. Map Ref.682738. There is plenty of room to park on the verge here off the road.

Dartmeet with its Cafe and Snack Bar, large Car Park and Toilets is 1.5kms away. Ponsworthy Post Office and stores is just over 2kms away. The Tavistock Inn at Poundsgate is just over 3kms away. *Short. 2½ miles. 4kms. Easy.*

Walk up east to the obvious granite cross standing on a rock known locally as 'The Belstone Bible'. This is a memorial to a young soldier killed in Palestine by a sniper in 1918 aged 19, Lieut. Evelyn Cave Penny.

Strike on up the hill north-east to Corndon Tor, known also as Belstone Chair, with its summit cairns. This is a fine viewpoint with Dartmoor unfolding all around with also glimpses to the South Hams. Walk north along the ridge to the other cairns; great mounds of rocks that mark Bronze Age burial places. A great many reaves, the boundary banks and walls can also be found on Corndon Down

Memorial cross on Corndon, Sharp Tor behind

running off east-wards. Continue on down the ridge slightly west of north until you can see walls ahead then swing west to the track that runs back down south to Sherwell, between walls to emerge on the road.

This whole valley up to Babeny is worth exploring. It is almost a green oasis of fields standing in the heart of the moor and surrounded by tors and open commons.

As you might expect in such a contained area there are several stories of the past to be found. At Higher Sherwell in the early part of the last century the owner turned his farm into an ale house where cock-fighting used to take place. It was known as 'The Cockler's Peep Inn'!

There is a stone near here called the Miller's Mile as it is exactly a mile from the mill at Babeny mentioned in Walk 26. On the opposite side of the valley there are the Flour Rocks where a pack-horse coming from the mill bolted one day and shed its load of flour turning the rocks white for some weeks.

The modern house with the name Rogue's Roost was built on the site of an old longhouse where sheep rustlers lived.

Granny White who was a white witch lived in the area with a mad son.

And so it goes on! Walk south, down the road, until you can see a way right that will take you clear of the enclosure walls across a stream to Yar Tor.

There are superb views from Yar Tor looking down on Dartmeet with its mass of ant like tourists and their motor cars packed like Dinky Toys in the Car Park. You can also look across to Brimpts and see the path you might have followed on Walk 26 and indeed you can see nearly all the route of that walk from Babeny up to the forest near Laughter Hole House.

There is a huge cairn on the summit that has been fashioned into an amazing hut circle like shape with a protected, curving, entrance passage.

It is an easy and quick walk back down to the start.

This makes a fine evening walk or for any other occasion when you have not got a lot of time. Of course if can be cut short.

28. Visits to Bowerman's Nose, Jay's Grave, Dunnabridge Pound.

There are three more things that might interest you in this section of Dartmoor that I have not been able to include in any of the walks.

The Bowerman's Nose. Map Ref.743805, not far from the road that runs across Hayne Down.

This fantastic, isolated granite tower is about 13 metres high. If you are a climber you can get to the top but the start is a little tricky! The name could be a corruption of the Celtic *vawr maen* which means large stone. However, a man called Bowerman did live near Hound Tor in the times of the Conqueror; I wonder if it was at the medieval village between Hound Tor and Grea Tor Rocks that you might have visited on Walk 21? Legend has it that Bowerman was a fine archer or 'bowman' and also a great hunter and one day with his hounds in full cry he galloped into a coven of witches in the middle of making fearful spells. They were so furious that the next time Bowerman went hunting one of the witches turned herself into a hare leading Bowerman on and on until he finally collapsed into a bog. With a great shriek the witch turned him into stone, as you can see. His hounds, which you can find at Hound Tor, were also turned to stone!

Next is Jay's Grave quite near the Bowerman's Nose. Map Ref.733799 on the Hound Tor to Chagford road.

Bowerman's Nose

Kitty Jay was a poor country girl who was seduced by the son of the farm where she worked some 200 years ago. Full of shame and despair she hung herself in the barn at Canna Farm near Easdon Tor. As was the custom of those days she was not allowed to be buried in consecrated ground so she was buried here at this crossing of old tracks.

In 1860 a Mr James Bryant intrigued by the tale but doubting its truth excavated the grave and found the bones and scull of poor Kitty Jay which he placed in a coffin and then reburied. He also raised the mound and stones that you see today. The strange mystery that surrounds all this is that there are always fresh flowers to be found on Jay's Grave. Who puts them there?

Finally Dunnabridge Pound is worth a visit. Map Ref.646746 on the Dartmeet to Two Bridges road.

This was originally a Bronze Age Pound and covers an area of some 2¼ acres. However, it was used into medieval times for holding the stray ponies and horses that were grazing illegally on the moor and had been collected together during drifts; a drift pound like Erme Pound.

Just inside the gate there is a fine stone seat which is called the Judge's Chair. Exactly how it got there and what it was and how it was

The Bailiff of Dartmoor's or Judge's Chair

used no one is sure but as you might expect on Dartmoor it is the subject of several stories and explanations. One is that it was just part of a prehistoric dolmen or burial chamber. Another says it was the pound-keepers shelter where he sat to do the paperwork concerned with the strays and drifts. Another says it was brought from the Tinners' Parliament at Crockern Tor. Finally, it could just be the seat for the stocks that were known to be here, probably for punishing those whose ponies had gone astray! I leave the choice to you.

NORTH EAST MOOR

Some of the walks in the next two sections are either likely to enter or pass very close to the ranges on the North Moor. Therefore please be careful and check that there is no firing on the day you want to walk there. Many, too, are walks that will take you into the heart of the moor so check on the weather before setting out and make sure that you have your map and compass and know how to use them!

You will also notice that the whole character of the North Moor is totally different to the South Moor and the Widecombe area where all the walks have been so far. In many ways it is a more remote, lonely moorland without the valleys and pockets of cultivated land with farms and other dwellings that you will have come across in the south.

29. Crockern Tor, Longaford Tor, White Tors, Brown's House, Flat Tor, Rough Tor, Wistman's Wood, Two Bridges.
(See map p.166)

START. Near Parson's Cottage below Crockern Tor. Map Ref.616755. There is room to park in the lay-by here or on the verge.

Princetown is 4kms away with all facilities of a busy, tourist village. There is a large hotel at Two Bridges just 1km away.

Long. 8 miles. 13kms. Hard. (You can shorten this walk at any time on the outward leg by cutting down to the West Dart Valley.)

Go through the gate and climb up steeply towards Crockern Tor, the place where the Stannary boundaries met and where the Tinners' Parliament gathered. (See the Introductory notes on the tinners.) There were supposed to be a 'a table and seats of moorstone hewn out of the rocks' here but there is no sign of them today.

You are on the beginnings of a ridge and it is a pleasant, ascending walk northwards, with the newtake wall down on your right, to Littaford Tors, Longaford Tor and Higher White Tor, the highest of the three at 527 metres. Longaford Tor looks like a small mountain from the road near Powder Mills and indeed the views from its summit are fine as if from a mountain.

Drop down slightly now to Lower White Tor and aim slightly west

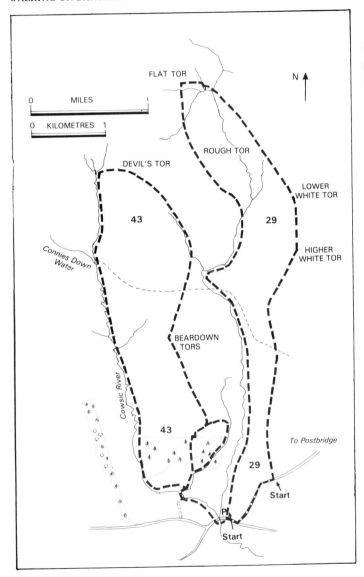

Two Bridges

of north to Brown's House across rather awkward tussocky ground and be careful to avoid Brown's House Bog to the east. I do not know what they got up to on dark Dartmoor winter nights but this is another house to which a morose and ungainly man called, I presume, Brown brought his pretty, young wife to keep her away from the attentions of other men! You will remember Dolly's Cot on Walk 26. It is a sour, remote area and any farming enterprise in this area must have been bound to fail. There is evidence that an attempt to make newtakes was started and then suddenly stopped; there are unfinished walls around. Brown's House soon fell into decay. It was used after that by peat cutters and moormen rounding up animals on this lonely moor.

You must now contour round the high ground north of Brown's House until you are in the valley of the West Dart. It is a fairly marshy area but on the eastern branch of the stream there is a tinner's hut and a lot of evidence of tin streaming and digging.

Turn west now to Flat Tor which as its name suggests is not very impressive and is where the flat bedrock is exposed on the side of the hill.

Cross over the streams, one of which is called Summer Brook, and climb up to Rough Tor. Though it is not a very high tor it can be seen from quite a few vantage points and the summit rocks form a strange oval shape enclosing a small area.

From Rough Tor descend in a long diagonal south-east steeply down to the West Dart, 60 metres below you. You have to cross the river so, from above, keep an eye out for a likely crossing place.

Once on the east or the true left bank follow the river down to Wistman's Wood. There are details of this interesting primeval wood (one of three stunted oak forests on Dartmoor) given in the section on Flora in the Introduction to this Guide. The name Wistman could be a corruption of the celtic words *uisg maen coed* meaning 'a stony wood by the water', which is exactly what it is. However the Saxons had a word *wealas* which meant a foreigner so it could be Wealasman's Wood or Welshman's Wood; the wood of the Celts whom the Saxons regarded as foreigners! It is a fascinating and mysterious place with a ghostly feel to it with its twisted trees, mosses and lichens all intermingled with huge rocks and boulders in which there are small caverns and grottoes. The Druids were said to have regarded this as a holy spot. In 1886 the main area of the wood was burnt by a fire that started here and the smoke from which could be seen for miles around. It could not be stopped and was left to burn itself out.

On the north edge of the central grove there is a huge triangular slab of rock, almost hidden in the surrounding clitter and trees, that bears the inscription to the effect that a botanist called Wentworth Buller felled a young oak in 1866 and that part of the trunk was presented to the Museum in Exeter.

Beyond the north grove and towards a final clump of trees northeast there are the remains of Wistman's Warren which was built in 1895 and you can also find the artificial burrows or buries around. The word Pillow Mounds to indicate these are seen on the 1:25,000 map.

Leave the wood now and follow the obvious paths south down to the old farm of Crockern. You could, if you wished, cut over the hill to your left, westwards, before the farm, to get back to the start but you may well have your mind on the hotel at Two Bridges - in which case follow the lane down to the quarry by the road and you will see the hotel on the other side.

After refreshment it will not seem a long walk back to Parson's Cottage and your car! It was known as Parson's Cottage, by the way, because the old building, long since gone, was built in the nineteenth century by the Rev. J.H.Mason the vicar of Widecombe who had land here. It was also known as Billy Clack's Cottage as another parson of that name once lived there.

30. Drift Lane, Roundy Park, Valley of the East Dart, Waterfalls, Sandy Hole, (Cut Hill, Fur Tor), Statts House, Beehive Hut, The Sheepfold. *(See map p.170)*

START. Postbridge. Map Ref.646788. There is a large Car Park on the north side of the main Moretonhampstead to Two Bridges road B3212. There is a National Park Information building here, open in spring and summer and Toilets. Postbridge has a Post Office and stores with petrol pumps. There is a pleasant pub and several small hotels and guest houses. For more information see Walk 26 Including Cut Hill and Fur Tor. *Long. 11 miles. 17.6Kms. Hard.* Leaving out Cut Hill and Fur Tor. *Long. (just) 7½ miles. 12.2kms. Moderate.* (However this is another walk that you can cut short, if you can get across the Dart easily.)

Cross the stile at the north-west end of the Car Park and turn right into the wide, grassy avenue which is known as Drift Lane. The name comes from the fact that this way was used during the round-ups of the ponies and cattle, known as drifts, as a route off the high moor. The wide end of the lane near Postbridge used to be the place where, at the beginning of this century, a local fair would set up with swings and coconut shies; what an event this must have been for the moorland children.

The East Dart which got its name in Saxon times is off to your right as you walk north-north-west.

Go through Drift Lane Gate at Acherton Trees and continue up the stony track with the wall on your right. There is a gate in this wall which will lead you towards the pound known as Roundy Park which must be all of 2 acres in extent. This is another example where a Bronze Age pound, and there are a few faint traces of ruined hut circles here, was used by medieval farmers who probably restored it and rebuilt sections.

Outside the wall of Roundy Park where it swings north-east you will find a large kistvaen, one of the best on Dartmoor. Two fragments of flint, some bone charcoal and a cooking stone were found in it. It is unlike any other kistvaen on Dartmoor having nine stones and could have been for a body rather than ashes and therefore from the New Stone Age rather than the Bronze Age.

Find your way back to the original track that will lead you on to a marshy area with several small streams coming in from Braddon Lake. There are fords across if you can find them. Ahead you will come to a clapper bridge over the old Powder Mill's Leat. To your right is

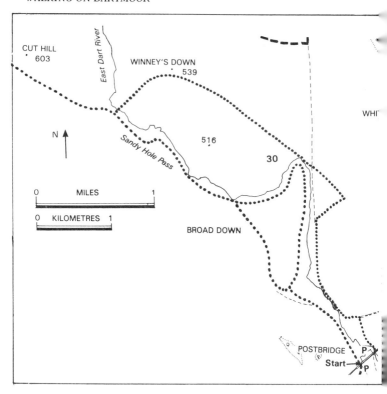

another huge enclosure said to be the largest on Dartmoor with over 40 hut circles in it; Broadun. You have a choice of routes here. You can either follow the leat round to the north above the river, which I prefer, though it is longer as the Dart takes a great bend just over 1km away, or you can strike up over Broad Down, north-west, and through Rowtor gate set in the wall of the enclosure and onto the open moor that way. If you follow the leat you will pass quite close to Broadun Ring, another Bronze Age enclosure but much smaller with only ten hut circles. Whichever way you go you will eventually reach the Waterfalls where the river cascades down over granite ledges and clefts and, further downstream, into a small gorge known as Broadun Hole.

170

The Clapper Bridge, Postbridge

If you wish to cut the walk short here you can cross the river above the waterfalls and then walk down the true left bank to the Beehive Hut; there is a sort of track. You will cross Winney's Down Brook and find yourself in a marshy area where the river takes a great swing from flowing north-east to south. Keep left to avoid wet ground to the Beehive Hut.

If you wish to keep going then follow the Dart up as best you can to Sandy Hole and Sandy Hole Pass. This is the point where the river leaves its birthplace, as it were, high up in the depths of the moor and becomes a young adult flowing in steeper, deeper valleys.

The river bed near Sandy Hole was excavated by medieval tinners to improve the flow to help take away the waste materials from their workings nearby. As the name suggests there is a lot of sand and gravel on the river bed here. You will also see sections where the tinners built walls to contain the river and again to increase the speed of the flow. (See the note in the Introduction about the tinners being responsible for silting up the port of Dartmouth.)

Again decisions about your route. You could now leave out Cut Hill and Fur Tor by aiming north-north east out of Broad Marsh towards the Peat Pass near Statts House.

If you want to go on then keep on up the river, past Broad Marsh and all the tinners remains, until a small stream comes in from the west and a little later another, Cut Hill Stream, comes in from the north-west. Near here is a crossing place called Kit Steps. This is all in the area where the river has another broad bend and changes to flow from the north.

Between these two streams there is good, hard ground more or less west to the peat pass called the North-West Passage below Cut Hill. The peat passes on Dartmoor often lie on natural routes over from one river valley to another and were used by the moormen driving their animals from one grazing area to the next or down to market. In many cases they have been enlarged and improved and one such man who did this was Frank Phillpots, a keen follower of hounds, who, between 1885 and 1905, cut some new passes and improved the old ones so that both horses and hounds as well as cattle could pass through more easily. A small granite post with a bronze plaque on it mentions this and Phillpots name.

The area around Cut Hill is difficult going if you get off track. The peat has been eroded into great gullies and gorges like some monstrous black glacier with deep, black crevasses!

The ridge out north-west to Fur Tor is obvious and easy after the peat. It is an amazing and noble tor standing in this remote and wild spot, jutting out from the surrounding blanket bog. The ground all around except on the south-east drops steeply away covered in a mass of clitter. Below to the north-west are several streams including the Amicombe Brook that flow into the Tavy just before Tavy Cleave. The views from the great pile of rocks are tremendous and you can see, for the first time on a walk, right into the heart of the North Moor to Yes Tor and High Willhays beyond. It makes a fine objective and you can feel justly proud if you have got here.

Retrace your steps now to the North-West Passage and Cut Hill and then back down to the East Dart which you should cross and then strike up slightly north of west to the Peat Pass near Statts House on Winney's Down. The house was built in the eighteenth century by a peat cutter called Statt and it is one of several small huts where the cutters could shelter and sleep during the turf cutting season. It has a curved north end and a square south end where the fireplace and alcove can be seen. About 40 metres away, south-south-east from Statts House, there is another smaller ruin which was probably a similar shelter.

You must walk now south-east across fairly level ground, leaving Winney's Down Brook on your right, until you find the wall which you must cross and get down into the valley of Lade Hill Stream. It is fairly marshy so if in doubt keep left, away from the main river, until you will see the pile of stones that form the remains of the Beehive

Hut. Even though not much is left here the shape is obvious and was probably built by the medieval tinners as a place where they could keep their tools and ingots of tin.

Do not stay by the river but strike south-east, slightly uphill, to a ruined wall and what looks as though it was once some large building. This is known as The Sheepfold and the courtyard covers almost ¾ of an acre. The walls are massive and you will see every three metres or so a large granite post let into them. The entrance was at the north end and at the south end there are the remains of a cottage. In the yard there are a few small pens used for cattle as well as sheep. It is said to have been built by a Scot to keep in his Scotch black-face sheep early in the 1800's. It was apparently burnt down in the 1820's.

To return to Postbridge you can drop back down to the Dart and follow it to where you must turn left to Ringhill Farm and the right-of-way across fields by the farm. Alternatively, there is a way down south-east from the Sheepfold which crosses Stannon Brook and follows the track, then a road and finally the right-of-way past Ringhill Farm and into the fields, where you go over Stannon Brook again, by a clapper bridge, to emerge on the road at Postbridge, by the two bridges.

31. Assycombe Hill, Chagford Common, Mine, King's Oven, Warren House Inn. *(See map p.174)*

START. Statt's Bridge near Warren House Inn. Map Ref.668806. There is room to park on the track that leads off north-north-west. The Warren House Inn is just up the road. See Walk 24 for details of this remote Inn. Postbridge is 2.75Kms away with all the facilities of a tourist centre. See Walk 26 for details.
Medium. 3¾ miles. 6Kms. Easy. This is another excellent, short walk that you could do on a summer's evening or when you have not got a lot of time. You could always start and end at the Warren House Inn!

Set off up the track from the bridge. I wonder if the name Statt comes from the turf-cutter who built his shelter high on Winney's Down? See Walk 30. You will pass a wheel pit on your right and the remains of a leat below the path. Soon you will come to a group of ruined buildings and quite a few gerts and pits. This is all that remains now of Wheal Caroline one of the most unproductive tin mines on Dartmoor which soon closed down and the buildings used later as a

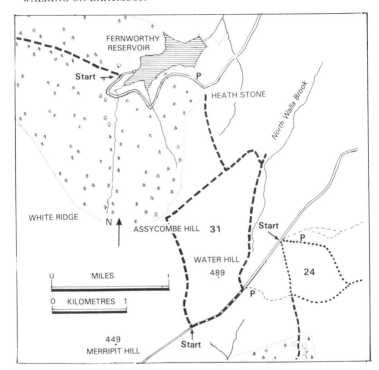

farm in the 1830's.

Be careful not to drop down to your left into the extremely wet area where the Statt Brook rises. It is a marsh that shakes and wobbles unnervingly if you try to walk across as it is almost a raft of vegetation floating on liquid. It was known as Caroline Bog but also part of the area was known as Coal Mires because excellent peat was cut here for use in the mines and also local farms.

After the ruins strike up towards the hut circles and then climb on to Assycombe Hill right on the edge of the forest. From here aim north-east more or less down the ridge and you will come to an interesting group of Bronze Age remains. First there is a double stone row about 130 metres long with nearly a 100 stones in it. At the south-west end there is a burial cairn. Archaeologists excavating this grave found bone charcoal and many fragments of a clay pot which was pieced together much later to make an urn some sixteen inches in diameter in which the cremated remains were once held. It has been dated as 1300 B.C. and can be seen in Plymouth Museum.

If you wish, you could add another 2kms to the walk by following the forest wall down to the Heath Stone standing in an area of Bronze Age fields. The stone probably started out as a megalith but was soon used as a boundary stone for the Dartmoor Forest and also as a waymark for an ancient track from Exeter to Tavistock. The carving on it is modern.

From the Hurston Ridge stone row strike out north-east to the remains of another mine. This was West Vitifer Mine. (The remains of the other Vitifer Mine was in the valley below the Warren House Inn mentioned on Walks 24 and 25.) You will find three circular washing troughs, or buddles as they were called, used for collecting the tin ore. The system employed used the same principle as the Holman Tables used in the modern, but sadly failing, Cornish tin industry or indeed also primitive panning for metals. After the ore had been crushed the tin bearing sand was heavier than the waste debris. The old tinners put the crushed ore into the buddles with flowing water. Attached to the central bosses, that you can see, were revolving arms with some form of brush on the ends. The arms turned round and round, powered either by water wheels or horses, stirring up the water enough for the waste material to be carried off, floating in suspension, while the tin bearing sand sank to the bottom to be collected. You can also see two wheelpits.

Climb up the steep hillside to the west by following the gully and a twisting track. On the top you should be able to see a path that will lead you south to the enclosures of King's Oven. You can just make out the ruins of a fairly large building of some 12 metres by 5 metres and, of course, the enclosure walls. It was thought that there was a tinners' smelting house here in early times. In the Perambulation of 1204 there is reference to The King's Oven and in a later description of Forest boundaries it is called Furnum Regis. The fact that the King is used in the title bears out the connection with smelting as tin was taxed and brought in a revenue for the Crown. (See the Introductory notes about the tinners.)

You are quite close to the road and the Warren House Inn here. Indeed you may have heard the sound of the generator thumping away if the wind is in the right direction; they have no mains electricity in this remote spot. The sound makes quite a good beacon to home in on if you are on Water Hill in the mist!

Anyway you may want to home in on a pint now before you walk back down the road to your car!

32. Fernworthy Circle, Grey Wethers, Sittaford Tor, Quintin's Man, Whitehorse Hill, Hangingstone Hill, Watern Tor, Teignhead Farm.

START. Drive to the extreme end of the road that runs through Fernworthy Forest. Map Ref.659839. There is plenty of room to park here but please be careful not to block the gate as forestry vehicles use it.

Chagford is 4kms away, an extremely pleasant little moorland village with all the facilities you might need, including some very good hotels within a few miles of the village.

There is a car park with toilets on the right by the reservoir just as you come into Fernworthy Forest.

Long. 9¾ miles. 14kms. Hard. As always there are opportunities to shorten this walk.

Set off up the broad waymarked forest track. Make sure you follow the signs and bear left at the fork that comes fairly soon after the gate. It is a gentle climb up through the forest and on stormy days the sound of the wind is like roaring surf in the pines. After about ½km you will see, to your right, a grassy bay and standing in it is Fernworthy Circle about 20 metres in diameter. This is one of the several Bronze Age circles that you will find on Dartmoor and on this walk you will be going to a far more impressive one. Keep on until you reach the crest of the hill and the track becomes narrower and starts to go downhill. At the end you will come to a wall with a gate through and you will suddenly be confronted with the open moor. I love this moment as you come out of the dark, secret forest and there it is, all sky and moor stretching away before you.

Turn left and walk straight down south. The edge of the forest will begin to drop away from you. You will cross first one enclosure wall and then another, part of the extraordinary system of walls that run far out into the heart of the moor in this area. They are a godsend for navigating mind you! Just over the second wall you will see The Grey Wethers stone circles. Bronze Age again and they are supposed to look like sheep grazing on the hill, hence the name. This is a name that occurs in several parts of Britain where stone can be mistaken for animals or people even, but only in mist I presume. There is a splendid story told of how a man called Debben, sitting in the Warren House Inn, over a pint, sold a farmer these 'grey wethers' which he was told he would find grazing near Sittaford newtake! He must have wondered why his dog could not get them to move!

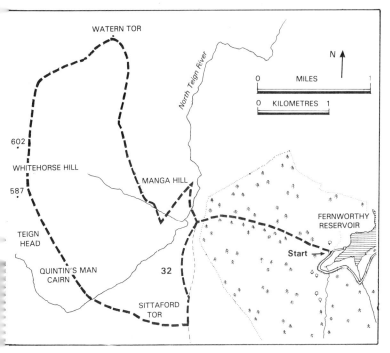

Sittaford Tor is the next point to aim for, just along the wall. There are fine views from here south and east. Standford Perrot, the son of the Dartmoor Guide James Perrot who more or less started the idea of Dartmoor Letterboxes, (see the Introduction to this Guide) was said to have driven a pair of horses with a carriage out to this tor!

Just south-west of Sittaford Tor the wall that runs north-west will take you on to Quintin's Man, if you keep on the west side of it. The bottom of the valley at Little Varracombe may be pretty wet but you should find a way over the infant Teign without much bother. Teign Head is only about 1km away. The name Quintin's Man suggests that there might have been a menhir on the summit at one time, but there is only an ancient cairn now.

You are now on a great whaleback ridge and you must go more or less north without the help of any walls! You will gradually climb on to Whitehorse Hill and you will probably be aware that the whole area was used for peat cutting for on this broad, fairly flat area the blanket bog produced excellent peat.

Nearly all this ridge is just short of the magical 2,000 feet height and indeed is one of the highest parts of Dartmoor, only topped by Yes Tor and High Willhays. Both White Horse Hill and Hangingstone Hill are just over 600 metres.

This is country where, if there is mist, your map reading and compass work will have to be spot on for it is very easy to wander off onto the wrong side of some of the slopes.

There is a peat pass just east of the highest point of White Horse Hill. (See Walk 30 for information about these passes.)

It is also interesting to note that, to the west, you are on the edge of a watershed here for down in the marsh you will find East Dart Head with the river flowing south and, only ½km away, Taw Head with this river flowing north to enter the sea on the north coast at Barnstaple.

Hangingstone Hill, as the name suggests, had at one time a logan stone weighing four tons. I say had for though it is still there on the north-west side, a long flat rock, it no longer moves. It was knocked off its pivot stone in the 1960's and although it was put back in place by the military so that, in fact, it still rocked, further vandalism later upset the balance and the one time logan stone no longer rocks.

You are now well within the ranges and you will have seen evidence of the military including the ugly observation posts built on this and other summits.

The views from here are tremendous with Exmoor and the Quantocks away to the north and north-east. Nearer you can see the Haldon Hills near Exeter and the Teign estuary to the south, while all around you should be able to make out some of the valleys and tors you might have visited on previous walks on Dartmoor.

Ignore the track running north and strike down really quite steeply north-east to Watern Combe and over the Walla Brook (you will find a Walla Brook in the Widecombe area too) to Watern Tor. Watern Tor looks really quite remarkable as if it is made up of thin layers of granite laid one on top of the other. This is known as false bedding and is caused by the granite cooling down gradually, almost one layer at a time, so that you have an effect of bedding plains or strata which, of course, are only found in sedimentary rocks; granite is igneous. Wind, water and ice do the rest and produce this extraordinary effect. At the northern end is the Thirlstone which means 'rock with a hole in it' and you will see why it has this name; there is a tunnel that leads through from one side to the other. Those of you who know the south coast of Devon will recollect that at Thurlestone near Salcombe there is a huge arch of rock on the shore there; the same name. Because of

The Tolmen on the River Teign near
Teign-e-ver Bridge

its unusual shape the Thirlstone is one of the boundary places
mentioned on the Perambulation of 1240.

If you walk south-east from Watern Tor you will find the walls
again. This one runs just west of south so follow it until you see
another wall running off south-east which you now follow. The going
is quite tussocky and awkward. Ignore the wall that runs east but
follow the main wall down to Manga Brook and on to Teignhead Farm.

I remember this ruin in the 1950's when it still was quite a
reasonable house with its roof intact. Yet another of the old moorland
farms that, as a young man, I longed to buy, renovate and live in. The
dreams of youth! The old farm built in about 1780 was never very
successful and was mainly used for summer grazing. The newtakes as

you will be aware, for you have almost walked round the boundary walls of them, were enormous and cover over 1,400 acres.

Down by the river, south-east from the ruined farm buildings, there is another small ruin that you might care to have a look at. Lying inside, easy to find, it has two troughs cut into a large block of granite, while there are two other troughs to be found one inside the other on the wall. I have read somewhere that this was not a blowing house for the tinners, in spite of what looks like mould stones, but probably a blacksmith's shop. If you do not wish to go down to this ruin then walk north-east from Teignhead Farm keeping your height and not following the path down to the clapper bridge over the river. You will come to a walled, funnel-shaped passage, quite narrow at the end called a stroll, which will lead you after about 140 metres to some more ruins. This is Manga House named after the brook, a farm built and occupied well before Teignhead Farm. There are three buildings here, one with three rooms and a fine yard. If you came here from the other ruin by the Teign you would have had to climb back up the hill first.

Now it is time to start back, so aim at the clapper bridge over the Teign, the first of many bridges, just up river, south, from Manga House. It is perhaps one of the finest clapper bridges on Dartmoor but it certainly is not a medieval one but probably built so that carts could reach the farms in the late eighteenth century. There are drill holes to be seen on some of the slabs and this system of splitting granite was not used until the late eighteenth century.

All that remains now is to wander gently back up to the gate into the forest and after a short climb it is all downhill back to the start.

33. Kestor Rock, Shovel Down, Teign-e-ver Clapper Bridge, Scorhill Down, Batworthy Corner.

START. Near Round Pound. Map Ref.664868. There are plenty of parking spaces off the road in this area.

Chagford, a pleasant moorland village is 3kms away with all the facilities you might expect in a small community. There are several good hotels in the area and the Youth Hostel at Gidleigh.
Medium. 3¾ miles. 6kms. Easy

Wherever you have parked you will see a large stone circle on the right of the road. This is Round Pound and when you reach it you will discover that there are two concentric circles in fact. The inner one was the wall of a large hut and the other radiating walls that you can

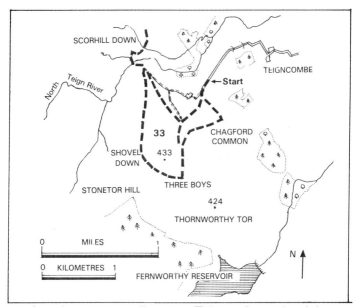

see formed pens or small courts. This, as I mentioned in my Introduction, was the site where there was definite evidence of early iron smelting; the only one on Dartmoor and therefore dates it as Iron Age or about 500 B.C. The whole area near here is covered with the remains of these people, huts and fields, and a whole community must have lived here at this time with an iron smelter's house with its own compound. Flints, arrowheads, knives and scrapers were all found in this area both on early excavations and on later ones after the last war. As there are no flints to be found on Dartmoor these early flint tools were probably made of chert, a type of flint found near Exeter and Sidmouth, and must have been brought from there.

You must aim south-south-east now towards Kestor Rock which is clearly visible. In fact, this rock with its low, squat shape can be seen from miles around and therefore the views from the top are excellent. Once on the top you will also discover one of the largest rock basins on a Dartmoor tor. This one must be all of 2¼ metres across. These basins are formed by erosion by water and frost not by the Druids as was originally thought! From the tor strike south-west aiming at the tall standing stone that you can see. This menhir is called the

Round Pound near Kestor
an iron age settlement

Longstone; not a very original name! It stands about ¼ metres high and when you look at it you will see the letters C for Chagford, G for Gidleigh and DC Duchy of Cornwall carved on it and, as you will have guessed, it forms the boundary marker for the two parishes and also the Forest of Dartmoor. Like so many of these ancient boundary markers it was mentioned in the Perambulation of 1240. But, of course, it was not put up for this purpose in that year but had been standing there from the Bronze Age and it was used by the people of medieval times as a convenient marker.

All around are a great many other remains of the Bronze Age, Beaker Folk. The name Beaker comes from the fact that the remains of clay urns and pots have been found in some of the graves.

In this area you will see double stone rows, a four ringed stone circle and kistveans and field systems with reaves. Just over 200 metres south from the Longstone there is a single block that once formed the cover stone of a dolmen. It has the name Three Boys which means obviously that at one time there must have been three stones left standing here; sadly no more. A stone row runs from the Longstone to where this burial chamber must have stood, which is usually the case.

If you aim north-west from the Longstone you should come across

The Longstone - Shovel Down

two more standing stones on the edge of the hill. These were the remains of another dolmen or burial chamber. Even if you do not find these stones then you must walk northwards towards the corner of the wall and the North Teign River. Here you will find the Teign-e-ver Bridge. This is a lovely spot with the river in quite a deep gully and all around mountain ash trees leaning over the water.

Just further west the Walla Brook enters the Teign and the peninsula between the two rivers is obviously an area that the tinners have worked. Indeed, like the East Dart at Sandy Hole there are sections where they walled up the banks of the streams to increase the flow of the water. There is another clapper bridge here, over the Walla Brook, which you must cross and then walk back downstream to the Teign and continue, for another 50 metres or so, past the confluence. There you will find the extraordinary Tolmen or 'Holed Stone' (from the Celtic *tol* a hole and *maen* a stone). It lies on the bed of the river and the hole is about 1 metre across. Like the rock basins it was said to have been made and used by the Druids but of course this again is natural water erosion. Like the Men An Tol stone on the Land's End peninsula in Cornwall this Tolmen is said to have magic properties, bring good luck, make wishes come true and even to cure the whooping cough if you crawl through!

Wallabrook Bridge

Return to the bridge and find a well made track to your right that will lead up the hill and over the Gidleigh Leat by yet another cart clapper bridge until you reach Scorhill Circle. This is a fine example of a Bronze Age Circle, standing in a splendid solitary place. It has a diameter of about 27 metres, with nearly 30 stones still left in position. The largest is about 2.5 metres high. Nobody can be sure what exactly the Bronze Age people used their circles for but it must have been some form of temple, or meeting place for worship or ceremony. This is a walk that has not taken you out into the deep moor but, if you have time, you could strike up west to Watern Tor or follow the Walla Brook to Wild Tor. The possibilities are endless.

However, if you want to keep this one short and just visit this amazing collection of prehistoric remains, probably the most concentrated group on Dartmoor - the cross, the clapper bridges over the leat, the Walla Brook and the Teign - climb up the hill to the wall south-south-east and follow it back to Batsworthy Corner, turn north and you will soon be back at Round Pound.

34. Cullever Steps, Oke Tor, Knack Mine, Steeperton Tor, Steeperton Gorge, Taw Marsh, Belstone, Nine Stones, Belstone Tor. *(See map p.190)*

START. Just above Cullever Steps. Map Ref.600920. You can visit the small and beautiful moorland hamlet of Belstone on this walk. There is a Post Office, stores, hotels and also a pub, so once again the timing of your walk will have to be carefully worked out!

Otherwise you will drive through Okehampton to the start which is out on the military road past Okehampton Camp. Drive through the gate to the east of the camp, over the ford and then continue up the hill. At the top take the left-hand fork and after about 400 metres you will see a track running off down to your left. Park here off the road and track.

Long. 7¾ miles. 12.5kms. Hard. Another walk that is easy to shorten but you might have to forgo a visit to the pub in Belstone if you do!

Set off down the stony track to the valley below. The little stream beside you is the Black-a-ven Brook and it runs over a series of small waterfalls and pools to reach the East Okement River.

This is Cullever Steps and is obviously an old fording place, but the present bridge is modern for military use. You will also see that the fording place is paved with granite slabs put here to make the crossing easier for the horse-drawn gun carriages, from the early days of the ranges. Do not take the track on your right but zig-zag up east for a while and then follow the track south by Winter Tor. Keep on climbing up the ridge; the track almost peters out, but the direction is easy to see and follow. The ground falls steeply away to your left and soon you will come to Oke Tor with fine views.

Beyond the tor the track is more obvious and after climbing a little starts to drop down to the steep-sided valley of the upper Taw. In the valley you will find the remains of Knack Mine which closed in the nineteenth century. It is also known as Knock Mine. Whether this name comes from the Celtic *Cnoc* meaning a hill, I am not sure, but there is another explanation of the name that I like. When a mine was abandoned the miners often spoke of it as being 'knacked'. So this was the knacked mine which became Knack Mine. There used to be a clapper bridge here but it was badly damaged by floods in 1890 and nothing much remains.

Cross the young Taw and climb steeply up north-east to Steeperton Tor. The views from here are extremely fine as you are now a long way into the heart of the moor, spoilt only by obvious signs of the military buildings around you.

This is the turning point now, and you should drop down very steeply north-north-west to Steeperton Gorge where the river rushes down in a deep ravine. You can make your way north along the gorge, beside the river, on the true right bank, but I leave it to you; it is quite awkward going. Soon you will emerge out of the valley after crossing Steeperton Brook and enter the wide Taw Marsh which could have been a lake in very early times. After the gorge there is a feeling of space and the sides of the hills, Cosdon Hill and Belstone Tor fall back.

You will see a great many mounds and gullies made by the ancient tin miners here. There are also quite a few modern buildings, hatches and concrete constructions that are all to do with extraction of water from Taw Marsh. I remember that I was called in during the 1960's, as I was an aqua-lung diver at that time, to dive forty feet or so into the pitch black, peaty water at the bottom of one of the concrete pipes here, to see if I could fit a clamp onto a high pressure pump that had become completely jammed on the bottom. After five dives, working in total darkness, I had to give up. Each time they tried to pull it up with a crane, the clamp that I had attempted to fix round the narrow neck of the pump, all that was sticking out of the gravel, came away. It is odd to have such memories of this lonely spot!

You should soon find a track on the right bank of the Taw which, after crossing Small Brook, will take you to a ford and stepping-stones at Horseshoe Bend where the river takes an enormous curve. If the river is in flood you may have to cross earlier. It is here that you could shorten the walk by climbing up west to Higher Tor and then exploring the ridge of Belstone Tor and the Irishman's Wall before dropping down west again, by the wall, back to Cullever Steps and up to the car.

As you walk north you will see some hatches; these lead into an underground pumping station; at least this is hidden.

Keep following the track north past the end of the Irishman's Wall. The story goes that an Irishman set about enclosing part of the moor in the early 1800's and to do this he brought over a large number of his countrymen, Irish labourers, who surprised everyone by working on the building of this wall bare-footed. The work went on and the commoners of Belstone and Okehampton said nothing and did nothing but clearly they were not happy about the possibility of being prevented from using such huge areas of their grazing land south of Belstone Tors. They let the Irishmen almost finish their task and then

Cullever Steps from Belstone Tor

they struck. They gathered in large numbers and set off to the wall which they then demolished in several places. The Irishmen disappeared and no attempts were made to close the breaches and so the cattle continued to graze on the commons. There is another modern building here, not underground, that is also part of the Taw Marsh water extraction.

Aim now at the corner of the enclosures where you will see the Sheepfold and dip with the river cascading by in an area known as Holloway's Fields. Walk along with the wall on your right on a rough track and if you wish to go to Belstone village then go through a gate near a house called Birchy Lake and onto the road that runs north. Down on your right you will see the rocky and beautiful, granite gorge of the Taw called Belstone Cleave. There is a crossing place below too that would lead you on to Cosdon Hill, sometimes called Cawsands Beacon, if you wanted to go that way for another walk.

If you do go into Belstone then there is a way back onto the open moor called the Higher Birchy Lake Gate which you can use rather than the other one which is the Lower Birchy Lake Gate or, you can come through the moor-gate near Watchet Hill Cottage, which is quicker still.

If you decide against a visit to the village then skirt round the edge

of Belstone Common until you are near Resugga and then strike up
south-west to the Nine Stones. Nine Stones they may be called but
there were, in fact, seventeen. Only twelve remain now. How nine
comes into it I do not know! They are also known as the Nine
Maidens, maidens being a corruption of the Celtic *maen* a stone! I
have also heard them called the Seventeen Brothers. In any case, if
you have been on some of the earlier walks you will know what I am
going to write next! Yes, these wicked girls or men (whichever you
prefer) were turned to stone for dancing on a Sunday and as punishment they are forced to dance and change positions every day at noon.
If you have visited the pub in Belstone you might well be able to see
this happen! They are, of course, all that remains of a Bronze Age
burial site. From here you can either go further west to find a track
that will contour round and then lead you back gently to Cullever
Steps or, if you are feeling strong, then go on up to the summits of
Belstone Tor. It is worth the climb as the views are tremendous.
Standing as it does on the north edge of the moor, you can see to
Exmoor. All around too the views into the moor, where you have been
walking, are fine and also down onto Taw Marsh and across to Cosdon
Hill. You can look down onto the wooded gorges of the East Okement
and also Belstone Cleave; yes it is worth the climb. If you do go to the
top then follow the Irishman's Wall west to Cullever Steps or find any
easy way down you wish.

The climb up the track to the car might be exhausting. I am sorry to
finish the walk with an uphill stretch!

THE NORTH WEST MOOR

35. Moor Gate, Black Down, Yes Tor, High Willhays, West Mill Tor *(See map p.190)*

START. Moor Gate near Okehampton Military Camp. Map Ref.592931.

There is room to park off the road anywhere you like here. If you wish to shorten the walk a little then you can drive some way along the road south-west towards Anthony Stile on the west side of Moor Brook and again park where you wish but off the road.

  You will pass through the small town of Okehampton with all the facilities that you might require on your way to the start by the steep and winding road to the Camp. If you can avoid the A30 in summer until the controversial Okehampton by-pass is built, I should, especially at weekends.

Medium.   6¼ miles. 10kms.   Moderate.

Any Guide to Dartmoor should include a walk up to the highest point of the moor. There are various ways to do it but this is the most obvious and straight forward. There is a maze of tracks in this area, many used and maintained by the military but as you might expect a lot of them are ancient tracks leading into the heart of the moor.

Having left the car somewhere by the wall of Okehampton Camp you walk along the road to what is marked as Anthony Stile on the map but where there is no stile and I can find no reason for the name! Here tracks branch off in all directions but you will need the one that goes south-west, not the one that runs south, to the east of West Mill Tor. There is a fine array of Dartmoor peaks ahead each one higher than the next.

Follow the rough track now as it climbs up Black Down, with West Mill Tor directly to your left. Keep right first and then left at the forks which should bring you down to the ford over the small Red-a-ven Brook. This stream has the distinction of having its source higher than any other on Dartmoor and indeed many rivers of the Pennines, at 550 metres, about 1800 feet. The trench with occasional sleepers and metal clamps, that you may have noticed to your left, was part of an

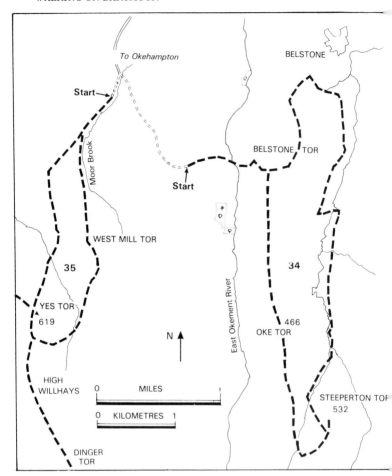

old tramway that carried moving targets for the military.

There is a steep climb ahead now to Yes Tor over fairly awkward ground with rocks and heather but I like the feeling of the direct approach.

If you feel this way is not for you then continue along the track after the ford and then strike up west-south-west to the broad ridge

190

between Yes Tor and High Willhays and you will probably see another track that you can follow to the col.

Yes Tor was thought, for many years, to be the highest peak of Dartmoor and it truly is a peak. But it was demoted in favour of High Willhays which was found by the Ordnance Survey to be a few feet higher, Yes Tor is given as 2,030 feet or 619 metres while High Willhays is 2,039 feet or 621 metres. With our maps changing to metric measurements the magic 2000 feet does not mean quite as much as it did but I suppose 600 metres will take its place. The odd name Yes is probably a corruption of East, while High Willhays is probably High Willes and indeed in 1532 was known as Hight Wyll. Both these peaks are the highest points not only of Dartmoor but the whole of England as far north as Kinder Scout in the Derbyshire Peak District which is higher at 2,088 feet.

Of the two peaks Yes Tor has the most magnificent views. To the north you can look away over a patchwork quilt of the fields, woods, farms and river valleys of North Devon and even North-East Cornwall. On fine days you will see as far as Exmoor and beyond to the Bristol Channel. On either side the ground drops steeply down to Red-a-ven-Brook or the West Okement River. To the south the view into the moor is not so good as it will be from High Willhays, where you must aim now, to the south.

Walk along the broad summit ridge, plateau even, to the rocks of High Willhays. It is not so impressive and I always feel that Yes Tor has every reason to feel jealous and cheated; it's much more of a mountain with a feeling of height. But I must not belittle the views south into the depths of Dartmoor from here, for these are perhaps some of the best that you will see. You will find the huge skies, the feeling of the lonelinesss of the wild primeval moor with its secret corners, deep valleys and tumbling streams. On some days you will have to lean into fierce winds with mist and rain sweeping across the landscape in fury. On other days all will be quiet and still in the hot summer sun with only the skylarks' bubbling trills to cut across the heavy silence.

Back north now to the col and then strike off east to find the track which you can follow all the way back to the start, but why not have just one more short climb and after Red-a-ven Brook aim north again to the little West Mill Tor, the small poor relation of Yes Tor towering above. Once on the top keep on north down to the track and the start.

36. Cranmere Pool. *(See map p.195)*

START.   Near the Observation Post. Map Ref.602878. Drive out on
the military road from Okehampton Camp. Take the right fork at the
top of the hill just before Rowtor and go via New Bridge to the start.

You pass through Okehampton on your way here and you will find
all the facilities that you might need in this small market town. Try to
avoid the A30 during summer, until the controversial Okehampton
by-pass has been built.

Medium.   3½ miles. 5.6kms.   Hard.

This walk does, in fact, lie just east of the 60 Eastings Grid Line and
should therefore belong with the North East Moor section but as I
shall be writing about a much longer walk to Cranmere that starts
further east, I have included it here.

Many parties will spit with rage at my including a walk that uses the
military road that runs, as you will discover, right into the heart of the
North Moor. My feeling is that if the road is there, why not use it,
however, much as you might disapprove of it. Of course you could
walk out to Cranmere from Chagford or Okehampton if you wish, and
why not, but if time is short or you may not be able to walk long
distances then this is one way to get to Cranmere fairly easily. Also the
road means that people who cannot walk at all can drive into the
depths of Dartmoor and see and feel something of the beauty and
excitment of this wild, lonely tract of moorland and share it with those
of us who can walk.

It is a great mistake to take a compass bearing from the Observation
Post and then set out straight for Cranmere! This approach will lead
you in and out of boggy areas as well as up and over endless peat hags!
Instead walk south along the rough track from the Observation Post
for about ¾km where you will see a lay-by on your right and then a
grassy track leading off south-west. This will bring you to a small pool
marked on the map as Ockerton Court but also known as Huggaton
Court or Pool. You will begin to get a feeling of being in the depths of
the peat country here.

Even though Cranmere lies to the south, do not be lured into trying
to get directly to it. The 1:25,000 maps show a peat pass to the north-
west of you and this is what you should aim for now. There is a gap in
the peat banks and a narrow footpath. You should find some marker
stones that will lead you into the peat pass known as Ockerton or
Huggaton Cut. It can be pretty wet going but will take you on down to
the upper part of West Okement River valley. The end of the peat

pass is marked by a stone on the right side and a small pile of rocks on the left as you come out of it into an area of reeds.

Turn left and go up the valley keeping along the edge of the black, overhanging cornices of the peat hags, still some way from the river. Ahead you will soon see a shallow tributary valley coming down towards you and the path will lead down to the confluence here of this side stream with the West Okement which is quite small by now. This is West Okement Ford.

Turn left and keep left following up the true right bank of the main stream through a gully and the obvious path will led you into quite a wide grassy trench with the peat banks on your left. A final climb up and over a peat bank will take you into the hollow which was once a pool called Cranmere; Crane Mere or Heron Pool. It is a pool no more having been drained long ago in the 1840's by a shepherd who had lost several sheep on it. It was first mentioned in the fifteenth century in the Itinerary of William of Worcester and it has always been a place that has caught the imagination of people as epitomising the remoteness and inaccessability of Dartmoor, though nowadays this is no longer true. Before it was drained it was a pool of some 200 metres in circumference. What a marvellous sight it must have been high up in the peat here. No wonder it was the haunt of wild duck, herons and other water fowl.

You will have read in the Introduction to this Guide about James Perrott, the Dartmoor Guide, who brought people here in the 1850's to leave their visiting cards in a pickle jar. Charles Dickens came with James Perrott to this spot, just one of the many who still make this pilgrimage. You will find the letter-box on the west bank with the huge area of eroded peat all round it where hundreds now come to sign their names and collect the stamp mark.

I cannot bring you to such a place without yet another Dartmoor legend! The pool is haunted by the spirit of a former Mayor of Okehampton, Benjamin Gayer, known often as Binjie Gear or just Binjie. There are various accounts of what he did but some say he was caught stealing sheep and hanged on Hangingstone Hill, near the scene of his crime, and that his spirit comes back to Cranmere either as a black dwarf or a black colt condemned to try to drain the water with a sieve. It is also told how Binjie found a dead sheep and used the skin to line the sieve and emptied the pool as you can see today!

This is a walk where you will have to go back the way you came so make a note of where the stones show the entry into Ockerton Peat Pass that will take you back to Ockerton Court and your car.

Having said do not try to cut across the peat or fen, if you are young, strong and foolish, if might amuse you to bog-hop in and out of the peat hags and gullies, like some fearful black glacier with crevasses, back on a straight course to your car! *Go carefully though, and watch out for the patches of quaking bog.* You will have to zig-zag a lot and you will find it exhausting. However, it will show you how difficult Dartmoor can be to walk in and what a good idea and how useful the peat passes are. The old moormen were not fools. Good luck!

37. Meldon Reservoir, Black-a-Tor Copse, Sandy Ford, Valley of the West Okement River, Cranmere Pool.

There are three ways to return; a) The way you came. b) Via Great Kneeset, Amicombe Hill, Kitty Tor, Corn Ridge, Branscombe's Loaf, Vellake Corner. c) Via Brim Brook, Dinger Tor, High Willhays, Yes Tor.

START. The Car Park at Meldon Dam. Map Ref.563917.

Okehampton is about 5kms away with all the facilities you might need. There are toilets at the car park by the dam.

a) Long.   *12¾ miles. 20kms.*   *Hard.*
b) Long.   *11½ miles. 18.5kms.*   *Very hard!*
c) Long.   *11½ miles. 18.5kms.*   *Very Hard*

This is one of the longest day walks that I shall be writing about and if you try either of the variations for the return then certainly one of the hardest. Although the alternative return routes are shorter, they both involve steep climbing comparable with walking in some of the true mountain districts of Britain. Return b. in particular will need good navigational ability and all these routes are very difficult in poor visibility. This was a walk that I used to do a great many years ago before the dam was built and still remember the deep, steep-sided valley of the West Okement River that is now hidden under the water.

I suppose one could argue that in themselves dams are beautiful and certainly that stretches of water in wild surroundings add to the beauty. I find all the reservoirs on Dartmoor have a charm of their own and now they have matured and mellowed, do not look out of place. But where I knew the area before the waters came, as I did here, I feel sad that it is man who has changed the landscape yet again; illogical emotions I suppose, you should either agree or disagree with the building of dams in National Parks.

Set off across the dam and find the path on the east side. It more or less follows the contours along the lake. You will see a small island

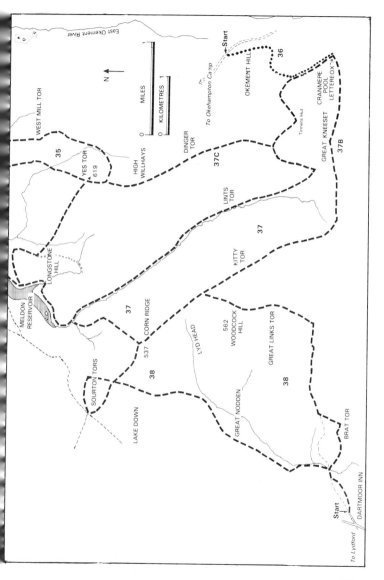

below that was man-made and the area around is marked as a Nature Reserve. A gesture by the dam builders to try to placate the conservation objectors when the controversies raged over the building of the dam and the flooding of the valley. The path we have been following drops to the river and you will see a modern bridge over it.

The river has formed a large alluvial plain here and the area is called Vellake Corner, crossed by a path which leads to a track.

Follow the track south with the river on your right. This is a delightful stretch as the West Okement comes tumbling down over rocks and falls, into deep pools, gullies and by boulders and islands all crowded in by a dense covering of trees. If you feel that you have time, go down and clamber around here for a while, even have a dip in one of the pools! This lovely part of the valley is called The Island of Rocks.

You will see, up to your left, Black Tor lying on the flanks of Yes Tor and High Willhays and soon you will come to Black-a-Tor Copse which takes its name obviously from the tor above. Like Wistman's Wood this is one of the three, stunted, primeval, oak forests of Dartmoor. It is mentioned as early as 1609 in a survey of that year and probably covered a much larger area than the 12 acres that it does today. For more details have a look in the section on Flora in the Introduction and also Walk 29 where I wrote about Wistman's Woods. I used to camp here in the early 1950's and it was a most tranquil and lonely place to be.

On the opposite side of the valley there are masses of granite called the Slipper Stones and, nearer the river, the remains of tin workings called Crocker's Pits.

Keep on up the river until you see a boundary stone sticking up which marks the end of Okehampton Parish and the start of the Forest of Dartmoor. By the stone there is a shallow crossing place called Sandy Ford. On the left a stream comes down to the main river called Lints Tor Brook and you will have seen Lints Tor itself for some time. Though the tor is not as high as Cranmere Pool, where you are going, because it is a more or less isolated peak the views from the top, right into the heart of the moor are fine, but you may feel that you have not got enough time to divert to climb it. A tinners' hut and some hut circles can be visited nearer the river if you wish.

Keep along the true right bank of the river and the valley begins to swing south-east after Kneeset Foot and then suddenly, below Great Kneeset, it reaches a bend and surprisingly turns almost north to Kneeset Nose. Obviously it is possible to cut off the corner here by going from the Foot to the Nose!

A stream comes in here from the north-north-east which is Brim Brook and which you will need to remember if you are going to return via Yes Tor.

On to Jackman's Bottom and the river, which is now only a small stream, is often hidden in a deep gully and you can only hear it rushing along, not see it. Soon it swings north-east and you will follow it round past another tinners' hut.

Beyond Vergyglade (or Vergyland) Combe you have now linked up with the details given in Walk 36 which will take you to Cranmere Pool itself and tell you something about the Pool that is now just a boggy hollow!

From Cranmere then it is time to decide which way to return. The way you came is very lovely and more or less downhill all the way and if you have time it gives you the chance to dawdle and look at things you may have rushed by or missed on the way up or to have a swim in the pools; in summer time!

Route b. probably has the greatest challenge. Set a course almost due west across the fen country towards Great Kneeset. You will find it hard going. On Black Ridge you should cut across the peat pass that runs north/south. Great Kneeset, 567 metres, lies on a spur and the views from the rock are magnificent. To the north you can look down the valley of the West Okement that you followed to get to Cranmere. To the south you can see Cut Hill and also Fur Tor peeping over Little Kneeset, while Amicombe Brook runs west down to Tavy Cleave.

Keep going west and drop down to the little tributary of the West Okement that meets it at Kneeset Foot. Once over the stream you have a long climb ahead just north of west to Amicombe Hill. This hill was also known as the *Preda de Aunnacombe* in 1346; *'preda'* being an old word meaning grazing lands within the forest.

There are also wierd stories told about the hill. Fires are sometimes seen at night, said to have been lit by the Evil One who is up there waiting for the terrible feuds to break out again between the men of Tavistock and Okehampton. Satan as ever waiting for a chance to stir up trouble!

You are now on a broad ridge with very steep slopes down to the West Okement River to your right and not so steep to Great Links Tor and Rattlebrook Peat Works to your left.

There are tracks along the top to Kitty Tor but do not be tempted to follow them down towards the west too far but keep along this high broad ridge at over 500 metres. Keep going just west of north past Lyn Head on a soggy plateau to Corn Ridge and Branscombe's Loaf.

The name Loaf is odd and could come from the fact that the tor does look like a loaf of bread. The fact that the other smaller rock nearby is often called the Cheese, bears this out. However there is a Celtic word *llof* which means a lump or excrescence and the name could have come from that. As so often with Dartmoor names, 'you pays your money and you takes your choice'! But there is another explanation. I am sure that you thought that you were going to get away without another Dartmoor legend. Well I am afraid that you are wrong! If you have done some of the earlier walks in the Widecombe area you will remember, I am sure, Walter Bronescombe, Bishop of Exeter who in 1260 allowed the people of the Ancient Tenements of Babeny, Pizzwell, Brimpts and so on to worship in Widecombe rather than Lyford. Well the Bishop was up here one day, though I am not quite sure why, and was lost. Suddenly an old man appeared who looked like a moorman and offered the Bishop some bread and cheese. He was just about to accept when he saw a cloven hoof sticking out from under the moorman's cloak. Yes, it was the Devil in disguise and the Bishop threw down the loaf of bread and the piece of cheese both of which turned instantly into stone as you can see for yourselves!

There is a prehistoric burial mound to the north-west, if you would like to look at it but, in any case, you have a steep descent down to Vellake Corner northwards from Branscombe's Loaf.

If you can get across the main river there you can join your original track back to the reservoir. If there are problems cross the small Vellake Brook that comes down from the south-west and get over the West Okement by the new Bridge at the head of the reservoir and then back to the start.

Route c. The other way back from Cranmere takes you on a long but fairly gentle climb to the highest points of Dartmoor, so, as well as visiting the most famous letter box, you will also be the highest person in southern England.

Follow your route back down the West Okement River to Kneeset Nose where you should then strike north-east up Brim Brook. On the east or true left bank you will see the remains of a tinners' hut. Opposite the hut start your climb up Dinger Tor, north-west, a single pile of rock just looking out westwards. A track comes as far as here that would take you back by the east side of West Mill Tor to Okehampton Camp.

You must now continue just west of north towards High Willhays.

You could divert, if you wished, further west to Fordland Ledge with its cairn and breathtaking view down the steep hill to Black-a-

Tor Copse and the valley you walked up some time ago.

Once on High Willhays you will see Yes Tor northwards along the broad ridge.

See Walk 35 for all the details of these highest peaks of Dartmoor.

From Yes Tor strike down north-west over the edge of Okehampton Common to Longstone Hill where you will find a track that will take you down to the path from the dam or go directly, steeply down to the path by the reservoir and so back to the start. You will have had a feeling of being in the high mountains on this walk and I hope you enjoyed it.

38. Brat Tor, Bleak House, (Great Links Tor), Rattlebrook Peat Works, Corn Ridge, Branscombe's Loaf, Sourton Tors, The Ice Works. *(See map p.195)*

START. On the common near The Dartmoor Inn, Lydford. Map Ref.527855. There are two pubs near the start. The Dartmoor Inn and, just up the road towards Okehampton, The Fox and Hounds which could also make a starting place as there is a way onto the moor here at Nodden Gate.

Lydford is very close with all the facilities of a small village. It is worth a visit as there is Lydford Gorge to see and also a castle which served as the Stannary Prison, even though Lydford was not a Stannary Town. The laws were severe and there was a saying 'hanging first and trying afterwards'. The last execution here took place in 1650.

Long. 8½ miles. 13.75kms. Moderate. By leaving out Branscombe's Loaf and Sourton Tors the walk can be reduced to 6 miles. 9.75kms.

There is a lane north of the Dartmoor Inn that will take you, through two gates, onto the open moor. Park off the track here. Do please shut the gates after you.

Set off along the track that runs, slightly downhill, north-east to the River Lyd. There are three ways to get across the river; by the bridge, the stepping stones or by the ford.

Two hundred yards to your right, along the river, there is another sad reminder of the Great War. Here there is a seat and nearby a plaque attached to a rock that reads. 'In loving memory of Captain Nigel Duncan Ratcliffe Hunter, M.C. and Bar, Royal Engineers, who was killed in action at Biefvillers, near Bapaume, on March 25th 1918, aged 23 years.' This young man clearly loved Dartmoor and on the plaque you will also find a short, poignant poem written by him on his last visit to Lydford. I will leave it to you to come here and read it for yourselves in this pleasant but sad spot.

Return to the bridge and take the smaller, steep path to the right of the main track that runs up to Brat Tor and Widgery Cross. When you arrive there you will see that this well known cross is made up of blocks of granite rather than being carved from one piece as are many of the older crosses that you have seen. This one was put up in 1887 to celebrate the Jubilee of Queen Victoria at the instigation of W. Widgery, the Dartmoor artist. The views to the west off the moor are fine from here.

Aim north-north-east now, just to the right of Arms Tor, and you will come to the miners' track that you could have followed from the bridge over the River Lyd if you had wished to miss out Widgery Cross. You will be in an area of familiar tinners' spoil heaps and gerts or gullies. As the track begins to swing north you will see, to your left, the two tors called Higher Dunna Goat and Lower Dunna Goat. Strange names and probably nothing to do with goats but Celtic words; *dan* meaning under or maybe *dun* meaning a hill and *coed* which means a wood. There is nothing much to be gained by climbing up to the two tors and if you do you will miss a chance to poke about in the ruins of Bleak House which lies on the far side, the left bank of the Rattle Brook. A splendidly apt name for this lonely and remote ruin where the manager of the Peat Works lived. Eden Phillpotts knew about this bleak house and described it in his novel 'The Whirlwind', in which he called it Dunnagoat Cottage.

Decisions to be made now. You can, if you like, walk west to climb Great Links Tor which standing, as it does, on the western edge of Dartmoor, gives you the most tremendous views across Devon and Cornwall to Bodmin Moor. The whole summit of the tor is made up of great piles of rock like some huge castle with a keep with the moor dropping steeply away below it. Or you could keep on north now up the valley of the Rattle Brook and you soon come to the huge industrial area of the Rattlebrook Peat Works. Obviously you will come down here after you have climbed Great Links Tor in any case.

This is a desolate and almost ugly place though, as so often is the case, nature has helped soften what man has done to his environment. The Peat Works were one of the few old industries that survived on Dartmoor until 1955 when the whole venture was finally closed down. For its start we must go back to 1868 when, with high hopes, a company was formed to cut peat up here and take it down off the moor. By 1879 a railway line had been built, with something of the same skill as the engineers who built the Foggintor and Swelltor Quarries Railway, which took the dried peat down to the main line of the old L. & S.W.R. at Bridestowe; you can still see the disused linking tracks and sidings. The climb up to the works was over 1,000 feet or 300 metres and there were cuttings, embankments, points, sidings and cross-over loops. You will be following a section of this track for part of the walk. Huge drying houses and boilers were installed high up here on the moor and thousands of tons of peat were sent away over the years. Sadly it was never really an economic venture and though many new companies were formed, each with new ideas and drive, they all failed. In 1961 the army were called in to demolish the old, disused buildings as part of an exercise. So ended another Dartmoor industry. This is an interesting place to potter around looking at the remains of the works but sooner or later it will be time for you to move on.

Decisions again! If you did not visit Branscombe's Loaf on the walk to Cranmere Pool, Walk 37, you can do that now and then go on to Sourton Tors and the Ice Works (this alone should make you want to go on to find out what on earth the Ice Works are)! If, however, time is short or you have had enough, then an easy, gentle route down the old railway line will lead you back to the start; north to start with and then south-west and, finally, south past Great Nodden. Or, if you prefer, go to where the infant River Lyd flows under the track, about 1.5kms from the Works, and you can follow that down to the start past amazing tinners' works. By the way, keep an eye out for the tinners' cache, like a little cave, quite close to the river after you have left the railway track.

But I shall assume that you are going on. Climb more or less north from the Works to the little rock of Hunt Tor and then north-east onto Woodcock Hill and the broad whaleback of Corn Ridge. Once on the plateau you should aim north-west towards Branscombe's Loaf. The views off to your right are very exciting. The slope down to the West Okement is one of the steepest on Dartmoor. Below, but you will not see them, are the Slipper Stones, huge blocks of granite that are said to resemble slippers. On the far side of the valley lies Black-a-Tor Copse that you may have visited on Walk 37 and above it rears Yes Tor and High Willhays, the highest peaks of Dartmoor.

Walk on now to Branscombe's Loaf and for all the details of this strange looking rock see Walk 37.

From here walk down past the cairn, a Bronze Age burial mound, towards the north-west. You might just stumble on a large stone circle but with many stones missing. It is quite close to where a reave (an earth and stone boundary bank) crosses a track.

You can now either aim straight at Sourton Tors, still north-west, or you can follow the track which you will cross anyhow round to the Tors. Off to your right, as your line of vision comes beyond the spur of Shelstone Tor north of Branscombe's Loaf, you will see Meldon Reservoir tucked in its steep valley.

On the north side of Sourton Tors, where the track will have taken you if you came that way, you will see a strange series of bumps, pits, mounds and buildings. These were once the Ice Works. I do not know on how many days they were able to produce ice but the idea was that water was run into the shallow pits that you can see and on frosty days it froze. The ice was then cut out and stored in specially dug trenches waiting to be transported down to Plymouth by horse and cart for use by the fishermen and fishmongers. This venture was started in 1875 and only lasted ten years or so. The position was ideal high on the tors here, facing north, in line with the bitter freezing winds but obviously only thrived before the days of modern refrigeration. But what a business, taking the ice all the way to Plymouth by horse and cart! Another failed Dartmoor industry!

Well, that is it! I hope the journey was worth it. Return to the track and follow it round and then south. Keep on it now, past the reave, onto Lake Down and Coombe Down. Here you will join the track of the peat railway which you must keep following under Great Nodden where there is an amazing series of tracks, sidings and points.

Off to your right you should be able to see King Wall and, running beside it, the King Way, an ancient track that leads to Nodden Gate. This was the old route along the north side of Dartmoor that was no longer used when the stagecoach roads were built in the eighteenth century.

You can either follow this or other tracks back to the start.

39. The Lich Way, Lynch Tor, Fur Tor, Sandy Ford, Watern Oke, Tavy Cleave.

START. Bagga Tor Gate. Map Ref.546805. There is parking space just inside the gate, off the track.

There is a Post Office and stores at Peter Tavy and also a pleasant pub. Tavistock is 6.5kms away with all the facilities you might need and in any case is worth a visit.

Long. 9 miles. 14.5kms. Hard. It is possible to shorten this walk by

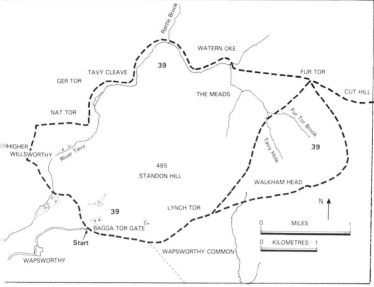

leaving out Fur Tor, but whichever way you go this is a hard walk into difficult, wilderness country.

The track that you can see ahead of you and indeed the one behind, running off to Brousentor Farm, are part of the Lich Way or the Path of the Dead which, you will remember you met on Walk 26. It was used by the people who lived in the Ancient Tenements near Bellever and Postbridge to carry their dead to be buried at Lydford in whose parish, rather surprisingly, they resided. This was one of several places where the Lich Way came off the moor for the last part of the journey to Lydford. I shall be writing more about the Way at the end of the walk.

For now then, set off east, along the track with the enclosure walls on either side that gradually drop away, and you will be aware that you are in a widening funnel formed by the walls, called a stroll. You may remember the one at Teignhead Farm. You will find them all round the edge of the moor where tracks lead off into enclosures and down to farms. Their purpose is obvious when you consider this is the way that the moormen and farmers drive animals off the moor.

At the end of the walls the actual track turns north but north-east of you there is Lynch Tor. While you could follow the track contouring round left it is best to strike over Lynch Tor and have a quick look at Limsboro' Cairn mentioned in the Perambulation of 1240. From the tor, and the cairn, set out across the heather and tussocks to the north-east; awkward going.

Soon you will see Fur Tor and you will begin to drop down to the River Tavy near Tavy Hole but do not stray too far to your right, unless you would like to add an extra kilometre or two by going round by Walkham Head, the tinners' huts on the upper Tavy and South Tavy Head and then to Fur Tor. This is real wilderness country and tussocky going but it avoids dropping down and then climbing up steeply to Fur Tor again.

By the way, if you go directly towards Fur Tor, when you reach the River Tavy, this is where you can cut the walk short by following the river down to Sandy Ford and ignore the steep climb up! If you wish to go to this peak of 572 metres then where the Fur Tor Brook joins the River Tavy attack the steep slope north-east towards the rocky tor standing on its ridge jutting out to the north-west.

Fur Tor is certainly worth a visit if you did not go there on Walk 30. For details of views from the summit have a look at that walk. This is one of the finest and remotest tors on Dartmoor.

Now it is knee punishing time! From Fur Tor drop steeply back down to the west, across Pinswell, to Sandy Ford where the Amicombe Brook joins the Tavy; watch out for the clitter rocks. It could be ankle breaking time too! You are in an area that was considered excellent pasture and around here was known, over 600 years ago, as the *Preda de Vurtorre;* preda was a word meaning good pasture land.

Cross the river at the ford, if you can, otherwise go back upstream and get to the north side. Follow the river down first west and then north-west. You will be aware of firstly a huge clitter but also a great many low walls. These are the remains of the largest Bronze Age village on Dartmoor, Watern Oke. In the area there are nearly 100 huts spaced out along the river for nearly a kilometre. This remote village from about 1500 B.C. was explored thoroughly in 1905 by the Rev. I.K.Anderson, who was vicar of Mary Tavy. He camped up here and found, with the help of many men who dug under his supervision, flints, pottery, charcoal and cooking stones.

After Watern Oke keep following the river until the Rattle Brook comes in from the north from Deadlake Foot. Walk 38 was just up the valley from here and you might be able to link parts of these two walks together if you have someone who would be willing to drive a car

Tavy Cleave

round to meet you. Here the River Tavy takes a huge bend and now begins to flow south-west and enters Tavy Cleave. This is one of the most exciting and spectacular places on Dartmoor as well as being really wild and beautiful. Nowhere else on Dartmoor is there such a deep ravine and the river to your left tumbles down over waterfalls, rock pools and past boulders and islands. To be here when it is in spate is an incredible sight. When you look at the depth of the gorge, it is hard to believe that Tavy Cleave was filled to the brim with snow in the great blizzard of 1881 and in more recent times too. It is rocky going down the Cleave but you should soon break clear and the path improves as you walk down to where a leat is taken off from the river by a weir in an area called Devil's Point. Up to your right still more huge rocks, this time Ger Tor.

You will have been aware of the Tavy all along but you will need to make a special note of how high the water is running for your return routes are affected by this.

There are two ways that you can return to Baggator Gate. The first will keep you on the open moor but could be difficult if the Tavy is in flood. In fact you would probably have to get on the true left bank before Tavy Cleave if you wished to follow this route home if the water was up at all. So for this way, get on the left bank of the river wherever you can and follow it down to opposite Ger Tor where the leat is taken off. From here begin to gain height up the steep slope and aim south to the old enclosure walls to the east of Standon Farm. Then, contour round south-east along the walls of Baggator Farm, which I gather is a residential youth centre. This is a frustrating route because you can see Bagga Tor itself south of the enclosures but there is no right-of-way through, though there are gates and gaps that would lead you directly to the tor and your car beyond. So keep going along Baggator Brook and you will see the extraordinary circular South Common Plantation on your right within the enclosure. Cross the Brook and follow the wall round as it swings south-east and then south-west; it is quite a long steady climb up. This will bring you back to the stroll and your outward route.

The better way is the second route. Follow the Wheal Jewel Leat from beside Ger Tor as it contours round below Nat Tor. You will soon see Nattor Farm to your left. Walk down to the track that runs to the farm and follow it to Lanehead. To be honest this is a most unattractive part of Dartmoor. The land to your right is flat, tussocky marsh, the hills have no features and the ugly Willsworthy range buildings and butts dominate the skyline. However, you will soon be in interesting and pleasant countryside. Turn down the lane at Lanehead and after ½km you will come to Higher Willsworthy on your left. Walk down the narrow rocky track beside the farm. Please shut any gates behind you.

You are now back on the Lich Way and it is obvious that this deep lane is an ancient track. Fairly soon you will come to a signposted stile on the right that leads you into a field. There is also a notice on the stile that tells you that the path is impassable in wet weather. It is now that your knowledge of the state of the River Tavy is vital. If you reckon that the river is high then the stepping stones that you will have to cross a little later on will be under water! If this is so then keep on down the lane until it drops steeply down a rocky section to a bridge at Standon Steps. *I must make it clear that there is no public right-of-way here, but if the river is flooded then there is no other way across without a very long road walk to Hill Bridge.*

Once over the bridge turn right and follow the left bank. In fact it is very marshy and you will need to keep just on the other side of the bank and line of trees in a field about 50 metres from the river. When you come to the wire fence on a wooded bank and wall turn right and go down to the river. You can climb round on rocks, right above the water, to emerge on marshy moorland. Keep on down the river until you hit the track coming across the river on the stepping stones I mentioned earlier.

Obviously it is better from all points of view to follow the Lich Way from the first turn off the lane and there are stiles, signs and yellow paint spots to guide you across and along fields. As you drop down to the river there are signs of the old track, deep in its gully, to your right and then on down to the river itself where you follow it. There is a faded yellow paint spot on a rock that will guide you to the final stile by the ford and stepping stones over the Tavy deep in a beautiful, rocky, wooded dell.

Even with the river low the stepping stones are not very good and there is one awkward gap so you may have to be prepared to get wet feet or take your boots off and wade!

There are some ghoulish names associated with the Lich Way; Corpse Lane and Coffin Wood. You have been in Corpse Lane and just to your right is Coffin Wood! It is said that they carried the bodies for burial at Lydford, from the Ancient Tenements near Bellever, just slung across the back of a horse in a canvas bag. To transport a heavy wooden coffin across the moor, either by horse or by manpower, would have been almost impossible. There were no wagons that could have been used or indeed would have stood up to the pounding on the desolate, rough tracks. But of course being decent, God-fearing folk they did not want to enter Lydford in this irreverent fashion with the corpse lolling about on the back of a horse. When they reached this wood where you are standing now, they had a coffin waiting and here they placed the body in it and continued in a more seemly, pious way. But it was still a long way to Lydford.

As before the path is well waymarked and it is a delightful walk through the trees with all around the signs of really ancient walls and tracks. You will join the concrete track that comes from Standon Farm for a while up a steep hill. Then the Lich Way ducks in behind Brousentor Farm up another and final deep, rocky lane overhung with trees and a stream flowing down it. This will lead you over the last stile onto the open moor and your car.

40. Higher Godsworthy, The Longstone, White Tor, Stephen's Grave, Wedlake.

START. On the corner where the road turns north to Higher Godsworthy Farm. Map Ref.530769. There is room to park here but please be careful not to block the road to the farm or access to the common. This is a cul-de-sac road that is not often used except by people who wish to get away from the crowds.

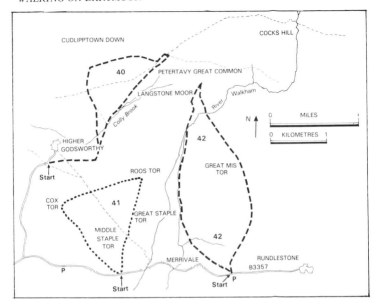

Merrivale with its pub is about 4kms away. Otherwise Tavistock with all the facilities that you might need is the nearest town while Peter Tavy is the nearest village with a Post Office, stores and pub. *Medium. 5 miles. 8kms. Moderate.*

This is a simple but pleasant little walk after all the long, hard trips I have described that take you into the heart of the moor.

Set off east with the enclosure walls to your left. Where the wall drops back north cut diagonally across to the corner where there is a gate. Before you go through the gate you might like to have a wander round the mass of Bronze Age Hut circles and reaves a little further east. Once through the gate again, aim diagonally across the fairly marshy area with reeds to another gate on the far side by the Colly Brook. Go through this gate by old Wedlake Farm and you will be on the open moor again. Turn right and wander up through the tinners' works north-east and, when the enclosure walls on your right stop, keep going until you will see the menhir called The Longstone. It is pretty marshy off to your right in the Longstone Mires so if there are problems keep left.

All these prehistoric remains were damaged by American soldiers

The Longstone

while training up here before D-Day. They turned a machine gun on The Longstone and you can see the bullet marks. It is the last tall stone (3 metres) of a row that is about 101 metres long. The row runs to what was a burial site where there is a stone circle some 18 metres in diameter which was also damaged.

From these remains walk straight west to White Tor. The views are great from here and you can see Fur Tor and Cut Hill, some of the places you might have visited on previous walks. The summit of White Tor is an extraordinary mass of natural rocks but circling the actual top area is a stone wall which, although it is now falling down, was obviously once very large. It formed the outer walls of what was an Iron Age Fort, one of the few hill forts from this period actually on Dartmoor. These early Iron Age people seemed always to be afraid of sudden attack and their forts were on hilltops and in fine defensive positions.

Keep going west and you will come to Little White Tor and more Iron Age enclosures and hut circles all of which produced charcoal, pottery, flint flakes and cooking stones when excavated in 1904.

Follow the newtake wall down south and by the Longstone Moor Track you will discover another standing stone. This is Stephens' Grave. Poor George Stephens was a young man from Peter Tavy who took his life in 1762, having discovered that the girl to whom he was engaged had been unfaithful. As with Kitty Jay, whose grave you may have visited near Hound Tor, suicides were not allowed to be buried on consecrated ground and so the wretched George lies here. It is said that at the moment that he was buried some linen that was hanging out on the line at Higher Godsworthy was whisked up into the air and was never seen again.

All that remains now is for you to walk slightly east of south back to the corner where the Colly Brook flows into the enclosures where you can go through the gates and back to the start the way you came.

41. Staple Tors, Roos Tor, Cox Tor. *(See map p.208)*

START. There is a Car Park on the north side of the Two Bridges to Tavistock road, the B3357 about ¾km west of Merrivale. Map Ref.541750.

There is a pub at Merrivale and all other facilities either at Princetown or Tavistock.

Medium (just) 2¾ miles. 4.5kms. Easy to Moderate. (Another short walk, easy going with good views; ideal for an evening in summer or when time is short.)

Set off north over the turf towards Middle Staple Tor leaving Little Staple Tor to your left. Although there is a lot of natural clitter you will notice that many of the rocks lying around have been split and partly dressed but then for some reason rejected. From the 1870's this area was a busy industrial site with large quantities of 'moorstone', in other words granite, being cut from the flanks of the tors here. Most of it was used for roads and pavements and can still be seen in London and many other cities including, of course, Plymouth. On the blocks lying about here you will see the lines of the drill holes that were used to split the rock. After a line of holes was drilled wedges were hammered in and the rock split along the line.

Further up the hill there are small roofless buildings and stone benches which were called bankers and this is where the sett-makers took shelter and worked out on the hillside. Their pay was one penny a sett and it was a really quick and skilled man who could cut sixty in a day so that he would earn five shillings.

Push on now up to Middle Staple Tor and then just east of north to Great Staple Tor. Staple from the Anglo-Saxon *steopl*, a tower maybe. The views from the top are enormous looking down south-west to Plymouth Sound (at night in clear weather you can see the Eddystone Light flashing ten miles out from Plymouth Breakwater) and west into Cornwall. The summit rocks are impressive and high like great battlements with a drive in between. There is, however, one curious rock called the Staple Tor Tolmen. You might remember that there was a Tolmen on Walk 33 on the River Teign. The word means a stone with a hole in it. To be truthful this one is not exactly a stone with a hole in it but rather a natural arch formed by freak erosion. As you will see it is formed by a great slab of granite nearly 3 metres long resting on two smaller rocks. As with the other Dartmoor Tolmen some say it was put there and used by the Druids for their mystic rites. It is extraordinary how the Druids get blamed for every odd shaped rock! For others it was supposed to cure whooping cough or rheumatism or just make your wishes come true!

North again and on to Roos Tor over some of the best and easiest walking ground you will find on Dartmoor. This is another splendid viewpoint looking as you can northwards into the heart of the moor but also west across the fields, woods and farms of west Devon and east Cornwall.

The map shows that there is a logan or logging stone here but although some of the summit rocks look as if they should move none of them, in fact, can be rocked. There are, however, some good examples of rock basins such as you might have seen on Walk 33 on Kestor.

Another pleasant stretch of walking over short turf, south-west to Cox Tor. (You could divert if you wished to have a look at the hut circles of the settlement to your right.) You will cross over a good path that ran from Higher Godstone to Merrivale and was used by the quarrymen walking to work each day.

Cox Tor is yet another place with superb views as it is the last high ground of Dartmoor and from here the slope drops steeply down west to farming land and Tavistock; the last bulging thrust of the igneous intrusion of granite.

All that remains now is for you to swing down off the scattered summit rocks towards the south-east where you will find tinners' works and gullies and some of their huts. It should be easy to walk back along the road to the Car Park.

42. Great Mis Tor, Langstone Moor Circle, Prehistoric and Tinners' Remains in Walkham Valley. *(See map p.208)*

START. Car Park on the site of the old school on the south side of Two Bridges to Tavistock road, the B3357. Map Ref.561748.

There is a pub at Merrivale otherwise all the other facilities that you might need are to be found at Princetown which is 3kms away.
Medium. 5 miles. 8kms. Moderate.

More details of this old nineteenth century school for the quarrymen's children can be found in Walk 17.

There is an obvious track that sets off north on the opposite side of the road from where you have parked. Follow this track up past Little Mis Tor. Keep on now towards the huge pile of rocks that makes up Great Mis Tor. This tor seen from the road conjures up all that most people think about Dartmoor landscape and tors. It epitomises the remote and savage beauty of this wilderness with the gaunt rocks crowning a distant hill. It is spoilt only by a flagpole on which flies a red flag when the ranges are in use! The views as you might expect are fine for at 538 metres Great Mis Tor it is the highest peak around.

There is a fine example of a rock basin to be found on the southern part of the tor; it has the name of Mistor Pan. Great Mis Tor was one of the boundary marks of the Perambulations of 1240. Rather surprisingly in another survey of 1609 they called the bound-mark 'a rock called Mistorrpan' rather than just Mis Tor. The basin is also known as the Devil's Frying Pan yet another example of the Devil up to no good on Dartmoor!

To the west there is an extensive and densely covered clitter slope, so that your descent to the River Walkham should be north-west.

On the north side of the river, which you should have no difficulty in crossing, you will come to Langstone Moor with its stone circle about 20 metres in diameter. Sadly this is another prehistoric remains that was used for target practice by soldiers training during the Second World War. See Walk 40. It seems ironic that the circle was restored in the 1890's only to be smashed down by troops in the 1940's.

Nearby, and you may well have passed through them on the way to the circle, there is a large group of hut circles and enclosures also from the Bronze Age.

Come back to the south and the River Walkham which you should now follow down its steepening valley. You will soon come to a weir by a small dam which controlled the flow of water into the Grimstone and Sortridge Leat that you would have encountered on Walk 18. It runs some 10kms to near Horrabridge to take water to an old mine there.

You are now approaching an extraordinary area within an enclosure wall that covers thousands of acres. There are a great many hut circles, enclosure walls and cairns that are worth wandering around.

On the map you will see the words Pillow Mounds which is the name given to the artificial rabbit burrows built for breeding on the Warrens and indeed there was a Warren here at Merrivale. But even more interesting are the three tinners' blowing houses shown on the 1:25,000 map and you can work your way down to them. In and near them are mould stones for forming ingots and mortar stones for crushing the ore. The third and last blowing house is the best of all and here you can see the furnace and an excellent mould stone.

As you will have read earlier in this Guide, the term blowing house comes from the fact that large bellows, powered by a water wheel, produced heat fierce enough in the fire to melt the tin ore. This is why the blowing houses were usually close to streams and, if you look closely, you can often see a leat that brought the water to the wheel, as you can here.

From the last blowing house cut back south-east fairly steeply to a gate that will take you onto the road and back to the start.

43. Beardown Tors, Foxholes, Crow Tor, Devil's Tor, Beardown Man, Broad Hole, Cowsic River Valley. *(See map p.166)*

START. Quarry opposite the Two Bridges Hotel. Map Ref.609751. There is usually room to park here but it is a busy, popular starting place for walks up to Wistman's Wood and geology students who come to hammer at the quarry face! There is the Two Bridges Hotel opposite otherwise Princetown is about 3kms away with all the facilities that you might need.
Long.   7½ miles.   12.3kms.   Hard.

Set off westwards along the road and over the modern bridge which crosses the West Dart. On your left, standing a little back from the road, is the pleasant eighteenth century coaching hotel which obviously has been added to over the years. It is typical of the larger moorland hotels where families would stay to walk, ride, shoot and fish in the pre-war years. I remember that a Preparatory School was evacuated there during the last war. The boys might not have had much contact with the outside world but what a place to be at boarding school.

You will also see the old, almost humped-backed, coaching bridge over the Dart. This was of course the only route across the moors in those days from Exeter with, as the modern road does today, branches running off to Plymouth and Tavistock beyond the bridge.

Where the granite posts and railing come to an end on your right you will see a marked Public Footpath and this is the way you must go between narrow walls to a stile. Over the stile there are fields, more stiles and a well marked path both with signs and yellow spots of paint, including one on a rock to show you the way across a field. The little Cowsic River runs just to your right at the bottom of a steep drop clothed with beech trees.

The path will lead you round to Bear Down Farm and up the drive, keeping to the left of the actual farm buildings. Through a gate a broad track runs north towards the forestry plantations. Follow this for a while. The right-of-way branches off right here and goes by the Devonport Leat, cuts through the edge of the forest and emerges on the open moor. Once here the path more or less follows the Leat until you need swing back north-west to Beardown Tors. You could, however, walk straight up north on the wide forest ride to emerge on the open moor and then continue north to Beardown Tors.

There are four main summit tors here, one of them with a flagpole for the red range flag. The views, looking south particularly, are good from the top. Your route now lies almost north and you should walk to the small outcrop on the ridge north from the easternmost of the Beardown Tors. Then go down steeply, but diagonally, to where the small Methern Brook runs down from the north to join the West Dart. On the way, though it is not obvious, you will cross the route of the Lich Path which came this way running westwards to Lydford and using Lydford Tor, just west of you, as an important marker in this bare and empty moor.

When you reach the confluence the area is called Foxholes. Foxes still have their earth in the rocks around. As romantic and as apt as this name is the old name of Dart Hole perhaps is a better one. Foxes may come and go but the Dart will never.

Cross over the Brook now and start the climb up to Crow Tor just east of north. There used to be a letterbox here with a splendid rubber stamp with a crow on it. I suppose the rocks could be said to resemble a huge squatting crow but otherwise I can find no reason for the name; no Celtic word this time!

You must now walk north-west and in the fork between the two final branches of Methern Brook you will find a tinners' hut and obvious remains of their workings up to your right.

Keep going north-west and after quite a steep climb you will arrive on a plateau with Devil's Tor at 546 metres standing on it. Quite close on the western side is Beardown Man, a splendid menhir some 3.75 metres high. Crossing tells an amusing story of how when he asked a moorman about the stone the old man replied that he thought the pillar represented the Devil and that the tor which is really quite small, 'was plenty good enough vur he'! What one solitary menhir is doing up here I am not sure, for there are no stone rows, burial mounds, circles or even huts really near except 1km down the valley south. As, by now, you will know, man is a corruption of the Celtic *maen* a stone.

This is really lonely, remote country up here and if you look north you will see as far as Fur Tor and some of the fen you will have visited on previous walks. You can feel the real desolation and mystery of the moor in places such as this.

You must now drop down west to the steep valley of the little Cowsic and on southwards, past the hut circles and enclosure walls I mentioned earlier. Beyond these Bronze Age remains Conies Down Water flows in from the right at Broad Hole where there is a ford. This is a crossing place for the Lich Way and was called The Traveller's Ford.

The stone row marked on the 1:25,000 map about ½km to the west of the ford on the Lich Way although not very remarkable is the highest on Dartmoor and therefore probably Europe, at over 500 metres.

Keep following the river down as it meanders about in its valley. Below Holming Beam on your right, an area famous for its whortle-berries and where many families come to gather them, and Beardown Tors to your left, you will find the start of the Cowsic or west branch of the Devonport Leat which you might have encountered on several walks on the South Moor. It is best to follow the Leat now on the path that runs beside it.

You are now back in the area of the Beardown Hill Plantations that you went through at the start of this walk.

You will discover that the large stone construction that looks like a bridge is, in fact, an aqueduct that carries the eastern branch of the Devonport Leat that you might have followed earlier. This branch takes its water off the West Dart just up from Wistman's Wood.

Just here, as a sort of 'Leatmeet', the two branches join at a small reservoir and flow on round, south, under the main road and out eventually to Nun's Cross Farm near Whiteworks. See Walk 14.

The Cowsic River now flows through a deep, rocky and delightful wooded valley.

Some of the rocks in the bed of the stream around here have inscriptions carved on them. This was the work of a Mr. Bray, who later became the vicar of Tavistock; he was the son of the owner of Beardown Farm. He decided that he wished to commemorate Theocritus and Virgil and other poets to give, as he put it, 'more animation to the scene'. He would paint the names on the rocks and then get one of his father's labourers to cut it out with a pick! There is also a fine little five span clapper bridge over the river here. Both this bridge and the one further down that takes the main drive over the Cowsic were damaged in the great floods of 1873 and again in 1890 and had to be extensively repaired.

You can now either follow the drive out and down to the main road or go back the way you came by the public footpath across the fields and back to the start and maybe some refreshment at the Two Bridges Hotel!

LONG WALKS

I thought that it might be a good way to end this Guide with details of four longer walks. Three are straight across Dartmoor and you will need someone to come and fetch' you at the end. The last and longest walk, as its name suggests, is circular, as it follows The Perambulation of 1240. You will probably need to camp or get off the moor to Bed and Breakfasts while on this last journey.

I shall not give details of the routes but merely tell you some of the main points along the walk so that you can plan it yourself by studying the maps.

Many of the places mentioned will have been featured on the Walks in the main part of the Guide and you can find out details and information in the relevant sections.

THE ABBOT'S WAY. Buckfast Abbey, Cross Furzes, Water Oak Corner, Huntingdon Cross, Crossways, Red Lake, Erme Head, Broad Rock, Plym Ford, Nun's Cross Farm, Siward's or Nuns Cross, South Hessary Tor, Princetown.

THE LICH WAY. Bellever, Bellever Forest, Higher Cherry Brook Bridge, Powder Mills★, Wistman's Wood, South of Foxholes, Lydford Tor, Traveller's Ford, Broad Hole, Conies Down, Bagga Tor, Brousentor Farm, Coffin Wood, Higher Willsworthy, Willsworthy Bridge, Yellowmead, Higher Beardon, Prescombe, Ingo Brake, Lydford.

★There is one area that you did not come to on the main walks and it is worth my giving a brief description of what used to go on here at Powder Mills. This is where they manufactured black powder, a type of gunpowder, in the nineteenth century. Work started here in 1844. Various buildings were put up, leats built and waterwheels were installed, all the brain-child of a man called George Frean. Gunpowder was in great demand in the quarries, some of which you will have visited, the tin mines and by farmers even, for clearing their land of large rocks. George Frean chose this spot partly for safety, and indeed there were several accidental explosions; partly because there was a good supply of water for the wheels used to powder the grindstones and because there were good routes out with the powder.

Alder trees were planted around the mills to act as a windbreak but also to provide wood for the charcoal needed with sulphur and saltpetre to make the gunpowder.

They tested the finished results in a mortar which can still be seen today near the farm which is now a craft centre.

In 1867 dynamite was invented and this was the beginning of the end for Powder Mills. By 1890 they were closed down but the ruins and the remains can still be seen lying up the little valley north of Powder Mills Farm, which you can visit as you follow the Lich Way.

THE MARINER'S WAY. Ivybridge, Near Addicombe ruins, Track of old Redlake Tramway, Abbot's Way east to Huntingdon Cross, Huntingdon Warren, Lud Gate, Chalk Ford, Scorriton, Holne, New Bridge, Spitchwick Manor, Lower Town, Leusdon, Ponsworthy, Jordon, Dockwell, Hamel Down, Grimspound, Hookney Tor, Bennett's Cross, Chagford Common.

You could go on to Bideford if you wished but this is the end of the Dartmoor section of the walk!

THE PERAMBULATION OF 1240.

I have mentioned this many times in the Guide and you will have visited quite a number of the boundary marks on the other walks but here then is the final challenge. Why not have a go at walking round the route taken by the twelve knights when they drew up the boundaries of the Forest of Dartmoor in the year 1240. What a journey it must have been for them.

I have given the start at Dartmeet because it is central and accessible but you could start at any point you wished. Obviously you need not do the whole round in one go, but you should manage it all in about 48 hours if you wanted to! After each bond-mark I have given the map reference to help you find them.

Dartmeet. 672731. O Brook Foot or Week Ford. 663724. Drylake Foot. 661710.

Boundary Stone on Sandyway. 659696. Petre's Bound Stone;
Ryders Hill. 660691. Western Wellabrook Head. 665686.
Western Wellabrook Foot. 665662.
Eastern White Barrow. 665652. Redlake Foot. 63661. Erme
Head Ford. 622669.
Eylesbarrow Cairn. 600686. Nun's Cross. 605699. South
Hessary Tor. 597723.
North Hessary Tor. 579742. Rendlestone. 574750. Great Mis
Tor. 563769.
White Barrow. 568798. Limsboro' Cairn; Lynch Tor. 566805.
Rattlebrook Foot. 561837. Rattlebrook Head. 561875. Steng-a-Tor.
568880.
Yes Tor. 581902. Cullever Steps. 606921. Cosdon Hill;
Cawsand Beacon. 636915.
Hound Tor. (North Moor). 629890. Watern Tor. 629869.
Hewlake Foot. 640860.
Long Stone. 660857. Heath Stone. 671837. Chagford Common.
671830.
King's Oven. 674812. Wallabrook Head. 676810. Wallabrook
Foot. 672747.

GLOSSARY OF DARTMOOR TERMS.

ADIT. Horizontal tunnel made by miners into a hill or side of a gully.
ANCIENT TENEMENT. One of the old farms on Dartmoor established in
Norman times, with certain rights and privileges.
BALL. A rounded hill.
BARROW. A huge mound of rocks usually near or on the summit of a hill
that marked the burial place of prehistoric man. See Cairn.
BEACON. Again a name for summit on which possibly fires, to act as a
signal, were lit.
BEAM.Several names on the moor have the word Beam in them. It refers to
mining and there is usually a deep, open working found nearby.
BEEHIVE HUT. Small circular stone huts that used to have a domed roof in
which the tinners probably left their tools and even ingots of smelted tin.
BLOWING HOUSE. A small stone building where the tinners smelted the
tin ore; see section on Tinners.
CAIRN. Usually an ancient burial place marked by a huge mound of stones
with the burial chamber in the middle. Most cairns or barrows have been
ransacked by treasure hunters or the stones taken away for more recent
buildings. Many of the old barrows occur in groups of three. There are a few
more recent cairns that have been built in modern times to mark paths or
summits of hills.

CLAPPER. A bridge made of huge slabs of granite resting on stone piers across rivers and streams. They are not prehistoric remains but were usually built on medieval pack-horse routes across the moor and between farms. The most famous Clapper Bridge is at Postbridge.

CLEAVE. A steep-sided valley or gorge.

CLITTER. A mass of boulders and rocks, usually covering a large area, found lying around and below a tor having been broken off by ice and general erosion.

COMBE. A small valley closed at one end. e.g. Widecombe. It comes from the Celtic word *cwm* found also in Wales.

COMMONER'S RIGHTS. The rights of certain farmers and landowners to graze animals on the open moor.

CORNDITCH. A wall with a ditch dug on the outer side to prevent deer and other animals entering the fields and eating the crops. Often seen near the remains of Saxon settlements.

DRIFT. The name given to rounding up the ponies and sometimes cattle on Dartmoor to make sure that all the animals gathered belong only to landowners who have grazing rights on the commons. Once rounded up the young animals are branded with the owners mark and some are sent to market

FEATHERBED. The name given to an area of marsh that wobbles and rocks over a large area when trodden on. Surface vegetation and moss, usually bright green, forms a solid skin over an area of liquid mud and slush. It is these areas that have given rise to the phrase the 'quaking bogs' of Dartmoor.

FEN. The areas of peat bog and bog-grass on the north moor.

FIELD SYSTEM. Prehistoric fields marked with low banks and walls called reaves.

HOLT. A small cave or lair of a fox or badger.

HUT CIRCLE. The remains of a circular, prehistoric dwelling, usually Bronze Age, made in stone that had a thatched roof when it was in use.

KISTVAEN. A stone coffin in which the remains, usually cremated, of Bronze Age people were placed. The kists were then often buried under mounds of earth or stones. There are many good examples to be seen on Dartmoor but all have been rifled by treasure hunters. Again from Celtic words *cist* a chest and *maen* a stone.

LEAT. A man-made water course to take water to mines and farms or in the case of the Devonport Leat down to the port for supplying ships. They were carefully built following the contours of the land but sloping slightly downhill so that they had a gentle gravitational flow.

LOGAN STONE. A stone or rock left by nature in such a finely balanced state on its base that it rocks if pushed gently.

LONGHOUSE. A traditional Dartmoor farmhouse with the human accommodation at one end and the animals at the other, all under one roof.

LYNCH. A rough track often running in a cutting below the level of the surrounding countryside.

MENHIR. The tallest and largest of the standing stones in stone rows or on their own, usually near burial chambers. Celtic *maen* stone, *hir* long.

MIRE. A Dartmoor marsh or swamp.

MOORGATE. A gate usually at the end of a lane leading onto the open moor.

MOORMEN. Men whose job it was to take cattle from one pasture to another across the moor.

MORTAR STONES. Found near Blowing Houses they were used for holding the tin ore for pounding and crushing; usually circular in shape.

MOULDSTONES. Also found near Blowing Houses they were used for forming ingots out of the molten tin; usually rectangular troughs about a foot long and three inches deep.

NEWTAKE. Reclaimed land taken from the open moor and then walled or fenced; a tradition started in Norman times with the tenants of the Ancient Tenements.

PEAT. Decomposed and compacted moorland vegetation in areas of high rainfall that can be cut for fuel.

PEAT PASS/CUT. A path or track cut through an area of peat hags, often forming a deep gully, used by the Moormen to take cattle and sheep from one area of the moor to another.

POUND. A walled enclosure for animals some dating from the Bronze Age. Perhaps the most famous is Grim's Pound.

REAVE. A low wall or bank marking the edges of boundaries or field systems. They still remain something of a mystery; some are prehistoric while others are medieval. Pronounced 'Rave'.

STANNARIES. These were the tin mining districts from early times and each district had a governing Stannary Town and there was a Stannary prison at Lydford. See section on Tinners.

STONE CIRCLES AND STONE ROWS. These obviously are what they suggest and date from the Bronze Age. The circles were probably places of worship while the rows often led to burial mounds. The longest row in Britain and probably the world is 4kms long near the Erme Valley on southern Dartmoor.

TURF-TIE. The banks where peat was cut for fuel. Each farmer had his own area and it was considered a great crime to cut peat on anyone else's Turf-tie. There was a rule that the green turf on the surface of the peat should be replaced after cutting to prevent large areas becoming a brown, peaty wilderness.

VAGS. Slabs of turf rather than peat cut for fuel with a specially shaped cutting spade.

VERMIN TRAP. As the name suggests it was a trap made of granite slabs with an ingenious trip-catch system that caused a slate to drop down to imprison the predator; often found near the Warrens.

WARREN. Farms, some of which are medieval, where rabbits were bred on a commercial basis. Specially constructed burrows can be found, near the buildings, that were used for breeding and keeping the rabbits.

WASTE. This is a name used only on South Dartmoor and is really another word for a Newtake but without the ancient implications and conditions of the old Newtakes. So they are small downs and commons that have been reclaimed from open moorland and enclosed by walls or fences.

Teign-e-ver Clapper Bridge

WHORTLEBERRY. *Vaccinium myrtillus.* Bilberry. Blueberry, Blaeberry and many other names are found for this small berry that grows in many areas of Dartmoor and which can be gathered in July and August.

Many of the old Dartmoor folk talked about gathering 'hurts' and it was often a marvellous annual outing for whole villages up onto the edge of the moor to pick the whortleberries in the old days. The berries were then sold in the markets while some were used in pies at home and when eaten with thick clotted cream made a splendid traditional Dartmoor dish.

USEFUL ADDRESSES AND TELEPHONE NUMBERS

Dartmoor National Park Headquarters and Information Office,
Parke, Haytor Road, Bovey Tracey, Devon. TQ13 9JQ.
Tel. Bovey Tracey 832093

The Dartmoor Preservation Association,
Crossings Cottage, Dousland, Yelverton, Devon. PL20 6LU.
Tel. Yelverton 853928

The Dartmoor Tourist Association,
8, Fitzford Cottages, Tavistock, Devon. PL19 8BD.
D.T.A. Phone-a-bed service. Tavistock 3360

The Devon Tourism Office,
County Estate Surveyors Dept., County Hall, Exeter, Devon. EX2 4QQ.
Tel. Exeter 53260

The West Country Tourist Board,
Trinity Court, Southernhay East, Exeter, Devon. EX1 1QS.
Tel. Exeter 76351

The National Trust,
Killerton House, Broadclyst, Exeter, Devon. EX5 3LF.

Nature Conservancy Council,
South West Region, Roughmoor, Bishops Hull, Taunton, Somerset.

Weather Forecasts,
Plymouth 8091 or 42534. Exeter 8091. Torquay 8091.

Youth Hostels Association,
Regional Office, Belmont Place, Stoke, Plymouth, Devon.
Tel. Plymouth 52753

Firing Times.
Notices in Police Stations, Post Offices and local newspapers, or
Tel. Okehampton 2939. Plymouth 701924. Exeter 70164. Torquay 24592.

BIBLIOGRAPHY

Crossing, William, *The Ancient Stone Crosses of Dartmoor and its Borderland.*
Crossing, William, *Guide to Dartmoor.*
Crossing, William, *One Hundred Years on Dartmoor.*
Crossing, William, *Amid Devonia's Alps, or Wanderings and Adventures on Dartmoor.*
Crossing, William, *Gems in a Granite Setting.*
Crossing, William, *Crossing's Dartmoor Worker.*
Gill, Crispin, (ed) *Dartmoor: A New Study.*
Harris, Helen, *Industrial Archaeology of Dartmoor.*
Harvey, L.A. & St Leger-Gordon, D. *Dartmoor.*
Hemery, Eric, *High Dartmoor.*
Hoskins, W.G. *Devon*
Langmuir, Eric, *Mountaincraft and Leadership.*
Perkins, John, *Geology Explained: Dartmoor and the Tamar Valley.*
Worth, R.Hansford, *Dartmoor.*

I have delved into the works of all these authors who have provided me with a wealth of excellent information and facts. Special mention must be made of William Crossing whose *Guide to Dartmoor* remains one of the most excellent and fascinating books ever written about the moor. The information in it is as pertinent and as fresh as it was when the second edition was published in 1912, except in a few areas where there have been physical changes caused by dams, forests, deserted and abandoned farms or whatever. My Guide is not intended in any way to oust or take over from Crossing's Guide for I have not covered the moor so extensively as he did. I have merely condensed and drawn together, in a modern idiom, a lot of the information given by Crossing with some of my own thoughts and comments thrown in for good measure.